Aloha, the bark

Unsung Titan of the Gilded Age

ARTHUR
CURTISS
JAMES

By Roger Vaughan

ISBN: 978-0-9970672-4-8 (Paperback)
Library of Congress Control Number: 2019933825

STORYARTSMEDIA

Published by Story Arts Media • storyartsmedia.com

Book Design: Joseph Daniel
Maps: Ben Smith
Cover Photograph: Newport Historical Society

Set in Sabon Lt Std. In the early 1960s, the German Master Printers' Association requested that a
new typeface be designed and produced in identical form on both Linotype and Monotype machines
so that text and technical composition would match. Walter Cunz at Stempel responded by commissioning Jan Tschichold to design a new version of Claude Garamond's serene and classical Roman.
The family's name is taken from Jacques Sabon, who introduced Garamond's Romans to Frankfurt.
Sabon has long been a favorite of typographers for setting book text, due to its smooth texture,
and in large part because Tschichold's book typography remains world famous.

PHOTO CREDITS: Mystic Seaport, Rosenfeld Collection 1, Redwood Library endsheets, 184, 186, 187;
Alexander Nesbitt endsheets; New York Historical Society 6, 192, 193, 289, 294, 317; Amherst College
Archives & Collections 8, 12, 17, 21, 166, 347; Yale University Sterling Library 25, 27, 28, 73, 74,
161, 293; Joseph Daniel 33, 135, 215, 238, 257, 347, 369; Seawanhaka Corinthian Yacht Club 36;
New York Yacht Club 36, 369; Atlantic Yacht Club 39; Wikipedia 42, 154-155, 211, 212, 246, 304;
IYRS School of Technology & Trades 45, 106, 107, 172, 196, 222; Mystic Seaport, Historic New
England, Nathanial Stebbins 48-49; Minnesota Historical Society 61, 64, 277; John Mecray 80-81;
University of Arizona Mineral Museum 85, 226; Phelps Dodge Corporation 89, 90, 95, 98, 101, 230;
Herreschoff Marine Museum 104, 177; *Harper's Weekly* 111; Minnesota Reflections 133; The Preser-
vation Society of Newport County 140, 323, 339, 357; National Park Service, Frederick Law Olmsted
National Historic Site 146-147; Newport Historical Society 149, 163, 204, 253; Library of Congress
174, 175, 201, 264; *Fortune Magazine* 183; Meriam Library CSU Chico 213; James J. Hill Center 219;
Arizona Historical Society 229; Sybil Waters Guthrie 238; Joan Malkovich 241, 242; Robin Anderson
242; Getty Images 247, 300; *Time* 249; Smithsonian Institution 265; University of Washington 278-279;
Rocky Mountain News 287; Ida Lewis Yacht Club 295, 296; Edward James Foundation 301;
Philadelphia Record 331; Robert & Oliver Manice 340; Frederic Remington Museum 349;
Newport Daily News 359; Dan Nerney 369

Please visit: acjproject.com for hardcover, electronic and audio versions of this book,
and for the companion film *Of Rails & Sails* on DVD or download.

POD Edition
Printed in the United States

For Kippy

Arthur Curtiss James driving the golden spike at Bieber, California, to complete the third and final transcontinental railway in America.

The American public is totally unfamiliar with the type of person Arthur Curtiss James represents. It does not place him. He is neither a Harriman, making his wealth a means to power, or a Junior Rockefeller administering his fortune as a public trust, nor yet an Astor withdrawn from the sphere of public influence.

He is something else, something more nearly comparable to a landed proprietor of nineteenth century English life, a man who has inherited a great property, who feels the responsibility of his inheritance, who intelligently increases it, but who does not make his holdings his career. Arthur Curtiss James is one of the first and perhaps the best example of the great funded proprietors Industrial Civilization must produce.

Yet at the end he will remain to the public the same shrouded figure he has always been—the least understood rich man in America.

From "Portrait of"
Fortune Magazine
February 1930
Vol 1, No. 1

Contents

Part 1

    1 – ECLIPSE   15

    2 – RAILS   84

    3 – ALOHA   103

    4 – MILESTONES   122

    5 – FEATHERING THE NEST   136

    6 – THE MASQUE   179

    7 – SECOND HOMES   189

Part 2

    8 – THE VISION   207

    9 – CONFLICT   218

    10 – AT HOME   236

    11 – AWEIGH   255

    12 – CONTROL   267

    13 – LIFE   291

    14 – DRIVING THE SPIKE   306

    15 – JOURNEYING ONWARD   322

    16 – LEGACY   343

Back of the Book

    Acknowledgments   358

    Appendix One – Associations   360

    Appendix Two – Genealogy   363

    Selected Bibliography   370

    Index   372

ARTHUR CURTISS JAMES

Part One

Eclipse

Scenario

It was one of those dreary academic teas held on a rainy afternoon during the 1894 spring term at Amherst College, in Amherst, Massachusetts. This particular tea was sparsely attended by the usual mix of faculty, students, and a few alumni. Not many had ventured out into the wet, chilly weather. The mud underfoot was tough on the women's delicate boots, the wind was turning umbrellas inside out, and the rain made a frightful mess of one's hair.

The tall young man in the room, whose neat beard distinguished him from the rest of the clean-shaven gentlemen, was Arthur Curtiss James, class of 1889. What had brought James to Amherst from his home in New York City, no one quite knew, but it surely had to do with college business.

Arthur's father, D. Willis James, was a committed champion of Amherst despite not being an alumnus. He was also a trustee, whose contributions to the college were very large. D. Willis was a partner and director of Phelps Dodge and Company, the biggest producer of copper in America. He was said to be one of the hundred richest men in the country. For his generous support of the school, D. Willis would be made an honorary graduate of Amherst in 1904.

Arthur was better known at Amherst as an alumnus than he had been as a student. He hadn't exactly set the place on fire as an undergraduate. He'd applied himself, done his work, and achieved his degree with good grades, but he wasn't much of a participant in the community. He had belonged to Alpha Delta Phi fraternity, and he had been a member of the Cleveland Club, which had supported Grover Cleveland for president in 1888 (Cleveland lost), but he had avoided most student group activities, including sports. Although he enjoyed playing tennis, his was the plight of a dedicated sailor who had been stuck in an inland college without so much as a large lake in the surrounding area. More significantly, he had shunned the limelight. Even as a student, celebrity was not for him. Arthur's reticence frustrated administrators, faculty, and many fellow students, all of whom saw in the friendly, quiet young man great potential for productive student leadership. Why, they surely had to wonder, didn't strong-minded, reasonable fellows like Arthur take charge instead of the half-baked, limelight-seekers who loved running for anything and everything, then made a mess of whatever they won? Instead, Arthur's remarkable degree of self-possession, his quiet confidence, sustained him very well without public approbation.

As an alumnus Arthur had been more active, mostly representing his father's various business affairs with the school. If faculty and students had been more aware that in 1893 Arthur, at the age of twenty-six, had been elected to the board of the Hampton Institute (Hampton University since 1984), a historically black college founded in 1867 in Washington, D.C., he would have attracted a bit more notice. Although there is no clear explanation of how Arthur had gotten involved with Hampton, there was a tradition of interest in black culture at Amherst. In the 1830s, two organizations within the Amherst

Arthur Curtiss James as an upperclassman at Amherst

student body—the Anti-Slavery Society and the Colonization Society—had conducted lively debates on the subject of race, but both had been dormant since the early 1840s. There had been three black students at Amherst when Arthur was matriculating there, which was noteworthy in the late 1880s.

Another influence on Arthur was surely the arrival in the Northampton area, in 1885, of the novelist and essayist George Washington Cable, whose poignant stories of Creole life in New Orleans presented strong advocacy for social reform. In 1884, Cable and Mark Twain had toured eighty-five cities, giving public readings from their works. But Cable's clarion call for civil rights had been denounced throughout the South, so he moved his family to New England. The presence of a figure of Cable's notoriety would have been difficult to ignore in such a small, interconnected, scholarly area as Amherst/Northampton. The very popular adult Bible class that Cable taught would have appealed to Arthur, as did the Home Culture Clubs that Cable had established during Arthur's undergraduate years to bring diverse people together through common enjoyments like games, cooking, sewing, and gardening. The clubs were supported by Arthur's wife-to-be, Harriet Parsons, and by both Arthur and Harriet as a couple. George Washington Cable was a very dapper fellow who wore stiff white collars, and whose stylized white mustache and trimmed beard were most unusual accoutrements for the day. Was it a coincidence that Arthur first grew his chin whiskers as a student?

There were other influences. Arthur's mother, who was a committed philanthropist herself, had a history of supporting the black community. In 1916, Ellen Stebbins Curtiss James would give $100,000 ($2.3 million today) to an organization benefitting "colored orphans." It's likely that Arthur had also been influenced by Robert Curtis Ogden, a reformer who had promoted education in the South. Ogden and Arthur's father had been associated by their interest in Union Theological Seminary in Upper Manhattan. D. Willis James had given Union the land on which it was built, a gesture that had cost him $1.6 million in 1867 ($26 million today). Both D. Willis and Mr. Ogden were on the board of the Seminary. Ogden was also a friend of Samuel C. Armstrong, who founded Hampton and was its president for many years. The depth of Ogden's connection with Hampton can be measured by the auditorium at the school that was named after him. But Arthur had joined the board of Hampton quietly, as he did everything. Not many knew about what would become his lifelong interest in and generous support of the black school.

Representing his father's interaction with Amherst may have gotten Arthur noticed, but what had really put his name on the alumni map was the notoriety generated by his marriage to Harriet Parsons, a girl from an influential family in nearby Northampton who had spent a year at Smith College studying music. Harriet's father, Sydenham Clark Parsons, was a druggist who had founded the New England branch of the YMCA. It was no secret that the proud Parsons family was less than enthusiastic about their daughter's extremely wealthy suitor from New York City.

The Parsons family was as old-school New England conservative as it got. Nearly all the Parsons were descended from a man named Cornet Joseph Parsons, an English Navy officer who had come to Massachusetts as a teenager in 1635. His ancestry could be traced back to 1290, in Muslo, Ireland. According to *Representative Families of Northampton; a Demonstration of What High Character, Good Ancestry and Heredity Have Accomplished in a New England Town*, Volume I, published by the Northampton Picturesque Publishing Company in 1917, Sydenham Clark Parsons, Harriet's father, was "foremost in the religious work of his day in Northampton, and he was also a strong advocate of total abstinence in regard to the use of intoxicating liquors." He was such an outspoken advocate that he was attacked physically more than once by those who disagreed with him.

Sydenham Parsons's death by suicide, at age forty-nine, had stunned the town of Northampton, and left his wife and four daughters in shock. Today, suicide is responsible for 10 percent of the deaths in the United States. In those days suicide was not only rare, but usually a condemning act for a Christian. The *Northampton Courier* covered the event in unusual detail, reporting Mr. Parsons had been unwell for a week, "much depressed in spirits and at times seeming to be 'out of his head.'" On the night of April 6, 1876, Parsons had avoided his caregivers, slipped out of the house, run half-dressed through an inch of April snow, and despite being a "very expert swimmer," had plunged to his death in the Mill River. The *Courier*'s account reported Parsons had frequently told friends "that some person was intending to injure if not kill him," and concluded: "The only assignable reason [for his suicide] is temporary insanity."

To lose one's father in such a dramatic way at age eight had to have been a life-changing event for Harriet. But as with so much about her life, the cloak of privacy has been well applied. No further mention of her father's suicide has been found in the documents that are available. There is no indication that Arthur knew the details of Sydenham Parsons's demise. Modern married couples tend to share the significant events of their lives, good, bad, or indifferent. In more formal days, that was not such a common practice. Given Harriet's extremely conservative upbringing, one cannot assume she would be forthcoming about such an uncomfortable event, even with her husband. But while often unreliable, gossip has always been an unrelenting means of communication. The Northampton/Amherst area is a tight little island, then and now. One has to assume that Arthur knew.

In any case, as Harriet's suitor, some fifteen years later, Arthur was respectful of the Parsonses's "good ancestry and heredity," but his background was equally strong, and also anchored in the British Isles. Indeed, his father, D. Willis James, was the son of New York-born Daniel James, who had settled in Liverpool during the early years of Phelps Dodge and Company, which at that time shipped American cotton to England and English metals to America. After the death of his mother, young D. Willis had come to New York in 1849 to work in that end of the business, eventually

Harriet Parsons

expanding into railroad and copper investments and becoming exceedingly wealthy. He was extremely pious and generous, while his English cousins were considerably more... lively.

The English side of the James family is a complex tale in itself, one set against the gilt-edge of mid-seventeenth-century England. Daniel James (who shared a stable with the Prince of Wales, who would later become King Edward VII) and his second wife, Sophia, had three boys: Arthur (John Arthur James), Willie (William Dodge James), and Frank. The three were half-uncles of Arthur Curtiss

James. Frank was killed elephant hunting in Africa. Mrs. Walter B. James (Helen Goodsell Jennings), wife of the esteemed New York physician who was Arthur Curtiss James's second cousin, presented her view of the various relationships in a chatty letter to her son, Oliver, in 1943 when she was eighty-four. She wrote:

> *Uncle Daniel left quite a fortune to these boys (Arthur, Willie, and Frank), thus enabling them to marry into the higher social circles.*
>
> *Arthur married Venetia Bentinck, who is related to the present Queen and her godmother. Arthur and Venetia had no children. Arthur had racing stables with King Edward.*
>
> *Willie married Evie Forbes, from a very old family, and I think her father had a title. She was a niece of the Moncrieffs, and very intimate with King Edward. He always stayed with them at West Dean, a wonderful place connected with Good-wood Racetrack. Willie Moncrieff had four sisters who married Dukes, one of them the Duke of Athol.*
>
> *Willie Moncrieff married a cousin of your father's, Edith Boyd. Their children Xandra and Edward were god-children of the King, and Xandra was named for Queen Alexandra.*
>
> *Audrey, youngest daughter of Willie and Evie, was very intimate with the Duke of Windsor, much to his mother's disgust. Audrey married Dudley Coates, a relative of the Coates Auchincloss family. He died and Audrey began her affair with Marshall Field.*
>
> *The English cousins, as you see, were half cousins of your father (Dr. Walter B. James, who died at age 69 on April 7, 1927) and always quite intimate friends of the family here.*

Northampton gossip sometimes included the word "wild" when referring to Harriet's boyfriend. There was no documentation for that description of Arthur other than his reputation as a sailor, an avocation that has always indicated to landlubbers a certain instability, along with a lust for adventure.

The marriage happened, nonetheless, on April 22, 1890. The *Northampton Gazette* devoted many pages to the event, beginning with this only slightly defensive introduction: "Northampton has seen in past years many elaborate weddings, in fact it has been somewhat famous for its celebrations of this character, but for extent and elegance none have surpassed that which is to take place here tomorrow evening."

The *Gazette*'s report went on to praise the solid character traits of both bride and groom, mentioning that Arthur had taught a bible class while at Amherst, and that Harriet had been a leading singer at a local church. Her grandfather, it was noted, was Captain Samuel Parsons, "one of Northampton's best citizens in former days." As for Mr. D. Willis James, the *Gazette* reported only that "he is reputed to be very wealthy."

While he couldn't stymie the *Gazette*'s copy, which included the name of the New York firm decorating the church (and all the other details, from the genus of the profusion of flowers to the colors of the silk bows), and the fact that the accumulation of presents for the bridal pair was so valuable it was being stored in the vaults of the three national banks in Northampton (descriptions of the silver items and jewelry and the givers' names were dutifully provided), and how the uninvited had been allowed into the church after the ceremony to view the elaborate decorations, and how people had climbed nearby trees to get a peek at the reception for 300 people, the fact that not one, single photograph of the event was published in the *Gazette*'s coverage smacked of Arthur Curtiss James's—and Harriet's—determination to curtail their celebrity as much as possible.

On this spring trip to Amherst in 1894, Harriet had not accompanied her husband.

Perhaps it was the inclement weather that had cast a pall on the nattily attired group assembled for tea, but conversation that day was decidedly forced and feeble. When Arthur began talking to an English professor he knew about the joys of Rudyard Kipling's recently published book of poems, the room brightened up. Called *Barrack-Room Ballads*, the Kipling book is a series of poems about the Victorian British Army. The enthusiasm in Arthur's voice indicated he was quite taken by it. He called the ballads brilliant, amusing. He praised Kipling's splendid way with the language, and also with dialect in this case. Arthur James wasn't someone you could hear across a room. His conversational tone was quiet, measured. It was his conviction, his enthusiasm that was contagious, that drew people in. He said one particular stanza from a ballad called "Troopin'" had become such a favorite he knew it by heart. Several pressed him to recite it, and he did, after clearing his throat, lowering his voice slightly for proper effect, and taking care to attend the rhythm of it:

> *They'll turn us out at Portsmouth wharf in cold an' wet an' rain,*
> *All wearin' Injian cotton kit, but we will not complain.*
> *They'll kill us of pneumonia—for that's their little way—*
> *But damn the chills and fever, men, we're goin' 'ome to-day!*

Arthur said he may as well give them the chorus as well, and he did:

> *We're goin' 'ome, we're goin' 'ome,*
> *Our ship is at the shore,*
> *An' you must pack your 'aversack,*
> *For we won't come back no more.*
> *Ho, don't you grieve for me,*
> *My lovely Mary-Ann,*
> *For I'll marry you yit on a fourp'ny bit*
> *As a time-expired man.*

Arthur's smile revealed strong teeth under his moustache, and his eyes twinkled with pleasure at the trickle of delighted appreciation that had greeted his recitation.

One couple moved toward Arthur and introduced themselves as Professor David Todd and his wife, Mabel. He was head of the astronomy department at Amherst. Mabel was a writer.

David was unremarkable-looking, slightly under six feet tall, with a bush of hair and the inattention to wardrobe typical of those with a scientific bent.

Mabel, on the other hand, provided an observer with considerable viewing pleasure. She was slim, attractive, dressed simply, but with attention to every lovely detail, including the elegant little flowers on the lapels of her jacket, painted by her hand.

Mabel's feminine charms were ample. Her pretty face was framed by thick brown hair that was piled in soft waves atop her head. Her face was fascinating. Her mouth was long and sensuous, anchored with dimples at each end, slightly out of line with her eyes, which only helped it conspire with them to achieve a look that wavered between expectation and acceptance. Her eyes were the irresistible magnet. They were ex-

Mabel Loomis Todd

traordinary, a bit too large, too round, and too prominent, wide-set beneath deep brows. At first glance they looked wrong. The eyes of a King Charles spaniel come to mind. But there was something beautifully otherworldly about them. They were totally arresting. Everything eyes can project, from sadness to love, astonishment, and rage, Mabel Todd's eyes could do to a startling degree. To have one moment of eye contact with Mabel—even across a crowded room—was to never forget that face, or the distracting power of those eyes.

Mabel Loomis Todd was a woman of many talents. She was a good painter, an excellent writer, a worthy pianist, a trained soprano, and a popular lecturer. She and David had married in 1879. Their daughter, Millicent, was born in 1880, the year before they came to Amherst. Mabel was one of a cluster of creative people trying to make sense of the Civil War's confounding aftermath. As Christopher Benfey wrote in *A Summer of Hummingbirds: Love, Art and Scandal in the Intersecting Worlds of Emily Dickinson, Mark Twain, Harriet Beecher Stowe, and Martin Johnson Heade*, a book that included Mabel Todd: "Social arrangements and practices that seemed natural before the war—from slaveholding to churchgoing—did not survive the carnage on the killing fields of Antietam and Gettysburg. . . . People tried desperately to hold on to familiar attitudes and emotions that no longer fit new realities."

Benfey continued: "War left behind a static view of existence, a trust in fixed arrangements and hierarchies. [Writers and artists] made a poignant effort to find a redemptive order amid traumatic circumstances . . . they came to see a new dynamism and movement in their lives."

Mabel Todd attracted both men, and women. The well-known American painter Martin Johnson Heade, with whom Mabel had studied, had fallen madly in love with her. In the spring of 1882 she had written in her journal, "What is there in me which so attracts men to me, young and old?" Perhaps it was a mystery to her, but she didn't hesitate to make the most of whatever it was. Heade had been putty in her hands. As Benfey wrote, she had arrived in the sleepy college town of Amherst "expecting to dazzle."

Not long after David had obtained his professorship and the Todds had arrived in Amherst in 1881, they had become close friends of the Dickinsons: Emily, her lawyer brother William Austin, known as Austin, and Austin's wife, Susan. Susan in particular had befriended Mabel to the extent that she had asked her new friend to help with the socialization of her son Ned, then twen-

David and Mabel Todd

ty-one, who suffered from epilepsy. It was a suggestion that would backfire on Susan. The assignment led to Ned falling impossibly in love with Mabel. As a regular visitor to the Dickinson house, Mabel formed a close but restrained relationship with Austin's sister Emily, the famously reclusive poet. Until her death in 1886, Emily liked to read her new work to Mabel, who was always asked to remain out of sight in the adjoining room. Mabel often played the piano for Emily, also from another room. In the end, she would edit all three books of Emily Dickinson's poetry. Mabel's presence in the Dickinson household had also led to a long, torrid, and eventually quite public love affair with Austin Dickinson, who also happened to be the Amherst College treasurer. It began in early 1883. The affair is exhaustively documented by Polly Longsworth in her book, *Austin & Mabel: The Amherst Affair and Love Letters of Austin Dickinson and Mabel Loomis Todd*. Martin Johnson Heade could only curse his luck.

Mabel Todd in mourning for Austin

As a willing participant in what these days might be called an "open" marriage, David Todd was no slouch as a philanderer himself. In the months leading up to his marriage to Mabel, according to Longsworth, Mabel "was coping simultaneously with a major disenchantment, one David had hinted at through his courtship letters, and now revealed." But Longsworth continues: "Mabel was no Victorian prude. David's virility and pleasure in physical intimacy were powerfully attractive to her." What most concerned Mabel, according to Longsworth, was the possibility that David had "low tastes." For Mabel, cultural superiority was of primary importance, a factor that would surely stimulate the fondness she would develop for Arthur.

As a student, Arthur had been exposed to his share of Northampton area gossip. It was a small town (population 4,500 in 1890), and the college student body totaled only 358 when he was there. Even if you ignored gossip, in a town that size gossip would find you. But gossip was of passing interest to Arthur. And Mabel's affair with Austin would not go public until Austin passed away, in 1895. At that time, a distraught Mabel publicly mourned her lover, always appearing in black dress, cape, and veil—much to Susan Dickinson's aggravation.

David Todd led the way to Arthur at the tea because he had overheard the quoted stanzas. He too was a devotee of Rudyard Kipling. He asked if Arthur knew "The Ballad of East and West," and if he realized Kipling had written the famous lines, "Oh, East is East, and West is West, and never the twain shall meet." Before Arthur could answer, David went on to quote from the ballad:

The Colonel's son has taken horse, and a raw, rough dun was he,
With the mouth of a bell and the heart of Hell and the head of a gallows-tree.

Arthur said he had always considered "The Ballad of East and West" to be one of Kipling's finest poems. He praised the prevailing theme of respect for bravery and courage in the poem, and contributed a favorite couplet of his own:

There is rock to the left, and rock to the right, and low lean thorn between,
And ye may hear a breech-bolt snick where never a man is seen.

As the two men chuckled at their shared pleasure, Mabel rolled those magnificent eyes at the friendly literary jousting between them, a stunning gesture fired at Arthur that abruptly brought the quoting of Kipling—and everything else—to a standstill.

Regaining his composure, Arthur asked the professor if there was any news from the heavens. Professor Todd said the news was a total eclipse of the sun scheduled for 1896; big news, actually, because while total eclipses take place every year or so in various parts of the world, many of them can only be viewed mid-ocean, which makes photographing the corona, the spectacular ring of fire around the edge of the blacked-out sun, most difficult if not impossible. The total eclipse in 1896 would best be seen from mid-Pacific Ocean. The last land-based viewing of a total eclipse had been in Russia, in 1887, a year after David and Mabel had climbed Japan's Mount Fuji to photograph a previous one. Much had been advanced in the way of viewing and recording techniques since then, and Todd said he and his team had begun prepping for the event.

Arthur asked where one would best view this 1896 eclipse. Japan was David's answer. Esashi, to be exact, a small town 1,100 miles north of Yokohama. Esashi would be smack dab in the center of the sun's narrow, 100 percent blackout path. David explained that Esashi was located on one of Japan's northern islands.

Arthur wondered how the astronomers and all their gear would make their way to Esashi. David said arranging transportation was, in fact, a problem.

Their conversation was interrupted by others making the rounds, and while Arthur exchanged pleasantries with various people one could tell his mind was elsewhere. As soon as he could do so, Arthur rejoined the Todds, taking them aside. He told David he had an idea. It was just the germ of an idea, really, but the more he thought about it, the more he thought it could work. He told David that he had a yacht, a schooner of 130 feet. It was called *Coronet*. He said the vessel was new to him, but it hadn't taken much sailing to know what a fine, ocean-worthy, capable craft it was. He said *Coronet* was a rather famous yacht, the winner of the 1887 transatlantic race to England, a yacht requiring a crew of fifteen or twenty. It had wonderful, spacious accommodations, and it carried plenty of food and water. He neglected to mention it did not have an engine, which was unusual for a yacht of its size.

Thinking out loud, Arthur said he could send *Coronet* around Cape Horn; in fact, she had been the third private yacht ever to round that wild and wooly Cape back in 1888, three years after she was built. Meanwhile, Arthur, his wife Harriet, and the astronomers, could take the train cross-country. The Great Northern Railway had been finished in 1892. His father's friend and partner, James Jerome Hill, had built it, and Hill might even be talked into lending them his private car for the trip. They could join *Coronet* in San Francisco and sail to Japan!

Professor Todd was overcome by this sudden, grand plan coming from Arthur James. Although he had never had him in his class, he knew Arthur had been highly regarded as a student. He knew well that the James family was a force, making huge contributions to the college. They were conservative, rational people; reliable, not known for hair-brained schemes or false promises. They were good Christians. Arthur was a shoe-in for trustee at Amherst in a few years.

David Todd was no sailor. He'd never so much as gotten his feet wet. The idea of a transpacific voyage on any vessel was anathema to him. But the difficulty of getting to Japan for the eclipse was extreme. He could handle photographing the corona. Figuring out how to get people, equipment, and himself to Japan was another question. Just the cost of such a trip would be a huge stumbling block. So he gave Arthur Curtiss James a quizzical look and asked him if he really thought such an extraordinary trip was possible. Arthur just smiled. He had already begun working on the logistics.

Today the storied schooner-yacht *Coronet* can be found on Thames Street in Newport, Rhode Island. If you didn't know about it, you would never see it because it is covered by a 200-foot-long shed located between the waterfront and a three-story, industrial-size brick building that houses the International Yacht Restoration School (IYRS). In 2018, as this is written, *Coronet* is not really a yacht, not quite. It is a yacht in progress, a replication of the oldest (1885) existing yacht of the Victorian era, and one of the largest surviving grand yachts ever built. The project started as a restoration, but only the keelson (a sturdy timber just above the keel) could be preserved.

Being in *Coronet*'s presence is always a moving experience. One normally views large yachts afloat as one views icebergs, because so much of them is underwater. But during a build, bottom work, or a restoration, the bottom of the vessel's keel is often at ground level, causing the hull of even a small yacht to loom over an observer because of the flare of its topsides. In *Coronet*'s case, the keel is at an adult's chest height, meaning the sheer (where hull meets deck) is a good 20 feet overhead. The facts that *Coronet* is 131 feet long, with a beam of 27 feet, and will weigh 160 tons when finished, complete the massive picture.

It's also a beautiful picture, first of all because the complex wood construction that is a classic yacht, with its sensuous curves and powerful structure, is a work of art. *Coronet* is a lovely, shapely creation from the drawing board of William Townsend. His is not a household name in the world of yacht design. Townsend drew shapely, extremely seaworthy schooners for harbor pilots in the mid-1800s, but his most notable yacht was *Sappho*, the 140-foot schooner that won the last two races of the 1871 America's Cup after defender *Columbia* had been damaged. With her clipper bow, *Sappho* was admittedly based on the lines of *America*, winner of the race around the Isle of Wight in 1851 that gave birth (and name) to America's Cup competition. *Coronet* was different, with an even more pronounced plumb bow than Townsend had been putting on his pilot schooners. But for *Coronet* he retained the low freeboard and graceful sheer line of *America* and *Sappho*. One hundred and thirty-three years later, rather than being antiquated, *Coronet*'s plumb bow happens to match the current trend in modern yacht design. William Townsend was at the front of a group of talented designers who would usher in the gilded age of yachting with their understanding of the synchronicity of beauty and performance.

Standing on the second-floor balcony surrounding the *Coronet* replication at IYRS, even in frames and only partially planked, one can marvel over the gorgeous flow of the yacht's stern quarter. The exquisite shape of the curved wineglass transom that measures 15 feet across becomes permanently imprinted on an observer's memory. For the current owner's pleasure, and at his bidding, the transom has been finished way ahead of its time. It has been painted white, the name having been carved into it, with each letter gleaming in gold leaf. It serves as an incentive to the builders, who must accommodate themselves to snail-like progress caused by erratic funding, skeleton crews, and the sheer heft of everything. One understands the owner's wish, because the finished transom gives observers a wonderful lift. On the surrounding balcony, just a few feet from the transom, and slightly below it, one has the aspect of being in a dinghy, rowing close under the stern of the great yacht at anchor. It's only a small, romantic stretch to imagine *Coronet* afloat again as it was more than one hundred years ago. It gives one shivers.

Some modern materials are being used in *Coronet*'s replication, but for the most part the lovely schooner is being restored pretty much as she had been built at the shipyard of Cornelius and Richard Poillon in Brooklyn, New York. The hull frames, more than sixty of them, are 24 inches on center and measure 10 inches wide, tapering to 5 inches at the top where they intersect with the deck beams. They are white oak from the Royal Danish Forest, timber available exclusively by application. Deck beams are 8-by-8-inch yellow pine, 10 inches thick at the ends. The planking, also Royal Danish white oak, is 3 inches thick. Each

Coronet, a work in progress at the International Yacht Restoration School

plank is 28 to 39 feet long, fastened by 1¼-inch black locust dowels, and secured by 8-inch, square bronze spikes. Just lifting one plank takes two strong people. Massive. It's all impossibly massive. The cutting and shaping of all that wood has filled the shed with a heavenly aroma. The antique yacht is like a patient etherized upon a table; unconscious, but definitely alive.

Coronet arrived in Newport Harbor on her own bottom in 1995. There wasn't much left of her back then. She had short, stubby posts where towering masts had been, and plywood deckhouses hastily nailed together. The old girl was falling apart everywhere. She was a sad sight, barely afloat. Thanks to the good work of a well-known maritime artist, the late John Mecray, and yachtswoman Elizabeth Meyer—best known for her restoration of the J-Class sloop *Endeavour*—who had helped John found IYRS in 1992, *Coronet* was placed in IYRS's hands for restoration.

The replication (or restoration) of any sizable classic yacht is an immense project. Anyone who has restored a house knows all too well the unhappy surprises that can lurk beneath layers of construction. Boat restorations are the same, only more challenging because of the perilous intimacy boats have with water. Given her size, age, and lack of adequate care, *Coronet* has stretched the known limits of restoration. There were no plans drawn when *Coronet* was designed—lines from half models were lofted on the shipyard floor—but a bunch of old photographs helped immensely. Research by Harold Rosengren, who was working at IYRS, and Commodore Henry H. Anderson Jr., done at the shipyard in Greenport, Long Island, and the Brooklyn Museum, verified that the half model of *Coronet* in the New York Yacht Club Grill Room, from which lines for the replication were taken, was made by a shipbuilder in Greenport. In the Rare Book Room of the New York Yacht Club library, Anderson and Elizabeth Meyer found the survey for her measurement rating by the club measurer that provided supplemental data.

One of the first things IYRS did was hire a structural archeologist who spent months on board recording every existing variation in color, every outline of a shape, every depression, every screw hole, and ultimately recreating the layout of the vessel, both above and below deck. Then the work of disassembling began. When workers were done removing timbers, planks, gear, fittings, and furnishings that were corroded, dried out, or rotted—including the piano—there wasn't much left. To revive *Coronet*, to make her seaworthy again, this "restoration" had to mean a virtually complete rebuild. That's why, more than twenty years later, *Coronet* remains a work in progress.

Why bother? Because of the history, of course. This is the oldest grand yacht extant! And the beauty. *Coronet* was famous in her day. In 1887, as a young thoroughbred, she beat the formidable, 121-foot schooner *Dauntless* in a race across the Atlantic. The owners of the two big yachts were prominent businessmen. Rufus T. Bush, for whom *Coronet* was designed and built, was an oil refiner who had made a name for himself by boldly testifying against the rebates the railroads were giving Standard Oil to transport its products. *Dauntless'* owner, Caldwell Hart Colt, was the heir to the famous firearms company started by his father. He would become a vice commodore of the New York Yacht Club in 1888. The *New York Times'* coverage of the race, and the $10,000 wager that was at stake, filled every inch of page one, catapulting *Coronet* to glory. A year later, *Coronet* rounded ferocious Cape Horn east-to-west—the so-called "wrong way" because of the prevailing westerly winds. After a succession of owners—including Arthur Curtiss James from 1893 to 1898—the schooner ended up in 1905 in the hands of a religious organization called The Kingdom, an apocalyptic sect that sailed her around the world on their evangelical missions until they gave her up to IYRS, ninety years to the day after acquiring her. The Kingdom had sailed *Coronet* twice to the Holy Lands and once around the world, but after its patriarch was convicted of manslaughter, and the death of six crew members from scurvy, *Coronet* had been mothballed in Gloucester before she was brought to IYRS.

* * *

Arthur Curtiss James and his father were *Coronet*'s fourth owners. D. Willis James bought the boat for himself and his son in 1893, when Arthur was twenty-six. The family lived in a fashionable neighborhood on East 39th Street near Park Avenue in New York City, where Arthur was born. Their summer home was in landlocked Madison, New Jersey. But those born to sail, like Arthur, find a way. Manhattan was a center for yachting and small boat sailing. We don't know where he learned to sail, but Arthur was clearly drawn to the Seawanhaka Corinthian Yacht Club, which was founded in 1871 aboard a yacht. In 1881, Seawanhaka members began to sail out of a facility on Staten Island before a proper clubhouse was purchased eleven years later on Center Island, New York, near the town of Oyster Bay. Arthur would join the club in January 1893 and be elected commodore in 1901, an honor that indicates a reasonably long, close relationship with an organization.

A year after being accepted by Seawanhaka, Arthur obtained membership in the New York Yacht Club in February 1894. Founded in 1844, the New York Yacht Club was considered the nation's oldest and most prominent yacht club, with a membership of old New York money, a fleet list of large and prominent sailing and steam vessels, a heavy racing schedule that included an annual coastal cruise, and possession of the America's Cup, the most exclusive trophy in international sailboat racing. *Coronet* was right at home in the club's fleet.

Arthur also belonged to the Atlantic Yacht Club in Brooklyn. Founded in 1866, the Atlantic was a very prestigious club, with an impressive clubhouse on Gowanus Bay (later moving to equally impressive quarters at Sea Gate). Atlantic boasted a membership list of the social elite that included J. P. Morgan, Sir Thomas Lipton, George Jay Gould, and a raft of New York's prominent families. Although it was best known for the quality of its sailors and for its excellent racing program, the club also

Seawanhaka Corinthian Yacht Club on Center Island in 1883 (*top*), and The New York Yacht Club Newport Station in 1895

gained a reputation for its theatrical productions. The club accepted Arthur as a member in 1895, when he was twenty-six.

This new boat, *Coronet*, was meant to be a father-son share, but the fact was that as one of two partners, and a member of the board, D. Willis was consumed with running Phelps Dodge, and developing the railroads that were so vital to hauling copper ore to the smelters. He had little or no time for sailing. Tim Murray, who as son of the engineer was born aboard *Coronet*, would become the yacht's caretaker. In *Coronet: Whither Away?* Murray compiled a history of her many owners based on the

Atlantic Yacht Club at Sea Gate in 1898, when Arthur was a member

logs of their cruises. According to Murray, D. Willis James was aboard just one time. He sailed with Arthur from New York to New London, Connecticut, in the summer of 1895.

Like so many wealthy men of his generation, D. Willis had started his son at the bottom of Phelps Dodge, in the mailroom. But that was more gesture than a job the young man was expected to fully embrace. Arthur's story does not take after that of Horatio Alger. Arthur's "accident of birth" had put him front row, center. No matter in what situation one is cast upon this planet—rich or poor, male or female, talented or bereft—there seems to be a certain amount of discomfort involved. The grass truly is always greener somewhere else, for everyone, it seems. The remarkable thing about Arthur Curtiss James is that he was born well suited to be wealthy and powerful. He was comfortable in his exclusive skin.

In February 1891 young Arthur had been made a director of the Copper Queen Consolidated Mining Company in Bisbee, Arizona, Phelps Dodge's biggest property, a move that extricated him from the mailroom. He had a lot to learn about the business, but he was not only a quick study, he took it seriously. Many are the tales of second- or third-generation wealth that end prematurely in death on the highway, or in a sanitarium. That would not be Arthur's fate. He was a chip off older, well-sculpted blocks.

Arthur's grandfather Daniel James had been a wholesale grocer in New York in the 1820s. He had gotten involved in Phelps Dodge when that company was in its formative stages by marrying a daughter of founder Anson Phelps, who had begun his career as a small businessman in Hartford, Connecticut. Phelps possessed a natural feel for business opportunities. As Robert Glass Cleland reports in *A History of Phelps Dodge*, Anson Phelps had expanded from selling saddles and harnesses in New England to doing business with plantations in the South. By the time Daniel James, then a young merchant, had fallen in love with, and married, Phelps's daughter Elizabeth in 1828, Phelps's business had grown to the extent that he owned a couple of square-rigged coastal packets of 200 or more tons that were carrying American cotton from Southern ports to Europe and returning to New York with iron, copper, tin, and other metals that were in high demand in the United States. Another of Phelps's daughters, Melissa, had married William Dodge, proprietor of a dry-goods store. Because the two sons-in-law shared Anson Phelps's elevated ideals, strong convictions, and devout religious beliefs, Phelps proposed the three of them form a family partnership. Thus, Phelps Dodge and Phelps, James & Co in Great Britain, were born. Daniel James and Elizabeth would go to Liverpool, England, and run that side of the business. Elizabeth would die in 1847. Daniel remarried two years later to Sophia Hitchcock, a relative of Tommy Hitchcock, a well-known polo player of the time. Daniel and Elizabeth's surviving son, D. Willis (his brother had died in a carriage accident), was sent to America to be educated, and to work in the Phelps Dodge company. D. Willis would marry Ellen Stebbins Curtiss, and they would become the parents of two children, Daniel Willis Jr., and Arthur Curtiss. Daniel had died at the age of ten months, leaving Arthur to be raised as an only child.

Cleland points out that Anson Phelps, William Dodge, and Daniel James were all raised in the English Puritan tradition and, that they adhered to the strict religious creeds of John Calvin and John Knox. They considered all of mankind to be depraved and unworthy. God had selected certain people for salvation. That selection, which happened to coincide for the most part with the degree of material success and power the selectee had attained, and the accompanying predestination, was unconditional. Those whom God selected would persevere in faith, and would be eternally secure. "The present generation," Cleland keenly observed in 1952, "harshly intolerant of such a creed, has little understanding of the authority it exercised on the thinking and conduct of its adherents, or of the contributions that those same adherents made to human welfare and social progress."

The three men were known for their strong sense of social duty. "They submitted their own souls," Cleland wrote, "to the same searching scrutiny that they applied to their business ledgers. Their religion was the most real and important thing in their lives. They saw the hand of God in every conceivable phase of human life."

Daniel James's son, D. Willis, who was born in Liverpool, England, and who attended the University of Edinburgh for a year, was brought into Phelps Dodge in 1853, when founder Anson

Phelps died. He was seventeen when he arrived in America. In five years he would become a partner in the company. D. Willis's 5 percent interest jumped to 12 percent when Anson Phelps's son died suddenly of smallpox, four years later. D. Willis's father died in 1876. Two years later, two other partners left Phelps Dodge to enter the banking business, while a third retired. That left William E. Dodge Jr.—son of another one of the three original partners—and D. Willis James, as the sole partners of the company.

D. Willis James

D. Willis James had an early interest in railroads that was stimulated by his father and other relatives, who always included him when they invested in American railroads. As Henry H. Anderson writes in his 2010 monograph, *James Railway System*, "by 1873, along with financier John Steward Kennedy of Jesup & Company, D. Willis had become a stockholder and director of two railroads in Iowa."

Historians give both William Dodge Jr. and D. Willis James high marks. Dodge is remembered as a courtly man whom employees called "The Earl," using his middle name as a British title they thought was fitting. James's presence in the office was said to be forceful, often irascible, but his outbursts were quickly over and forgotten. Together, the two men are lauded for their virtues of integrity and fair dealing. "They refused to prostitute their authority," Cleland wrote, "as sole directors of the affairs of a great company, for selfish or discreditable ends. They gave generously to philanthropies of every kind, as their fathers and grandfathers had done before them." Also like his father and grandfather, D. Willis was a deeply religious man who regarded his wealth as a trust. The quote most often attributed to D. Willis James is, "Wealthy men ought to give until they feel it."

When copper was discovered in Arizona, in 1880, the man selected by Dodge and James to evaluate various claims was a chemist by the name of Dr. James Douglas. Little did Dodge and James know how well Douglas would enhance the leadership model that had been forged at Phelps Dodge. Douglas was a brilliant chemist, a scholarly man who was perfect for the job he was assigned. But he was also another devout man who would end up leading Phelps Dodge, first as director of the biggest mine in Arizona, later on as president of the company. Unlike many of his contemporaries, James Douglas promoted fair wages, shorter working hours, and more leisure-education time for his employees. He believed in "all the essential rights and the intrinsic dignity of human nature."

It's clear that a most unusual, effective, and very humanitarian situation had been established at Phelps Dodge over the first sixty years of the company's existence. Arthur Curtiss James had been raised in line with the same principles his father and others had applied to the company as well as to their own lives, and the son had wholeheartedly subscribed to them. D. Willis was both father and mentor to Arthur. As an only child, Arthur had strong relationships with his parents. Being part of Phelps Dodge was appealing to Arthur James. The railroads the company was developing were of particular interest. He was most influenced by James J. Hill, one of the great railroad innovators of the day, who was both a close friend and a trusted business associate of his father's.

But Arthur was young. That he would have a career in the Phelps Dodge hierarchy, if he wished, was a foregone conclusion. But it wasn't quite the time. His father was in charge, running things capably. From him, both day and night, Arthur was getting an education about all issues on the company table. Such privileged information had surely led to insights about the folly of participating in the business too soon. Stories of bitter father–son struggles over policy in the boardroom were already legendary. Why risk that? And this confident young man had nothing to prove. He was already a member of the board, and the boss's son! He didn't need to make waves in the company to prove his worth. His inheritance, both personal and corporate, was assured.

If one of the great yachts of its day hadn't been rigged, crewed, and ready to sail at (and under) his command, it might have been different. In his wisdom, had D. Willis James craftily provided *Coronet* as an irresistible alternative for his sailing-obsessed son? Since his graduation from Amherst in 1890, Arthur had been taking courses at New York Nautical College to earn his master's papers. Since childhood he had been reading books about ocean voyages under sail. He was hopelessly drawn to the sea.

Arthur had been given *Coronet* in October 1893. Just four months after remarkably pronouncing the 160-ton, 133-foot, two-masted tops'l schooner-rigged vessel that was without auxiliary power to be "an ideal type in which the young and inexperienced sailor could gain experience," Arthur, his wife Harriet, and three friends, had departed the Brooklyn, New York, waterfront where *Coronet* was moored, for a cruise to the West Indies. As one of his guests wrote in his report of the trip, "Only Jake would consider a 130-foot schooner to be a perfect training vessel for the inexperienced." "Jake" is what his friends called Arthur on board. Superstition about leaving port on a Friday was not the only caution dismissed by the young and inexperienced Jake. It was two degrees below zero. Snow had fallen the previous evening. Weather bulletins indicated a blizzard was brewing. *Coronet*'s salty old Captain Crosby pronounced it a "dirty day." None of that diminished Arthur's enthusiasm for going to sea.

According to the report of guests Arthur Francis and William Kingsley, at 8:00 a.m. on February 16, sail was made. With double reefs, *Coronet* tore through the Narrows at 10 knots. They turned south, and in three hours logged 36 nautical miles. "Such a following sea there was," the guests wrote, "that *Coronet* seemed to be chasing herself, and was awash from stem to stern." They wrote of the helmsman being lashed to the wheel, of lifelines being strung. They wrote of Jake and Arthur Francis holding fast to the quarter rail, and being surprised "by a perfect deluge of green water, wresting both from their hold, and hurling Jake to the binnacle which he fortunately grasped."

Arthur at the helm of *Coronet*, with Captain Crosby in the background

That night was said to be a frightful experience for inexperienced yachtsmen, several of whom prayed they might live to see terra firma again. It was tough sledding for the veterans as well. The mate had called for volunteers to work aloft, not wanting to order men to do so. With the temperature hovering in the low 30s, one can imagine all passengers were questioning the decision to willingly sail into such trying conditions.

By morning the wind had abated and the air temperature was up a few degrees, but wind against the Gulf Stream current produces a most uncomfortable seaway. The passengers huddled below until dusk. When they finally ventured on deck, it was with trepidation. "Jake alone was master of the situation," the guests wrote. "We agreed it would take a diabolical mixture and an unearthly upheaval to disturb his equanimity."

Mr. Crosby might have been *Coronet*'s captain, but when Arthur was on board, he was not just the owner, he was Master of the yacht. Being Master was a great source of pride for him, and rather than cause him to sit back and give orders, it gave him license to lead by example in all departments. He was everywhere on board, putting in many hours on navigation, shooting sun and stars with sextant and doing the mathematics to ascertain the yacht's position. He stood regular watches with the crew. He kept precise logs that stated position, conditions, course and speed, and very little else. He constantly examined all aspects of the yacht for wear and tear. On Sundays he read the religious service, which was attended by the paid hands as well as guests. He loved steering the yacht, "fondling the spokes as one would caress a pet dog," one guest noted. And as host, another guest wrote, "he hides his feelings during difficult times, and braces everyone up by being encouraging."

That Arthur was a gregarious host was lucky. It is evident from the frequent bouts with seasickness mentioned that many of the guests aboard his various yachts were friends, not "sailors" accustomed to the rigors associated with venturing upon blue water. Even a luxurious yacht like *Coronet*, with its piano, library, hand-carved furnishings, gourmet galley, and a raft of creature comforts equaling those found in the most comfortable homes, was at the mercy of Neptune's whims. Those whims can be downright violent at times.

It warmed up, eventually. The Jameses and their friends enjoyed the rest of their cruise south in more typical fashion: playing card games in the evening; playing quoits on deck and reading during the day; exalting over turmoils of porpoises frolicking in the bow wave; bathing on deck for the men; swimming;

and lowering the dinghy during periods of dead calm for the thrill of rowing a small boat in mid-ocean. Their landfall was the island of Barbados, where the guests reported that "Jake's oily persuasion" got the better of the officious harbor master, and that "his suave manner with all officials was certainly irreproachable, and occasioned good natured bantering."

The party inspected sugar plantations, took photos of "little naked pickaninnies" running beside their carriage "begging 'Just one penny,'" watched island birds, and were introduced to the West Indian Swizzle, a mix of coconut milk and gin "and heaven knows what else which produces a most peculiar sensation in the head." They visited several islands, including tiny Dominica. There, during a trail ride, Arthur—distracted by the beauties of the nature island's lush flora and elusive fauna—was thrown off his "fiery steed" when it bolted for home. Only his pride was damaged. That was repaired upon leaving St. Thomas for the trip home, when he swung his yacht gracefully around in close quarters, made sail, and departed in grand style, causing his guests to admire "the beautiful yacht and her masterly management."

The trip home was uneventful until they encountered a northeasterly gale off Cape Hatteras that ultimately forced them to turn and run with it under bare poles. In nine hours they were blown 90 miles in the wrong direction before they could resume their course to Brooklyn.

It was after that initial voyage that Arthur visited Amherst and encountered David and Mabel Todd over a cup of tea.

The depression of 1893 was in full cry. It began when the Philadelphia & Reading Railroad went into receivership just as world agricultural prices were falling. These events triggered the failures of hundreds of banks and businesses, and several other major railroads dependent on a Pennsylvania company that, by 1870, had become the largest corporation in the world. A domino effect kicked in, starting with the stock market plunging, causing foreign investors to withdraw funds. Meanwhile, the

Coronet, **with a bone in her teeth**

agricultural depression already plaguing the West and the South deepened. This worldwide financial crisis would last four years before recovery began.

Depressions raise major havoc with the workingman. The wealthy may be inconvenienced by a depression, but they are not terribly threatened. Their wealth is usually diversified in "safe" repositories. For the extremely wealthy, even the inconvenience is minor. So it was that Arthur and Harriet and their friends kept sailing.

They took *Coronet* north that summer into the lovely Bras d'Or Lakes on Cape Breton Island, Nova Scotia. That trip was notable for two reasons. First of all, they spent two lively evenings with Alexander Graham Bell, who was then forty-six years old. After inventing the telephone in 1876, Bell had begun summering at Baddeck in 1885, on the north shore of the northern-most Bras d'Or Lake, with his wife Mabel, "Ma" Bell, and their daughters. Bell's family had emigrated from Scotland to Canada twenty years before, but he did much of his work in Washington, D.C. He moved to little Baddeck on the north shore of the northern lake just a year after visiting the town. Bell said he had traveled the globe, but Cape Breton surpassed all he had ever seen "for simple beauty." Bell had quickly set up shop in Baddeck to further his experiments with sound, teaching the deaf to speak, lighter-than-air craft, and hydrofoil boats.

The quality of the exchange between the considerably younger Arthur and the esteemed inventor on those evenings— one at the Bells' home, the other aboard *Coronet*—can be measured by the sendoff that ensued the morning when *Coronet* sailed away on the tide. "We saluted Mr. Bell as we passed his house," a guest on board wrote, "and were answered by his launch whistle, a large bell on the piazza, and several small guns. We fired a second cartridge, and the shore demonstrations were renewed vigorously."

The other notable event that summer in Bras d'Or was *Coronet* running aground. The pilot was responsible, electing to tack through the narrow St. Andrews Channel instead of the wider, Great Bras d'Or Passage to the west. Today, a local yachtsmen says he wouldn't even take his 35-foot lobster boat through St. Andrews, which is often more narrow than *Coronet*'s length. But the buck always stops in the skipper's cabin. Arthur was not pleased, and Captain Crosby's language was said to be "eloquently profane." No injuries were sustained, so gently did the big schooner engage the bottom. But there was concern about the yacht. Luckily she had fetched up on sand instead of on the rocks on the other side of the passage. It was decided two of the guests would be dispatched to North Sidney to arrange for tugs to free the yacht. The grounding of such an impressive vessel so close aboard galvanized everyone in the area. Soon dozens of people were gathered, kibitzing about the best way to free *Coronet*, wondering how they might help, and generally creating a social event out of an unfortunate, but apparently benign, situation.

"We became particularly interested in one of them, a Captain Livingston," a guest wrote. "He furnished the horse and buggy, to say nothing of his oldest daughter as driver, that conveyed the men to North Sydney." The rest would have plenty of time to kill, since North Sydney was a good 40 miles distant. "We went to Livingston's house," the guest wrote, "and saw his wife and nine children. Mrs. Livingston was much alarmed about her daughter, who had ridden to Sidney with two gay young Americans. And with good reason, for [the two men] constantly referred to their drive with Julie and her horse, Penny." In the parlance of the day, "gay" was characterized solely by cheerfulness, or being lightheartedly excitable.

The flooding tide, combined with some kedging, eventually freed the yacht. The tugboats arrived too late to be of assistance, but they towed *Coronet* around to North Sydney, where everyone aboard could collect telegrams and letters.

There were two other trips on *Coronet* before the yacht would be sent around Cape Horn to San Francisco, where Arthur, Harriet, the Todds, and other scientists from Amherst would join the boat for the voyage to Japan. *Coronet* made a second trip to the West Indies in March 1895, and to the Gulf of St. Lawrence in July. Both were social events with guests on board. Fun was the primary order of both trips, with Harriet and friends doing silly things like welcoming Arthur and the shore party back on board by playing "Yankee Doodle" on kazoos made of combs, and stuffing paper into one another's boots on April Fool's Day.

The irritable rash of seasickness while underway was only a temporary deterrent. The West Indies trip included a stop in Bermuda. As one guest unashamedly bragged of that visit, "In the evening we trimmed the deck with flags and lanterns, and some people from the hotel came on board. We put on lots of airs with the landlubbers and patronized them tremendously. But when the people cleared out we all got together and said how nice we all are, and how much we like each other and love the *Coronet*."

Arthur continued to preside over Sunday services, but he did so with a suitable lack of formality, "clad in the lightest flannels, minus necktie, with sleeves rolled up." They went on to Jamaica and Cuba this time, roaming "interesting" streets by donkey cart, and enjoying their roles as tourists.

As they left for the Gulf of St. Lawrence in July, Arthur and Harriet took advantage of the calm weather to sit below and take stock of their shipmates. Under the heading "Live," they listed a crew of sixteen men plus Captain Crosby. This heading was categorized as "useful." Then came "guests," categorized as "diverting but supernumerary." Among the more humorous entries were Andrew P. "Pete" Alford, a fraternity brother of Arthur's from Amherst, "commonly called Pete, whose chief duty was to smile and look pleasant, bring cushions from below for the ladies, spin yarns of his experiences in the woods, which frequently degenerated into 'though I once shot a deer'; Hon. Charles Falconer Sterns, sometimes inelegantly alluded to as 'Push,' whose duty was to charm the ladies with his gallant com-

pliments and military bearing, and in the performance of such
duty he was never found neglectful; and Howard Wilson, known
as 'Tug,' who alone on the stock sheet might have been designated as 'useless.'" The Gulf of St. Lawrence report was signed by
the initials "HW"—Tug himself.

Fishing was one object of the St. Lawrence trip. They made
their way through the Strait of Canso, which separates Cape
Breton Island from Nova Scotia, and on to the little village of
Paspébiac in northern New Brunswick. They had picked up a
pilot in Port Hawkesbury, on the Strait. The man came aboard
with a flourish and such a lively line of patter that *Coronet*'s
guests conspired to have some fun with him. "We were rather
ashamed of ourselves," HW writes, "when we evoked his sympathy by pretending that Pete had come aboard as an alternative
to another term in a Keeley Institute." Keeley centers were, at
the time, well-known for the treatment of alcoholics. Much to
the delight of his mates, Pete warmed to the assigned role by
expounding on the temperance lectures he had received on previous visits to Keeley. A sudden northeaster brought a temporary
halt to the hilarity.

Arthur again proved his mettle as a host by finding three
local Indian guides in Paspébiac who said they could put them
on some fish on the nearby Bonaventure River. In birch-bark
canoes, no less. Peter, the head guide, was said to look as if he
just stepped out of a tale by James Fenimore Cooper. Another,
Gerome—a name the visitors immediately changed to Geroni-
mo—said he was one hundred and one years old. Perhaps it was
that slight manipulation of the truth that caused him to be the
random victim of Miss Bessie Stokes's errant cast in her determined attempt to catch the largest trout in the river. Her "red
ibis" lure lodged itself "in the red man's trousers just where it
was most awkward to extricate the barbed hook." HW confessed
he laughed so hard he fell into the bottom of the canoe. On the
way back to the boat, Peter Alford shot a couple of ducks, one of
which was later determined to be a "web-footed crow."

The *Coronet* cruises proved to be great fun, but they were also relatively safe, coastal exercises that allowed Arthur to gain experience with the vessel he would soon be sailing across the Pacific Ocean to Japan. Arthur's five years of classes at New York Nautical, during which time he exhausted the school's course syllabus and eventually passed his master's exam, counted for a lot, but there is nothing like putting one's hands on the real thing when it comes to seamanship and navigation. When the real thing is a schooner of 160 tons and 131 feet, with scores of lines, a crew of sixteen, half a dozen guests, thousands of square feet of sail, no engine, a very slow response time, and a mind of its own in many situations, having hands-on is imperative. *Coronet*'s main boom was 79 feet long. One can barely imagine the damage such a formidable cudgel could do when driven by several thousand square feet of canvas filled with wind if it had been allowed to become out of control. In Captain Crosby, Arthur had a great teacher. Crosby was also a man whose salty manner and direct approach to situations coincided with Arthur's own, direct handling of events. Given the choice of sightseeing ashore, or staying aboard to tinker with his vessel, Arthur would have opted for tinkering every time if he could.

But he also acknowledged the social aspect of yachting, as he once wrote: "One of the most delightful experiences to the yachtsman on summer cruises in home waters is the harbor life in such ports as Bar Harbor, Newport, and the other resorts. . . . To many this social life is the highest idea of yachting, and were it eliminated, the chief charm of the sport would be taken away."

By the end of 1895, Arthur had a detailed plan in place for sailing *Coronet* across the Pacific to Japan for Professor Todd and his crew to observe and photograph the eclipse of the sun. Step One had been to put the yacht in a shipyard for two months to undergo a meticulous examination, with overhaul conducted as necessary. For example, a small spot of some sort, an imperfection of less than an inch in diameter, was noted on the foremast. That was sufficient to cause the mast to be replaced—an enormous job. A complete set of new sails totaling more than 8,000 square feet was ordered.

The total solar eclipse would be visible in Siberia and northern Japan on August 9, 1896. Step Two was to dispatch the schooner for San Francisco, which Arthur did on December 5, 1895. Captain Crosby would be in charge of that lengthy, potentially challenging segment of the trip, which would be more than 100 days under sail by the most informed predictions. It turned out to be 117 days. Even with his privileged status at Phelps Dodge, that was more time than Arthur could afford to be away from his duties at the company. It had to have been a difficult moment for James as he watched his yacht disappear down the Narrows until it was out of sight. Rounding Cape Horn is one of those exclusive feathers every blue-water sailor would be proud to wear in his cap.

Captain Crosby's terse account of that trip, again, the wrong way, amounts to roughly three and a half words per day. It reports the longest day's run, a respectable 274 miles; a variety of ships sighted; the sea state, which one February day Crosby said was "calm as a kitten's eye;" and the appearance of King Neptune to subject a man named Thompson, son of an astronomer at Amherst who would be making the trip to Japan, to the usually gross, humbling ritual of crossing the equator. Captain Crosby referred to Thompson as "the Tired Boy" for some unknown reason. Later on, the captain tells of having "great fun" luring the Cape Horn pigeons and albatross with hook and line, and of Tired Boy shooting one of the big birds. Crosby seemed surprised to experience fifteen days of bad weather after that lapse of respect for nautical lore. If the captain had read Coleridge's *Rime of the Ancient Mariner*, published in 1798, he would have known to hang the bird—"instead of the cross, the Albatross"—around Tired Boy's neck to appease the gods of the deep. *Coronet* encountered a four-day northerly storm 100 miles from San Francisco, but in the main it was an uneventful, accident-free passage. The yacht dropped anchor in San Francisco on April 1.

Arthur, Harriet, and their party of the Todds, fellow astronomers, and a few friends, had been packed and ready, but had waited for word that *Coronet* had arrived San Francisco before they embarked for the West Coast. For Mabel Todd, the idea of a trip away from Amherst of seven months' duration was initially quite disturbing. But Austin Dickinson had been taken ill in the spring of 1895 and had died that August. In addition to her grief, there were complex and emotional legal issues initiated by Austin's wife and sister attempting to block Mabel's inheritance of land and financial securities left to her in Austin's will. The lawsuit had opened the floodgates to her affair. The trip to Japan had turned into a welcome respite. She had organized several magazine assignments around the voyage, and she planned a book-length treatment of the expedition.

According to Mabel, "the College Glee Club gave the Amherst yell" as the party left New York by train for San Francisco on April 6, 1896, in a snowstorm. The rail routes east of the Mississippi had been well established by then. The overnight run from New York to Chicago was routine. The major trunk lines connecting the major cities of the East Coast to Chicago—the Baltimore & Ohio, the New York Central, the Pennsylvania, and Canada's Grand Trunk railroad—had been well-traveled by 1875. The trip westward from Chicago would be more of an adventure.

The early railroads of the 1830s and 1840s had been frightening, dangerous. There was nothing friendly, or quiet, or comfortable, about a large steam boiler, with a wood fire burning under it, clanking along on steel wheels rolling on iron track. By 1896, rail travel had been developing for nearly seventy-five years, but while passengers no longer had to endure a storm of hot cinders and thick smoke bellowing from the engine's stack, the ride continued to be rough and jolting. The railroad had been a mad concept, one only the most zealous visionaries could have believed in. Until a British engineer named George Stevenson created a locomotive driven by steam technology in 1815, and the idea took off, goods and people had been moving quite pleasantly at the speed of a walking horse along a network of canals wherever possible. Canalboats were slow, but who cared? And the challenge of railroad construction, starting with the acquisition of land and rights of way needed, was enormous. The stuff of construction was immense, heavy—the rails, the crushed stone, the wooden ties and spikes. The roadbed had to be robust to bear the weight of the massive locomotives and heavily-loaded cars. It took thousands of men to lay track. Strong men, rough men, men desperate for work.

The first transcontinental route had been completed across the country's mid-section in 1869, when the Central Pacific and Union Pacific railroads were connected at Promontory, Utah. Arthur was two years old at the time. Together, along with some hundred miles of track laid by the Western Pacific Railroad (in California), the two lines had bridged the 2,327-mile gap between Council Bluffs, Iowa, and Sacramento, California. From Council Bluffs, seven different railroads served the Eastern Seaboard.

That transcontinental accomplishment (powered largely by railroad pioneer E. H. Harriman) was crowned by the driving of a golden spike at Promontory on May 10, 1869. Some have called it the greatest achievement of the nineteenth century. It was one of those outrageous, impossible undertakings that can only occur during times of ultimate pioneering at its most celebrated, at its most grandiose. At such seminal times, manic overreaching—the stuff of "progress"—is given carte blanche. Logic and reason succumb to blood, sweat, and tears; greed, bribery, and corruption. "Patriotism" is generally invoked. All were essential elements in building the 2,327 miles of railroad track across two ranges of "impassable" mountains, the Sierra Nevada and the Rockies. It required labor from three thousand Irish and ten thousand Chinese who died by the hundreds in the brutal heat, in the freezing cold; in pitched, racially motivated skirmishes with one other; and in grisly encounters with Indians who were trying in vain to protect their homelands. It took a cast of generals, including Grant and Sherman, led by President

Lincoln, the Commander in Chief himself, and scores of brilliant engineers with big-project experience learned during the Civil War. Laying track at the rate of five miles a day, blasting twenty or more tunnels through solid rock, building scores of bridges and trestles, they did it in only six years.

The connection at Promontory was wildly acclaimed nationally by the press, and confirmed in the record books as an important, historic milestone. The government issued a commemorative, three-cent postage stamp about the event. But as a "transcontinental" route, the Promontory connection must be accompanied by an asterisk. The Union Pacific terminated at Omaha, on the west bank of the Missouri River. Passengers had to debark and board a ferry to Council Bluffs, on the east side, where they could continue by rail after boarding one of several trains traveling east. Or vice versa. Travelers would have to wait until March 1873 for a railroad bridge to be constructed across the river.

In 1881 the second transcontinental railroad opened when the Atchison, Topeka & Santa Fe Railway met the Southern Pacific, providing a route to Southern California. Two years later the Northern Pacific was completed from Minnesota to Seattle, Washington. The Canadian Pacific completed the northern route across Canada in 1885. From those four options, the James party had decided to travel west via the Great Northern Railroad, a route that had been established by James J. Hill.

There were many reasons Arthur wanted to take that route. It had only been completed three years prior, and it would take him and his party through a remote part of the country that had been seldom seen. In the modern world of virtual reality we can trek through the wildest jungles, climb mountains, and explore the deepest ocean trenches in high-definition color at the press of a remote button. In the 1890s, even poor-quality, black-and-white still photographs were scarce. One saw things with one's own eyes, or not at all. The Great Northern route would afford wonderful sightseeing across the high plains and through the northern Rocky Mountains.

And James Jerome Hill was a family friend. Six years younger than D. Willis James, Hill was born in Canada. Despite losing the use of his right eye in a childhood accident, Hill attended school till the age of twelve when his father died, then became a bookkeeper in Kentucky. Moving to St. Paul, Minnesota, in 1856, he got involved in steamboat transportation on the Mississippi and in the coal business. In the 1870s he took advantage of the failure of local railroads after the Panic of 1873 to begin a northern railroad empire. The value of his railroad grew from $728,000 in 1880 to $25 million in 1885. His motto was simple: "work, hard work, intelligent work, and then more work."

As an only child, Arthur Curtiss James had been privy to Hill's presence on his frequent visits to the Jameses' family homes, exposed to the glow of Hill's eminence as one of the great railroad innovators of all time. When he got older and began learning the business, Arthur's respect for Hill's accomplishments soared. Hill became one of Arthur's idols, a mentor. His high regard for Hill, and his understanding of Hill's ultimate, unfinished dream of making his railroad empire transcontinental by bringing it into San Francisco, inspired Arthur James to dedicate himself to fulfilling that dream with great purpose.

It is impossible to look into the history of railroads in the United States without James J. Hill's name coming up. Hill was called "the Empire Builder" with good reason. His railroads ran from Chicago to Puget Sound, from Canada to the South. While other entrepreneurs built their rail networks around existing population centers, Hill grew populations around his railroads by providing financial incentives to farmers and miners from overseas to come work America's fertile land, where rail transportation would be waiting to serve their needs. He built it, and they came, because he encouraged the formation of settlements by reducing fares for immigrants. Unlike his rivals in the business, Hill never sought federal land grants to subsidize his railways. While his competitors indulged in personal animosity leading to costly legal fights, and focused on political and financial matters, Hill, a self-taught scientist and engineer, studied proposed routes; planned where and how track would be most efficiently laid; insisted that his engines be the most powerful and that his bridges be built of granite; and demanded his engineers design shallower grades (1 percent maximum) and more gentle curves. His great-grandson, Anson Beard Jr., wrote about Hill in *A Life in Full Sail*; "A leader without snobbery or Gilded Age social aspirations, on occasions when his train was snowbound [Hill] was known to join the crew in shoveling off the tracks." Hill had his own car, but he thought it was snooty to call it a "private car." Instead, he called it a "business car."

Hill was equally brilliant with political and financial matters, plowing profits back into his companies, and forging productive relationships with the top financiers of the day—men like D. Willis James, John S. Kennedy, and J. P. Morgan. His principles were simple, but proved to be sound. Hill said that a railroad produced train-miles, the number of which determined its expenses. Ton-miles—what it charged for hauling freight—determined earnings. Therefore, the fewer train-miles it logged, and the more ton-miles it sold, the more money the railroad would make. Hill expressed annoyance over the typical station-master of his day, who would sit in his office tending to paperwork when he should have been on the platform making sure the most freight possible was packed into every car.

Hill was a taskmaster who drove his crews hard, pushing for track to be laid at several miles per day. He was also not beyond participating in financial schemes and manipulations that pushed the boundaries of legitimacy. But he lived by a strong ethical code. For example, in 1897 he would purchase a failing railroad and associated timberland in northeast Minnesota. A huge deposit of iron ore was discovered beneath the timber. It was such a large deposit the land eventually became known as the Mesabi Iron Range. Hill thought it was a conflict of interest for him to own the iron ore and also ship the product on his railroad. He sold the land at cost to the Great Northern, so profits

James Jerome Hill

would be distributed among all shareholders. That decision of Hill's was said to have cost his family more than $750 million.

In summation, Beard writes of his grandfather: "He had an internal drive to succeed; competitive urgency; the will and energy to be an active builder rather than a passive participant; to be a giver, not a taker; to put ethics before profit; to develop vision beyond the near future; and to share the wealth with those who are less fortunate."

Hill would also become a yachtsman. In 1900 he would purchase a 243-foot steam yacht, renaming her *Wacouta*. For a committed, like-minded young man like Arthur Curtiss James, it would have been difficult to find a better mentor.

Arthur was right about Hill loaning him his business car, "A1," for the trip to San Francisco. Having the car made the trip as comfortable as possible. Writing in *Coronet Memories*, Harriet James (who was then twenty-seven years old) described the car as "large and airy, with two staterooms having comfortable brass beds." Arthur and Harriet took one stateroom. The Todds took the other. The remaining members of the party spent their days in the business car, but slept elsewhere on the train. The business car also managed to hold twenty personal trunks, along with various pieces of astronomy gear. Harriet complained about the rough tracks of the Chicago, Burlington & Quincy between Chicago and St. Paul, but she was delighted at the results of the first rehearsals of the quartet of singers she had organized for the trip, a quartet that included soprano Mable Todd. "We congratulated ourselves on having the car," Harriet wrote in her journal, "and realize how delightfully easy it is to cross the continent in our way."

The portion of the trip from St. Paul to Portland on the Great Northern did not initially live up to expectations. They found the scenery quite dreary as they passed through North Dakota: Fargo, Grand Forks, Minot, Williston—the town James Hill had named for his friend, D. Willis James—and Ft. Buford. In her book about the trip to Japan, *Corona and*

Coronet, Mable Todd mused poetically on the "impressive and illimitable levels of North Dakota and Montana. Strange to weirdness and unutterably lonely, snow often fell across the treeless wastes, no trace of spring brightened the gray scene, and twilights descended in ghostly fashion, as the edge of the visible world softly faded."

As they passed through the (then) two-million-acre Ft. Peck Indian Reservation, where the flatlands were dotted with many teepees, several in the party found it odd that no Indians were drawn to observe the train's passage. The one Indian woman they saw was chopping wood, and never looked up. "The passage of the train made no impression on her," Harriet observed, forgetting, or oblivious to, the enormous destruction the building of the railroads had wreaked upon the Indian culture. "During the night we will finish the prairies," Harriet wrote, "and I must say all will be glad."

Traversing Ft. Peck, Mabel Todd saw a bit more out the same window. Todd saw "spiritless communities. . . . companies of Indians in vari-colored rags galloping on rough ponies from nowhere to nowhere," and how "a brawny squaw, chopping wood with vigorous strokes, was watched with silent approval by a row of braves."

In Montana, spirits lightened as the train rolled along the picturesque Flat Head River; through the town of Kalispell situated at the base of snow-clad Rocky Mountains; and on to the Kootenai River with its "dashing falls." Snow began falling as the train entered the Cascade Mountains. Soon it was a blizzard. "Heavy though the storm was," Harriet wrote, "we could see the mountains half way to their summits, the beautiful pines laden with snow, the telegraph wires covered with it, and the track entirely screened from sight. On either side were banks of snow or deep ravines through which the mountain brooks were cutting great crevasses."

In the interest of sightseeing, and to secure a more powerful locomotive to negotiate the multiple switchbacks that would

Snowblower clearing a high-plains blizzard

take them over picturesque, 4,000-foot Stevens Pass at night, the Great Northern parked the train until morning at Cascade Tunnel Station. There was no tunnel in 1896, but the station was located where the tunnel entrance would be located. Eager for any break in the inactive routine, Arthur was quick to accept the conductor's invitation to observe the big railroad rotary plow tossing snow several hundred feet to either side. The blizzard did not let up. Stalled trains in front of them caused such a delay that Arthur was concerned their engine might be getting low on water in the boiler. Soon he was leading the charge among the male passengers to organize a bucket brigade from a nearby spring.

"Arthur finds a ladder," Harriet writes. "Mr. Thompson climbs onto the engine in order to pour pails of water into the tanks; Dr. Adriance, Arthur Francis, and Alfred run back and forth from engine to stream, while Mr. Garrish stands at the foot of the ladder and hands the pails to Arthur. The keenest enjoyment was depicted on the faces of all, and even when the snow turned to rain they still worked on."

It would turn out that the blizzard the James party encountered was the last straw. The long-contemplated Cascade tunnel was begun in 1897 and opened in 1900. That tunnel (since replaced) was 2.7 miles long, eliminating many switchbacks.

Harriet James was good at describing scenery and events, but those who expected more about the people on the trip, amusing or telling anecdotes, or stories about their activities and relationships, would be disappointed by her periodic reports. Her entries were governed by the manners of restraint that had pervaded her upbringing.

Hill's Great Northern had taken the party to Seattle, and their car, "A1," was sent on to Portland, crossing the Columbia River on a large railroad ferry. The Great Northern itself would not begin direct service to Portland until 1899, but thereafter would expand its Northwest network. That meant the remaining 635 miles to San Francisco would be a forty-hour ride attached to a Southern Pacific train to Oakland, followed by a ferry ride across the bay to San Francisco. Harriet James sorely missed the comparatively smooth ride on Great Northern tracks. "We never received such a shaking," she writes. "It was almost impossible to sleep, and we were glad enough to escape being thrown from the track." But once in San Francisco, before they loaded their baggage aboard *Coronet* and cast off into the Pacific, she gave the readers of her journal this final caution: "You must all of you read between the lines for those messages which come from our hearts and cannot be written."

Without getting specific, Mabel Todd offered a bit more: "Half unconsciously, the company studied one another, deciding that it was a harmonious combination... and likely to remain so."

* * *

The significance of the unpleasant Southern Pacific segment was not lost on Arthur. He too was practically thrown from his bed thanks to the SP's very rough roadbed. And he felt the train slow as the engine struggled to pull its load up grades that far exceeded James Hill's 1 percent maximum. He knew they were traveling on the west side of the Cascade Mountains, and he appreciated the folly of the Southern Pacific's decision to build on such challenging terrain. He knew there had to be a better route to exploit the potential of San Francisco with its deep-water port. He also knew the Southern Pacific had no connecting service running east to Chicago in the northern tier of the United States. Its route through the southern tier was long and tortuous.

At the same time Arthur agreed with James Hill's decision not to extend the Great Northern south at the time. It would have been prohibitively expensive. Hill's decision in 1914 to connect with San Francisco via the Great Northern Pacific Steamship Company from a terminus he established at Astoria, Oregon, at the mouth of the Columbia River—just 100 miles from his Portland terminal—would make sense to James. It also happened to be Hill's only recourse. Hill's determination to extend the Great Northern south into California had been blocked in 1911 by E. H. Harriman, owner of the Southern Pacific Railroad. Hill's steamships competed very favorably with the Southern Pacific for both passengers and freight, but James knew the time would come when a new, improved railroad link would not only complete Hill's transcontinental dream, but it would make financial sense. His lookout for that opportunity would never lapse until satisfied.

Arthur James's foreword to Mabel Todd's book, *Corona and Coronet*, is titled "Deep Sea Yachting." It begins:

To the yachtsman truly interested in his hobby, who enjoys a home on the rolling deep for its own sake, deep-sea cruising affords a wider scope and more perfect enjoyment than can possibly be obtained from short trips on inland waters. . . . It is not until "Farewell" has been taken and the first course set for a distant port, that the true lover of the sea begins to feel the exhilaration of life on the ocean wave. Newspapers are not wanted. Telegrams are impossible. Worry is left behind, and the yachtsman enters upon an indefinite period of perfect content-ment. Details of managing the vessel, the study and practice of navigation and seamanship, even settling the quarrels of sailors and cooks, are simply pleasant pastimes.

By the time all the gear was loaded aboard *Coronet*, "Fare-well" was extended on April 25, 1896.

Arthur wrote: "*Coronet* was once again in her element, out of sight of land, with boats lashed securely on deck and every-thing snug below and aloft; prepared for anything which might be in store for her on the 4,000 miles of sea that must be covered before reaching Yokohama." To hold the trade winds and assure perfect summer weather, they kept between 18 and 20 degrees north latitude.

"Day after day the awning was set on the quarter deck and the yacht kept on her way with scarcely more motion than would be experienced in Long Island Sound," wrote Arthur. "The long Pacific rollers lazily following, and even the flocks of goonies slowly circling astern seemed to express the spirit of the tropics, and bid us enjoy southern seas to the utmost."

To allay the symptoms of seasickness, some of the passengers resorted to a medication called Fraser's Remedy, taken by injection. The ingredients of Fraser's Remedy are long lost, but during the period it was common to "self-medicate" with "remedies" based variously on alcohol ("spirits"), cocaine (Coca-Cola), opium, and other stupefacients, as well as many concoctions reported to ward off foreign diseases and stomach upsets. Days aboard were spent reading, playing quoits, napping, exercising, playing chess, learning to tie knots under the watchful eye of the mate, and helping the as-tronomers prepare their gear for the upcoming eclipse. Exercising, for the men, meant hauling themselves up various lines hand-over-hand. For the women, and the men as well, exercise also meant walking. They quickly calculated that walking from the mainsheet block at the stern to the gig (small boat) lashed on the foredeck, and back, sixty-one times, equaled one mile. Exercise was taken seriously then, as "physical culture came to the fore."

Chess was played on a board of ribbons woven upon a cushion that was constructed by one of the crew. Pins on the bottoms of the chess pieces insured stability whatever the heel angle of the yacht. Tea was served on deck at 5:00 p.m. each day, weather permitting.

Arthur taught navigation to those interested, while Mabel taught the gentlemen, including Arthur, to sing. "Arthur receives many words of encouragement," Harriet writes, "but persists in behaving so obstreperously during lessons he still remains in Class B." Everyone but Professor David Todd seemed to be enjoying the passage. Todd was "miserable most of the time," Harriet writes, "and is by far the poorest sailor on board." David would often excuse himself from the table at mealtime to rush on deck in hopes that a breath of fresh air would keep his meal from being (once again) tossed upon the seas.

Arthur was in his element, often spending the night on deck, helping the crew gather rainwater for the tanks, standing watches, steering, and in constant communication with Captain Crosby and the mate. On Sundays, as always, he read the religious service.

They stopped at Honolulu for two weeks. Arthur and Harriet fell in love with the place to the extent that the rest of their yachts of significance would have Hawaiian names. Many were the visitors to *Coronet*, including a delegation from the Young Men's Christian Association who appeared at the request of Robert Ross McBurney, the esteemed secretary of the New York City YMCA for thirty years. [Today, the main branch of the Manhattan YMCA is named for McBurney.] With Arthur's support, Harriet would come to embrace the YMCA—founded in 1844 to "win young men to Jesus with any means in accordance with the scriptures"—as one of her major philanthropies. The Jameses and their guests had a great time visiting the various islands, marveling at the active volcanoes, and dining with the first president of the Republic of Hawaii, Sanford Dole, who would serve from 1894 to 1898, and his wife, Anna P. Cate, who hailed from Castine, Maine. In 1899, Dole's cousin would found the pineapple company that now bears the family name. As a man who had grown a beard when almost all his contemporaries were clean-shaven, Arthur was amused and amazed by President Dole's prodigious white chin whiskers, which extended nearly to his belt.

Coronet moved on toward Yokohama on May 25. All was well until they were 200 miles from port. Then the barometer began to fall. "Constantly increasing wind and a heavy sea indicated we were on the edge of a revolving storm, the center of which appeared to be traveling rapidly along the coast," wrote Arthur in his foreword to Mabel's book. "Under short sail, *Coronet* was kept on her course until nightfall, but the rapidly falling barometer warned us it would be unwise to approach land until the disturbance had passed. A storm at sea may be a grand sight, but a little of it goes a long way."

The typhoon moderated, leaving a heavy seaway in its wake. That night, they encountered the light on Mile Head that marks the entrance to Tokyo Bay. It wasn't long before Arthur had his first exposure to the Japanese culture. "Yokohama pilots are an unknown quantity," he wrote. "No response came to our repeated signals, and we were obliged to navigate the channel unaided. The Japanese fishermen sail their unwieldy junks without lights, and without the slightest regard for rules of the road. Their immense square-sail is an impenetrable wall between the helmsman and anything which may be ahead of him. A lookout is an unheard-of precaution, so it was only by rare good fortune that we avoided running down a number of them in the darkness."

Keep in mind that *Coronet* did not have an engine.

Arthur was charmed by some of the remote Japanese ports that had never before been visited by foreigners, and he recognized that the remote fishing villages offered an opportunity to study the Japanese character that was then untouched by Western civilization. And he loved sailing in the Inland Sea. In the foreword he wrote: "The ten days in the Inland Sea were altogether too short a time to explore its intricate channels, and even to sail past the thousand mountains and thickly wooded islands which form a barrier to the Pacific and give the Sea its name."

Mabel left for Esashi by steamer from the port of Otaru in late July to join her husband and his fellow astronomers, who were setting up for the eclipse. She was unhappy about missing the trip Arthur had planned to visit small coastal towns on the Inland Sea. He had chartered a small steamer that would be better suited to the tricky navigation involved than his big schooner without auxiliary power. But Mabel, a student of astronomy, had her responsibilities to David to be carried out during the eclipse. And she had to write about it, of course. She made her way to Esashi on a series of "tramp" steamers, loving the adventure involved. "How Esashi could be reached (on this steamer) was misty, but enticing," she wrote in *Corona and Coronet*, "as I rather hoped it might be necessary to travel a few days by packhorse over hitherto untrodden wilds, a few Yezo bears in the background and the 'hairy Ainu' as hosts."

Mabel did not encounter any bears, but she did spend some time among the remarkable Ainu tribespeople who lived on the northern island of Hokkaido (Esashi was on Hokkaido, but far to the south). She wrote with enthusiasm about the little-known, gentle Ainu, who once fancied themselves as the center of the universe. While she found some of the towns she passed through along the way "dirty and sordid," she chose to focus on the "blossoming white lilies and purple hydrangea" that brightened them.

Meanwhile, Arthur and his party on the chartered steamer SS *Miyako Maru* ran into more "adventure" than they had bargained for. It began with the confines of tiny cabins, cabins without standing headroom, and the hard, straw mattresses they were given to sleep on. "Our washing facilities are all outside our stateroom," Harriet wrote, "and much of our dressing is necessarily public." The party was initially "greatly amused" by the *Miyako Maru*'s twenty-six crewmen staring at every move of these strange foreigners. But amusement soon turned to concern. Arthur related the experience in a letter dated August 1, 1896, that he posted to Mabel in Esashi. It would be the first of many letters he would share with Mabel over the years. He always addressed Mabel formally, as Mrs. Todd, and signed off with his full name.

My Dear Mrs. Todd,

We have just returned from the Inland Sea having had a most delightful trip. I wish very much you could have been with us as I think that even your exalted opinion of the Japanese character might have had a rude shock. The polish and veneer of the semi-civilized people in the treaty ports is very interesting, but as soon as one sees the masses as they are all such illusions vanish with the greatest rapidity. I never was thrown in with more absolutely unprincipled and disgusting specimens of humanity as we met in the small towns along the sea coast. Even the crew of the ship which we chartered were of the very worst type, and for two nights we had to keep watch with our revolvers in our hands to prevent their robbing us. One night, from the Captain down, all hands were absolutely paralyzed with Saki, and the orgies that were carried on on the vessel were not the results of the highest kind of civilization which you think so much superior to that of Europe and America. We did not dare lie in the harbor, and the white men on board—that is our party—took charge of the vessel and ran all night through the sea, running from the bridge to the engine room in a vain endeavor of keeping the officers awake and attentive to their business. I think that this would have been an experience you would have enjoyed, and would have been a valuable chapter of picturesque and progressive Japan. In spite of this, however, the scenery was beautiful and we enjoyed the trip greatly.

On my return I have found your letter and have written to

Kobe to have the one you sent to the consulate there forwarded. I also found a letter for you from Nishimura at the Grand Hotel which I opened. It said that your packages had been forwarded but were delayed on account of the washout of the road. The Grand Hotel people here promised to take charge of them when they arrive, and I will see that they are brought on board. I am much disappointed that Mr. Ibashi is not going to send a steamer to Yezo as this will absolutely put a stop to our going to see the eclipse. On Monday we are going up to Miyanoshita for a few days, and from there to Nikko. I have written to Professor Todd in regard to his plans after the eclipse and await his answer and suggestions with interest.

All join in kind regards,
Very sincerely yours,

A C James

The washout of the road Arthur refers to was collateral damage caused by a seismic sea wave, as high as 115 feet in places, that struck the northeast coast of Japan's main island on June 16, 1896, six days before *Coronet* dropped anchor in Tokyo Bay. The 8.5-magnitude earthquake in the town of Sanriku turned out to be one of the most destructive seismic events in Japan's history. For vessels at sea, a tsunami is just a very large wave that passes under the keel. When a vessel gets close to shore, or happens to be in port when a tsunami arrives, all hell breaks loose. *Coronet* had dodged a bullet. The death toll from the 1896 tsunami was near 27,000.

Arthur, Harriet, and their remaining guests were unable to make it to Esashi for the eclipse. The steamer they had planned to take was suddenly unavailable. Their disappointment was somewhat relieved, after the fact, by the incredible news that it had not been possible to properly document the phenomenon. "Corona scarcely visible," David Todd telegraphed from Esashi. "Have taken a few pictures." The years of preparation by the astronomers, the miles traveled by land and sea, all the planning, logistics, and the seven months set aside for the trip, had all been diminished by the onset of clouds: Mother Nature at her most dismissive.

Professor Todd's observation camp at Esashi, Japan

While the total eclipse was a disappointment to astronomers, Mabel Todd's description of the event would give the *Coronet* party second thoughts about having missed it:

Grayer and grayer grew the day... a penetrating chill fell across the land as if a door had been opened into a long-closed vault... it was a moment of appalling suspense; something was being waited for—the very air was portentous... unearthly light enveloped all... dimly seen through thin cloud, it was nevertheless beautiful beyond description, a celestial flame from some unimaginable heaven. Simultaneously the whole northwestern sky, nearly to the zenith, was flooded with lurid and startlingly brilliant orange across which drifted clouds slightly darker, like flecks of liquid flame, or huge ejecta from some vast, volcanic Hades.... Well might it have been a prelude to the shriveling and disappearance of the whole world.... No human being spoke. No bird twittered. Even sighing of the surf breathed into utter repose, and not a ripple stirred the leaden sea.

Drawing of 1896 eclipse

The sail home was relatively uneventful. Harriet's journal indicated that David Todd was bearing up well under his disappointment with the eclipse. In *Corona and Coronet*, Mabel wrote: "The astronomer patiently waits and works for still another eclipse. His life is a consecration to the best and highest. His joy over one new fact wrested from sun or star is more than the mere merchant's over an additional fortune made. He must possess the potential of a hero, the calm of a philosopher, even the uplift of martyrs of old. He often knows 'the finer grace of unfulfilled designs;' but his hope springs eternal."

One can only wonder how that cruel stroke of bad luck affected a weary psyche that had already been compromised by his wife unashamedly flaunting her affair with a neighbor's husband, by his own frequent philandering, and with the knowledge that unpleasant legal documents were awaiting Mabel's return to Amherst. In addition, after the goal of the extraordinary effort having been compromised, David Todd was faced with several more weeks on the high seas, a prisoner on a vessel whose motion made him constantly nauseated. In her book about Mabel's affair—*Austin & Mabel*—Polly Longsworth writes, "During his late fifties David's behavior grew increasingly erratic, which led in 1917 to his being eased off the Amherst faculty into early retirement." A few years later he would be institutionalized for the rest of his life.

Arthur had opted for the fastest great-circle course from Tokyo to the Golden Gate, a dreary, month-long, upwind slog through a vacant sea void of news, telegrams, or letters. As Mabel ruefully put it, "What better chance to make acquaintance with that stranger too seldom met—one's innermost self." How she fared with that project was indicated in part by a report from Harriet, who wrote that "Professor Todd had inadvertently told Mrs. Todd she talked too much, and tonight she announced she would not speak through dinner. We did everything to make her talk, and had great fun over it."

Coronet was not the only one in its element. Arthur was so pleased to be back at sea he assumed a full watch schedule, often retiring at 8:00 p.m. and going on deck at midnight. Or he would come off watch at 4:00 a.m. and sleep until 11:00 a.m., when he would have breakfast and take the noon sight. There was a new mate on board, and Arthur thought it best not to leave him alone on watch. There were occasional spates of heavy weather, with the yacht pitching and rolling, slamming into head seas under storm sails with such a jolting it was impossible to sleep. Arthur was in the thick of all the seamanship involved in keeping the yacht safely moving apace. And when the doctor had to remove a tumor from a crewman, who assisted but Arthur James. He later told Harriet, "I believe I ought to have been a doctor."

Arthur also revealed a bit of romance in his soul. On September 6, Harriet discovered some boxes in her stateroom and found that the entire party had showered her with birthday gifts from Japan. "I afterward discovered that one day in Tokyo when it was very necessary for Arthur to return to the yacht, he had not gone straight there," she wrote. "Instead, he had stopped at the Seibiken, where he found a lovely inlaid box, and some very handsome vases." One night when he was on the dog watch, 10:00 p.m. to 2:00 a.m., Harriet said he came to her cabin after midnight, woke her, and asked, "Do you want to see something pretty?" She got up and put on a warm wrapper. He escorted her to the deck, where she was bathed in the light of a waning but

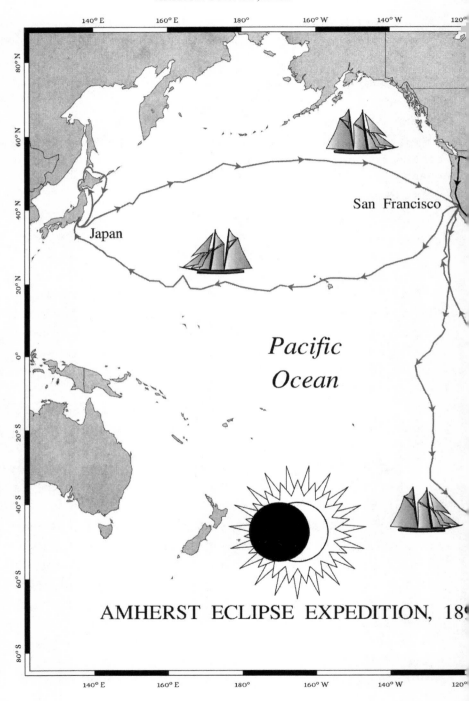

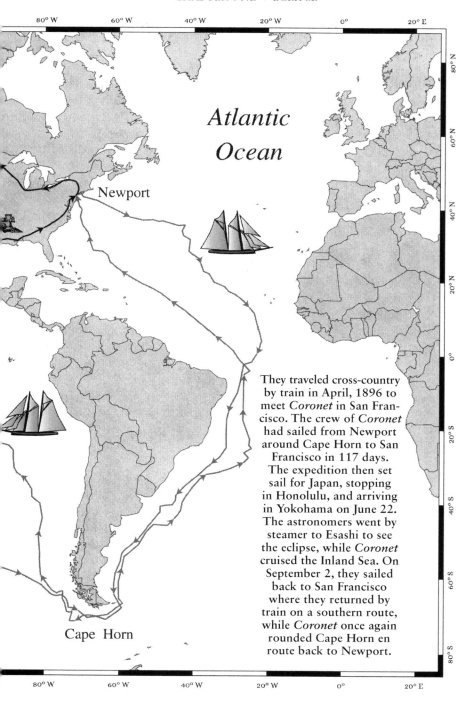

Atlantic
Ocean

Newport

Cape Horn

They traveled cross-country by train in April, 1896 to meet *Coronet* in San Francisco. The crew of *Coronet* had sailed from Newport around Cape Horn to San Francisco in 117 days. The expedition then set sail for Japan, stopping in Honolulu, and arriving in Yokohama on June 22. The astronomers went by steamer to Esashi to see the eclipse, while *Coronet* cruised the Inland Sea. On September 2, they sailed back to San Francisco where they returned by train on a southern route, while *Coronet* once again rounded Cape Horn en route back to Newport.

bright moon revealed by an evaporating bank of clouds.

In the foggy, wee hours of October 2, 1896, *Coronet* raised the light on the Farallon Islands, and soon after, a light at the entrance to San Francisco Bay. Arthur would write in the foreword to *Corona and Coronet*, "The yachtsman who has never known the pleasure of making a light after a long and difficult voyage has something to live for."

Once again, Arthur would have to absent himself from *Coronet*'s trip around Cape Horn, the right way this time (west to east, with the prevailing wind). It was time to reacquaint himself with Phelps Dodge. But among his duties before he boarded a train home, was to make sure his acquaintance, George B. Spaulding Jr., was all set to sail back to New York on *Coronet*. Three years younger than Arthur, George Spaulding had grown up as a minister's son in Syracuse, New York, graduated from Yale in 1893, and attended divinity school. Perhaps he and Arthur had become acquainted while he was serving as assistant pastor at the Madison Square Presbyterian Church, not far from the Jameses' Park Avenue home. His name, or the name of any other Spaulding, does not appear on the guest lists of other voyages of *Coronet*. That he was quite young was evident by his need to obtain his parents' permission in order to make the Cape Horn voyage.

It is clear that Spaulding had been overjoyed by the invitation, and made sure to get himself to San Francisco in time for departure. His enthusiasm for the trip, both the expectation and the reality, is evident in the one hundred pages he wrote about it. That's about a page per day, considerably more than Captain Crosby's account of the first voyage around the Horn. Spaulding's firsthand description of the yacht as it was in 1896 is a treasure in itself:

As an ocean home, she is palatial. She has all the beauty common to such pleasure yachts in burnished brass work of rail and binnacle, figured ground glass skylights, and tapering, gilt-lined head.... Two skylights run, each for 12 feet, one above the saloon, the other above the passageway, fore and aft, between the staterooms. The domes of these openings, curving handsomely in polished mahogany and heavy, curved, plate glass panes, give a noticeably elegant appearance above decks.... Below there are book shelves well stored with the latest works of travel and fiction... a folding desk, a Chickering upright piano, and a tiny tile open-grate fireplace with brass trimming and chimney piece.

The yacht's stability is seen from her great spread of canvas. A toy beside the great merchantman [moored nearby at the same San Francisco dock], she can carry as much upon her two slender masts as the largest vessel upon its four. The great foresail and mainsail were raised, each of more than 800 yards. The fore and main gaff topsails were set. The heads of these, fitting to the working, not the racing, topmasts, taper to the luff at 135-feet above the deck... and the jibs, jib topsail, flying jib, jib and fore stays'l. Under these, some intimation of the yacht's riding can be gained. Even with a discouraging breeze, she rises upon the long swells like a sea bird.

A keen observer, Spaulding was fascinated by Captain Crosby. That was lucky, since Spaulding had to spend one hundred days or more within 130 feet of the captain, whose life had taken him from Maine coasting schooners, to service in the Civil War navy, to a decade in command of *Coronet.* "He is a born story teller with opinions based on some fact, much fancy," Spaulding wrote. "The combination makes him whimsical. He is a reprobate undenied, yet not altogether hateful." Spaulding writes that Crosby also had strong political views. He was pro Grover Cleveland, which had to please Arthur. "Some weird tales he tells me," Spaulding wrote of Crosby, "if not all elegant, yet bound to illustrate a truth." Spaulding went on, complete with dialect:

Captain D.S. Crosby is a true sea dog—an old campaigner, grey in the service. He has the sterling mark, "rugged," on him.

Marine artist John Mecray's 1976 painting of *Coronet*

A genius at words, he owns and constantly uses an unabridged compilation of the provincialisms and archaisms of all places in all times. "Have yer ever read that book—what is it, 'Afore the Mast'?—'Two Years Afore the Mast'?" he puts to me. "Eh? Well that fellar never saw the sea. Ef he did, he's a mighty poor scholar!"

"They's lots of things you read about the sea that's never on 'em. It riminds me o' when I was among the Europeans at the Cowes Regatter. A lot of 'em came aboard, Lady Reade and her Earl was among 'em. When they come to go the Earl offered me a soverin. 'No,' I says—'I thank you.' 'Aw well,' he says, 'paws it round among the good fellows.' 'No sir, thank you,' says I, 'we don't allow them to take anything. We are all Americans here!'.... Afterward he gave me his card and asked me to come to lunch with him and his lady. Which I did.... Now ef I'd taken the soverin, it wouldn't ha' been 'Come to lunch!'"

Spaulding also got to know First Mate Andrew Berthold, extracting his story as any good journalist would. Only about thirty, Berthold had spent half his life at sea, sailing in merchant ships before joining *Coronet* as quartermaster under a previous owner. When the yacht was sold, he ended up working ashore as a coachman for a while, gaining regard by saving his employer's house when a fire broke out. His employer, a music teacher, trusted him with accompanying his female students home safely after their lessons. "Dey lik-ed me and haf die laugh on me for die t'ings I say," Berthold remarked. A series of connections led the upstanding young man to Arthur's notice, and Arthur, showing the keen judgment of people that would be so critical in sustaining his life style, brought Berthold back aboard *Coronet*.

"Why! [Mr. James] has done more for me dan my own fader could do," Berthold told Spaulding. "He paid my tuition for a course in navigation in die College ob New York, die same course dat Captain Jams took himselb." In Japan, "Captain Jams, he recommend me to Professor Todd, and let me go up into die countres mit him."

Berthold was a hit in Esashi, mainly because of his natural diplomatic tendencies, and his penchant for humor that delighted the Japanese. "Dey lik-ed me. I am so funny," he said. "I talk lots of Chinese," Berthold told Spaulding. "Know only few words, but keeps talking. Eet come out so funny! Dey all laugh. Dey likes you to make dem laugh." Professor Todd told Berthold he should stay in Esashi, that he would be a big man in town and introduce European ways. Berthold said no thanks. "I moost stay by die yacht. I can go dere again."

Coronet made New York Harbor on February 6, 1897. Spaulding wrote:

The basin was crowded with all sorts of craft, three-deep to the dock and butted with ice. We waited unendingly for an opening. At length I heard a hearty ring: "Where's Spaulding?" shouted down the companion stairs. I dashed out to meet it, and it turned out to be Captain Arthur James. He gave me a hearty grip and was wanting to know everything and I trying to tell a part of it. We had been reported by telephone from Fort Hamilton, and he hurried down and crawled through coal yards, eager as a boy over his toy sloop. Dr. Adriance, who went on the yacht to Japan, followed him. We were soon with the old man in the messroom over four bowls of soup.

Rails

After reprovisioning in San Francisco, *Coronet* had set sail for New York on October 15, 1896. Five days before that, Arthur, Harriet, the Todds, and fellow astronomers had boarded the Buenaventura train of the Southern Pacific Railroad that would take them home via Bisbee, Arizona, a dozen miles from the Mexican border. At the time, Bisbee was the home of the Copper Queen mine, one of the world's greatest copper camps. Phelps Dodge had taken over Copper Queen in 1885.

The heavily mineralized nature of the area had been accidentally discovered in 1877 by US Cavalry soldiers who were in pursuit of a band of renegade Apaches. Having camped one night at a waterhole in the rugged, hilly terrain near Iron Springs, soldiers had noticed outcroppings of lead and iron. The water had a metallic taste. Word traveled fast in the local saloons, and soon prospectors began filing claims in the general area. One claim that would exceed its supposed potential was called Copper Queen. That property was lost one afternoon by one of the owners who had wagered his share that he could outrun a man on a horse. Alcohol had been involved. Given the fact that

Copper Queen would produce 8 billion pounds of copper, 2.9 million ounces of gold, 77 million ounces of silver, 300 million pounds of lead, and 380 million pounds of zinc before it was closed in 1975, that wager would end up costing the owner's family in excess of $20 million.

Copper Queen mine smelter in 1880

Phelps Dodge was not feeling flush in 1885, having made investments in several mining properties that didn't pan out. But Dr. James Douglas, the chemist Phelps Dodge had hired to evaluate the mining potential of southern Arizona, found a vein of high-grade copper ore at Copper Queen and provided an argument so compelling for purchasing the property that Phelps Dodge wrote a check. It was the best move they ever made, and as has been mentioned, the person of Dr. Douglas was an equally fortunate find for the company. Douglas became president of Copper Queen, the Copper Queen Consolidated Mining Company, as it was officially called, in 1885.

It was at that point that Phelps Dodge began focusing its activities on mining, a direction Arthur would later help engineer.

As Robert Glass Cleland wrote in his *History of Phelps Dodge*, James "successfully shunned publicity, and let others serve as the leading figures in the company, but he played an extremely influential part in determining its policies and guiding its course."

It would have been an acceptable path of lesser resistance for a man fresh off a long voyage at sea to have taken the northern route back home in the comfort of a private car. Instead, Arthur and his party were bounced along the Mexican border with temperatures hitting 100 degrees in the railroad cars, and with dust "sifting in through double windows, and powdering the little parlors," as Mable Todd described it. But for Arthur it was an opportunity to check in on the Copper Queen operation, then in its eleventh year.

The trip to Bisbee had been delayed because of an ominous headline in a San Francisco newspaper not long after *Coronet*'s arrival: "Bisbee Washed Away by a Cloudburst." The headline turned out to be overstated, but the history of Bisbee had given it potential credibility. Serious summer cloudbursts were frequent in that mile-high territory where the Mule Mountains rose above 7,000 feet. In July 1890, twenty minutes after a deluge had begun, a wall of water had rushed down the funnel-shaped canyon, washed away four houses, filled many cellars with mud and debris, and killed two miners. As Lynn Bailey wrote in *Bisbee: Queen of the Copper Camps*, "When thunderheads gathered over the Mule Mountains and the crash of thunder reverberated through the canyons, everyone headed for high ground and prayed their property would be spared." Arthur and his party suffered through several days of anxiety until, finally, the telegram from Bisbee came through: "Bisbee safe—no one killed."

Both Mabel and Harriet wrote about the bleakness of the southwestern terrain they observed from the train. "In the Yuma desert a bush is not an incident merely, but an epoch," Mabel wrote. They both also described the amount of standing water they encountered that had been dropped by the sudden, violent rainstorm that had caused the rash headline. Both noted the groups of tramps they encountered. This from Harriet: "[The tramps] clung to the trucks beneath, stealing rides of a few miles at imminent risk to life and limb; they climbed to the roof of the train cars, and were continually dislodged, even from our own observation platform."

For the last 60 miles the James party had transferred to the Arizona & South Eastern Railroad, which the mining company had built in 1888 to '89. It might have been the business portion of the trip, but when there was fun to be had, this group of young people didn't hesitate for a moment. David and Mabel Todd were the oldest among them, and they had only recently celebrated their fortieth birthdays. With a director of the company that owned the railroad on board, the sky was the limit. Harriet wrote in her journal: "After breakfast, Mrs. Todd had her wish fulfilled, and rode on the cow catcher. Professor took his seat near her, and Arthur and I established ourselves in the engine cab. After all we are only grown children, for it was quite as much fun to blow the whistle or ring the bell as it would have been in childhood's days."

The Todds' ride on the cowcatcher was brief. While that perch was free from bugs, ash, and cinders, many were the cows. The animals' disregard for the train was evident by the many bovine skeletons seen bleaching in the sun beside the track. The cows would hold their ground to the last possible moment, sometimes beyond, endangering both themselves and those who would ride on the catcher.

After logging many miles across the barren desert landscape, coming upon the attractive town of Bisbee was a pleasant surprise. Thanks to the employee-welfare priority of Dr. Douglas, his "kindly authority," and the abundance of water released by mining operations, the town of Bisbee was striking for its display of lush grass, many flowers, and trees. At the time, the town boasted a work force of around seven hundred men, a population of three thousand with families included, with twenty-two nationalities represented among them. The town supported two physicians, a clergyman, and a decent library run by a graduate of the Pratt Institute.

But mining operations, and the smelters required to process ore into product, have never been environmentally friendly. That was not much of an issue in 1896, but looking past the flowers, Mabel Todd took a twenty-first-century view of the situation as the train entered the town: "Tall chimneys and pipes spouting greenish vapor became frequent, and one enormous smoke conductor eight feet in diameter and 700 feet long, lying at a steep angle up the mountain and pouring its incessant volume of Sulphur smoke off, far above the little town—this was Bisbee. No growing thing, not even the hardy cottonwoods, can live in the Sulphur-laden air, even with the worst of it carried off by the great flue. . . . the air cannot, even now, especially in certain directions of the wind, be called favorable to agriculture."

Arthur was eager to spend time with Dr. James Douglas, whom he had met briefly in Phelps Dodge's New York office when Douglas had been engaged to evaluate mining potential in Arizona. Arthur had been a thirteen-year-old student at the time who just happened to be at home on break when the meeting with Douglas occurred. Allowed to attend, he had immediately felt admiration for Douglas, and had been impressed by this man's confident approach to the dangerous task he had agreed to undertake. Douglas was a chemist, a scholar who would eventually become president of the esteemed American Institute of Mining, Metallurgical and Petroleum Engineers. But he was also a physically strong, self-reliant man ready to tackle whatever the Wild West held in store. And in the 1880s, the brutality and rapaciousness of the Apache Indians toward pioneering interlopers was so well known that their name had been applied to the cut-throats and robbers of Paris. Shortly before Douglas's first trip to Arizona, the Apaches had attacked a stagecoach on the very line he would travel, massacring the passengers.

Douglas was an impressive figure. He had grown up on a 60-acre farm on the St. Lawrence River, near Quebec. His early desire to become a Presbyterian minister had been derailed by a sudden lack of faith in institutional Christianity. Robert Glass

Bisbee, Arizona, in 1890

BY ROGER VAUGHAN • PAGE 89

Cleland wrote that Douglas returned to university and studied chemical geology under the founder of that scientific specialty, Thomas Sterry Hunt. Together, they invented the Hunt-Douglas electrolytic method for extracting copper from its ore, a process Douglas later spent nine months installing in a mine in Chile. Douglas also installed the process (and became superintendent) of a refinery in Pennsylvania, a venture that failed. But it was that association in Pennsylvania, involving mines in Arizona, that first brought Douglas to the attention of Phelps Dodge.

There was more about Douglas's life, much more, "a curious medley of novel and adventurous experiences," as Cleland puts it, that included a two-year tour abroad, and a term as surgeon on a Greenland whaling ship. Familiar with his story, Arthur often imagined Douglas's iron will, and the deep religious convictions upon which it flourished, garnering grudging respect from any Indian leader who might be his captor.

Dr. James Douglas

Douglas had initially been brought to Phelps Dodge in New York to advise Earl (William E.) Dodge and D. Willis James about the sense of building a smelting works on Long Island. Douglas had told the two men that with the falling off of mining in the Alleghenies, and with western ores being smelted at the mines, building a smelter plant on Long Island was a bad idea. But Douglas, who had been evaluating mines in Arizona, did express enthusiasm about a mining claim in Bisbee, Arizona.

Douglas was no salesman. While strongly advising the investment, he did not spare describing the risks involved. "I explained to my clients," Douglas was quoted in *James Douglas: a Memoir*, by H. H. Langton, "that they would have to put in jeopardy not only the price of the prospect—for there was no mine—but far more in proving it either worthless or valuable, and if it turned out the latter, a law suit might be their first asset. [This because laws defining ownership of meandering, underground strips of ore were still being heavily contested.] Had they not been able and willing to lose with a good grace, I should have advised them to throw up the offer."

Having considered themselves able and willing, D. Willis and Earl Dodge had taken the risk in 1881 with a mine called Atlanta, next to Copper Queen. Two years later, Douglas had sunk a test hole that led to nothing of consequence. "Had it been followed for 200 feet," Douglas wrote of that test, "it would have led us into the big ore body a year in advance of its discovery." But it wasn't until 1884, with D. Willis and Earl Dodge struggling to maintain "good grace" after having spent $60,000 of their company's money on exploration that had not yielded one carload of ore, that James Douglas drove a test shaft that hit pay dirt. "The last $15,000 to be dropped into the mine was with much misgiving put at my disposal," Douglas wrote. "Long before it reached the 400-foot level, the gloom which overhung the company had been dissipated, for at 210 feet the shaft penetrated a very rich ore body." With the Atlanta and Copper Queen working the same vein, they merged in 1885. Phelps Dodge took ownership in 1886.

Arthur had kept track of what Douglas had accomplished in Bisbee since then, and that too was impressive. Mining is nasty, backbreaking work performed deep in the earth under trying circumstances. In the late 1800s, the air in the tunnels was foul, the heat could be numbing ("the sweat came out of the tops of your shoes," as one miner put it), and safety standards even in the best-run mines were laughable. Until 1886, when the newly developed generator began producing electricity, the miners worked by candlelight! Each man carried his own metal sconce, and a supply of "smokeless" candles. Such work unsurprisingly attracted rough-shod, hard-bitten, often desperate men. Violence was their second nature. The predominantly Cornish miners at Bisbee were clannish, proudly independent, and a volatile handful for any authority figure. All the more reason why James Douglas was held in such high esteem by Arthur James, Arthur's father, and the other officers at Phelps Dodge.

James Douglas was open with Arthur. It was Douglas's innate candor at initial meetings with D. Willis James and Earl Dodge that had led to his engagement. Douglas's keen business acumen, along with his prowess as chemist and metallurgist, along with his reliable analyses and candid reports of situations, had made him a valuable asset for the company. In a day when communications were slow, and distance provided an all-too-convenient shroud for the shady, honesty and loyalty were highly valued within organizations.

Douglas was quietly proud of his mining camp's reputation as the best one in Arizona. He paid the highest wages, and sought out the best labor. Camp morals, according to Lynn Bailey, were controlled through Douglas's "wise and stern discipline." Bailey wrote, "Any employee found drunk or gambling was instantly discharged." Douglas was also cautious. He lived with the high-risk element of the mining work every day. He had no time for celebration. All his time was spent keeping the lid on the many boiling pots he was tending: relationships with other mining companies in the area; safety issues; keeping workers' wages as high as possible; making sure workers' children got good academic and religious educations; maintaining a happy work force through good communication; and by addressing problems before they became nasty issues. As Robert Cleland noted,

"Douglas regretted profoundly that the rise of great corporations was fast destroying the close personal relations that had been possible at one time between employers and employees, and urged that some means be found to counteract this growing evil." When men work as hard as these men work, Douglas told Arthur James, the slightest problem can become a crisis in a flash. Douglas believed the workers and their families deserved to have good lives.

There was another issue, of course: unionism, born of a growing separation between management and workers. The union movement was young, chaotic, but gaining momentum. Everyone knew that like every them-or-us situation, it was going to get ugly. In the Phelps Dodge scheme of things, there was no place for labor union supremacy or domination. The best way to sustain that scheme of things was to keep a happy mining camp. Bisbee, in 1896, was as good as it got. The union issue wouldn't flare up in Bisbee for twenty years—after James Douglas had retired.

In 1899, Dr. Douglas would avert a certain crisis by not invoking "the law of the apex," the 1872 mining law that gave owners of land where a surface outcropping of a vein existed, rights to follow and mine the vein wherever it went. This controversial law had led to lengthy litigation in many cases, and nasty showdowns among miners. Copper Queen was in a crowded neighborhood of rival mines. Invoking the law of the apex would have raised havoc. Dr. Douglas led the way in following the more common law. "We agreed among ourselves," Douglas wrote in *A Memoir*, "to have free access to each other's mines, and therefore anything that one discovered should be open to inspection of his neighbor, so that the development of one would be the development of all."

There was a well-supplied store in Bisbee, one started by locals in the 1880s, that had been taken over by the mining company. The Bisbee store would be the start of the Phelps Dodge Mercantile Company that would open similar "department" stores in all the towns where their mining or smelter operations took place. The Mercantile Company was the Walmart of its day, "buying at lower prices on a large scale to supply townspeople and mine employees with a wider selection of better and cheaper goods," from nails and fencing, ammunition and dynamite, to clothing, feed, food, white silk parasols, Navajo blankets, and steeple-crowned hats.

It wasn't long before Arthur and others in the party so inclined were at the store being outfitted in work clothes for a trip into the mine. The women donned "wash dresses." They ventured to the 400-foot level, experiencing the overwhelming sense of being suspended deep in the dark, hollow silence of the earth, feasting their eyes on other-worldly blue, green, and white caves that had been revealed by mining operations, and marveling over the rich veins of ore being harvested. In one chamber, "candles held close revealed a fairy grotto," Mabel Todd wrote. "The roof and sides were of softest green moss like velvet, so delicate that a finger touch brushed it away—and every leaflet of rich copper."

That evening they had a tour of the smelter, where the roaring Bessemer furnaces were processing 230 tons of ore a day. Workers glistening with sweat shoveled precise amounts of coke into the mix to produce a brilliant, continuous river of molten copper. That night, Arthur and friends followed the small, open train full of the glowing by-product to the slag heap a quarter mile away to watch the sparks shatter the darkness when it was dumped over a precipice into the valley 100 feet below. "It is as beautiful as fireworks," Harriet wrote, "but more useful as the slag-hill becomes solid ground in a short time." Solid ground useless for anything but walking upon, but in 1896, who cared?

For Arthur Curtiss James, the stopover in Bisbee had been well worth taking the long and more uncomfortable way home. Being able to see the Copper Queen mining operation firsthand—getting friendly with Arizona dirt and mud in the process—and being schooled on the nature, potential value, and politics of the various neighboring properties (and the character of their own-

Inside the Phelps Dodge smelter in Bisbee, Arizona around 1900.

ers), would be immensely useful. But mainly, in James Douglas, Arthur had found another mentor worthy of joining the hallowed ranks of his father and James J. Hill.

Heavy rains had delayed their trip to Bisbee, and more rain caused washouts in the roads, delaying their departure. "Arthur decides," Harriet wrote, "the only sure way of traveling and meeting engagements is by sailing vessel."

A mine's heavy reliance on the railroad was also reinforced by Arthur's visit to Copper Queen, and served to justify the high regard he held for rail transportation. Everything a mine requires for its operation is voluminous, and also heavy: timber, fuel, explosives, and big machinery, to mention a few essentials. And hundreds of thousands of pounds of ore need to be shipped on schedule to the smelter. Transportation continues to be a mine's most expensive problem. Arthur was already quite convinced that rail was the future of the country, but nurturing his early dream of fulfilling James Hill's goal of a transcontinental route was one thing. In Bisbee, Arthur had the opportunity to learn in detail how hard James Douglas had worked to solve the relatively miniscule need of a 30-mile rail extension between Bisbee and the town of Fairbank, there to join the Southern Pacific's line that ran between Tucson and El Paso, Texas.

In the early days of Copper Queen production, ore was hauled to the town of Benson by large-wheeled wagons that held five tons. Three wagons would be hooked up in tandem and pulled by the proverbial twenty-mule team. The system was woefully inadequate. The mine was producing around 10,000 pounds of copper a year at the time—or roughly 40,000 to 50,000 pounds of ore. In 1883, there had been the possibility that the Atlantic & Pacific Railroad (predecessor to the Atchison, Topeka & Santa Fe) might build a new line through Bisbee. When that didn't happen, Phelps Dodge decided to build a railroad of its own. Its line from Bisbee north to Fairbank, where there was a Southern Pacific railhead, was finished in 1889, the year Arthur graduated from Amherst. They named it the Arizona & Southeastern Railroad. It had cost $400,000, big money at the time ($10 million today). It also reduced the cost of freight from $6 to $1 a pound, and could move almost unlimited tonnage. It was later extended to the rail head at Benson to give Copper Queen access to the Southern Pacific Railroad as well as the Santa Fe.

Back in 1882, Phelps Dodge had underwritten the construction of a smelter for the Detroit Copper Company in Morenci, Arizona, about 120 miles northeast of Bisbee. Phelps Dodge would assume full ownership of Detroit Copper's Morenci mine the year after Arthur's trip, and James Douglas would take over management. To improve access, the company built the narrow-gauge Morenci Southern Railroad down the mountain to link with the New Mexico & Arizona Railroad at Guthrie in 1901. This was another 30-mile extension further north, close to the New Mexico border, and through much more mountainous terrain. It required the construction of four "loops," or spirals, a track pattern that rises on a steady curve until it has passed over itself, gaining vertical elevation in a relatively short, horizontal distance. One such loop on the Morenci-Guthrie route was built almost entirely in a tunnel.

On another trip to Arizona in 1900, Arthur had a firsthand look at the Morenci-Guthrie construction. What he saw amazed him, and provided more fuel for his railroad obsession. He became even more assured that with rail, anything was possible. Arthur wrote: "After seeing this road I do not wonder at all at its cost. It is by far the most difficult piece of railroad building I have ever seen. . . . It winds back and forth up the side of the mountain, through looped tunnels and over immense trestles. Twisting and turning upon itself in a most wonderful but immensely costly way."

Arthur's keen interest in the railroad end of things was as well-known to Earl Dodge as it was to Arthur's father. In 1901, the elders James and Dodge had conspired to put Arthur's passion to work when Phelps Dodge's railroad properties were merged to create the El Paso & Southwestern Railroad.

**The development of railroads played a pivotal role in
Phelps Dodge mining operations.**

Phelps Dodge's railroad building had expanded as its other mine properties' requirements for transportation became critical. They had found that waiting for existing railroads to accommodate their pressing needs was not good for business. As head of Phelps Dodge's Arizona & Southeastern Railroad, Walter Douglas—son of James Douglas—had been negotiating with the Southern Pacific to route its proposed new line through a point that would be convenient for Phelps Dodge shipments. When that negotiation had fallen through, Phelps Dodge took even more action. "The men who had developed a mining empire in the wilderness were not afraid of large undertakings," Robert Cleland wrote. They had the means. All their properties were growing. Copper was being produced at 11 cents a pound and selling for 19 cents.

When Phelps Dodge's El Paso & Southwestern line was established, Arthur James was made first vice president of the new venture. Shortly after that, Arthur helped spearhead a project to build a 215-mile line to El Paso, Texas, a decision that rocked the Southern Pacific and started a battle between the two companies. The Southern Pacific made the first move, cancelling all joint tariffs with Phelps Dodge, and imposing a maximum rate of 14 cents per ton-mile on the material Phelps Dodge needed for building the new line.

To reach its goal in Deming, Arizona, where they could join with the Santa Fe, the El Paso & Southwestern had to cross the tracks of the Southern Pacific to bring in the supplies it needed to begin building the line to El Paso, Texas, site of the refineries. The Southern Pacific blocked that crossing. What happened next was a team effort engineered by James Douglas in Bisbee, and his son, Walter, and Arthur Curtiss James, who were at Phelps Dodge headquarters at 99 John Street in New York City. The plan was carried out at the crossing by a crew led by a resourceful construction engineer named Darbyshire. That Darbyshire understood the vital nature of his mission was evident by his initial telegram to the team: "Am afraid that we cannot get any of

our material over tonight unless we use some force, and lock the
S.P. crew up in a box car." He reported two watchmen guarding
the crossing day and night, and reported a switch engine parked
on the crossing.

A few hours later, the team received another wire stating
simply that the job had been done. It would be a while before
James and Walter Douglas, and Arthur, would receive the details
of the mission. One can only imagine the restrained enthusiasm
expressed by this trio of conservative overseers when they received word how the job had been accomplished.

What Darbyshire and his crew had done was to flag down
all Southern Pacific trains, then piled rails and other impedi-
ments across the tracks to block the trains' further progress.
"By the following morning," Robert Cleland writes, "five hundred cars of equipment and materials... had been run across the
Southern Pacific right-of-way and left safe on the tracks of the
EP&SW for delivery to the construction crews. Douglas and the
partners of Phelps Dodge officially disapproved of Darbyshire's
actions, but there is no record that he, or anyone else, lost his
job in consequence of the irregular maneuver."

The battle wasn't over. Southern Pacific continued blocking Phelps Dodge's effort to extend its line to El Paso. In court,
the Southern Pacific obtained an injunction against the crossing, successfully blocking a right of way Phelps Dodge needed,
forcing the company to spend an additional $1.5 million ($38
million today) on an alternative route. But the rail line got finished in 1903. By then, the powerful railroad baron, E. H. Harriman, had taken control of Southern Pacific. Realizing he would
be alienating a very good customer by continuing to harass the
El Paso & Southwestern, Harriman made overtures of peace to
James Douglas. As Carlos A. Schwantes wrote in *Vision & Enterprise: Exploring the History of Phelps Dodge Corporation*,
Douglas would extract a stiff price to forget past differences:
"Douglas would refuse to extend his hand in friendship until a
chastised Harriman came to his office bearing a check for the

difference between the 14 cents-per-ton-mile the Southern Pacific charged him for shipping construction materials, and the lower rate that had previously been in effect." There were additional costs Douglas demanded be repaid by Southern Pacific. "Only on receipt of this generous settlement did [Douglas] relent."

All in all, the El Paso & Southwestern experience provided a significant initial chapter in the railroad career of Arthur Curtiss James. His mentor, James Douglas, had showed him the way.

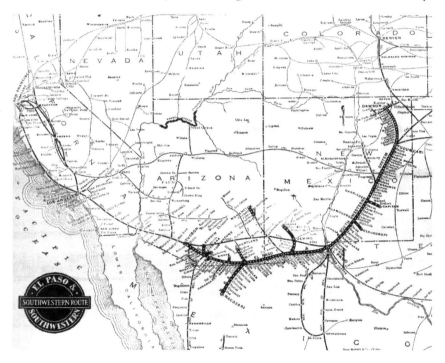

And working alongside Douglas's son Walter, Arthur discovered that apples can in fact fall far from the tree. Walter Douglas had inherited his father's tough side, but not his belief in the intrinsic dignity of human nature. This would create a problem later on.

Arthur's next venture as vice present of EP&SW would involve the acquisition of another railroad—the El Paso & Northeastern—that ran between El Paso and Dawson, in northern New Mexico, where there were coal mines. The railroad was in bad shape, nearly bankrupt, but James Douglas thought the coal mines made it a worthwhile purchase in a forced sale. "The coal mine itself," he wrote in a memo, "can supply all the coal needed for the next hundred years . . . we have a blanket of coal at least five feet thick extending in one direction for ten miles and in the other, eight miles. This can all be mined by tunnels in the hillside." The El Paso & Southwestern acquired the El Paso & Northeastern in 1905.

By 1906, the El Paso & Southwestern had reached Tucumcari, New Mexico—where it connected with the Rock Island RR (Chicago, Rock Island & Pacific). Arthur James would become a director of the Rock Island line in 1906, and eventually a member of Rock Island's executive committee. By 1910, the El Paso & Southwestern could boast 1,000 miles of track in an arc following the curve of the Mexican border, with Tucson as its western terminus.

Aloha

3

One thing serious sailors have in common is their never-ending lust for boats. Like car guys, or those preoccupied by the opposite sex, serious sailors never, ever tire of looking at (or dreaming of) the objects of their passion. Water is such an unstable medium that the challenge it offers yacht designers is infinite. Combine water with wind and you have two very unstable mediums disharmoniously working to beset whatever vessel one tries to design. There is all manner of water, from the deceptively innocent-looking pond, to lakes large and small; from broad, cranky rivers and stormy bays to the legendary perils of the open ocean. Many vessels have been built for these various waters, and it is safe to say that all of them could fail at some point or another. Mother Nature will always win if she wishes. Serious sailors know that, but for them, the combination of wind and water is impossibly seductive. They find the enduring pleasures it offers to be well worth the risk. Armed with due respect, and a vessel all their experience tells them is as fit as possible for the job, they venture forth with confidence. Serious sailors who are wealthy build their dream boats, and often amass a fleet. That's what Arthur Curtiss James would do.

In the winter of 1896 and '97, not long after the Japan trip, Arthur got in touch with a budding naval architect by the name of Clinton Crane, asking him to design a small sailing lifeboat for *Coronet*. There is no indication that Arthur was a friend of Crane's, but serious sailors used to regularly promote kinships from afar with a designer based on the vessels he produced. That sort of thing happened more in the days before wind tunnels, test tanks, and, ultimately, computer modeling began making vessels look so similar. Before the science of determining the most efficient shapes for vehicles moving through air (automobiles in particular) or water took over, the art of design prevailed. Just as any eight-year-old boy worth his salt could tell a Ford from a Chevrolet a quarter mile away in the 1950s, serious sailors could identify a Herreshoff, a Burgess, a Crane, an Alden, or a Fife from the subtle curve of a sheer line, the rise of a bow, or the flow of a stern quarter. The look of every yacht in those early days bore the designer's unmistakable signature.

Clinton Crane

Crane was regarded as an "amateur" designer who drew yachts for himself and his friends. His body of work would eventually rank him among the most noteworthy naval architects. He started a small design shop, but quit to run the family's mining business, the St. Joseph Lead Company in Missouri. Crane's involvement with mining surely had something to do with Arthur's inclination towards him as a designer. Crane was president of St. Joseph Lead for thirty-four years, and he was a member of the Phelps Dodge board of directors as a "renown mining engineer." Somehow, he made time to design a bunch of beautiful, significant yachts, including several 12-Meters including *Gleam* (US 11), and the J-Class *Weetamoe*. Crane was also from Oyster Bay, New York, and a member of the Seawanhaka Corinthian Yacht Club. Even without all the connections, the talent Crane's lovely designs revealed would alone have been sufficient to attract Arthur's attention. In any case, Arthur tried him out with the little lifeboat for *Coronet*.

In his book, *Yachting Memories*, Crane wrote that the lifeboat for James was his first professional order as a designer: "The boat was to be designed with a self-bailing cockpit and watertight compartments, so she might be a lifeboat and yet be so designed that she would be fun to sail when *Coronet* was in port." The only indication that the lifeboat was a success was Arthur James's subsequent request to Crane for the design of a seagoing auxiliary yacht to replace *Coronet*. "This yacht was to be a steam auxiliary of 126-foot waterline," Crane wrote, "rigged as a brigantine, with square yards on the foremast and fore-and-aft sail on the main." That's quite a leap, from a 15-foot sailing lifeboat to a 126-foot, full-rigged brigantine.

As a designer, Crane was interested in producing the fastest possible square-rigger. Yachts of the size James had requested were indeed the fastest sailing vessels in the world at the time. But Crane knew that in order to support the larger rig he envisioned, he would have to reduce the interior living space to accommodate the more robust gear that would be required. "I am sure that as she finally came out," Crane wrote, "with the smaller rig and more comfortable quarters inside, the James [sic] enjoyed the *Aloha* more, but it was a little disappointing to the designer."

The first Aloha (*above, and opposite*) was a 160-foot, full-rigged brigantine.

Aloha was built of steel by the J. N. Robins & Company shipyard (having merged with Erie Basin and Drydock Company) in Brooklyn, New York, and launched on June 22, 1899. The *New York Times* covered such events in those days. The *Times* reported the yacht was 160 feet overall, and would carry 13,000 square feet of canvas. Her beam was 29 feet, 6 inches, she had 16 feet of depth below decks, and her sides were full, allowing for a main saloon that measured 15 by 25 feet. There were watertight bulkheads throughout, but no mention of a piano. Two items in the report were extraordinary for the day. First, the yacht's funnel was of the telescoping variety so it could be lowered when under sail. The other was even more noteworthy: *Aloha* had a feathering propeller, with blades that folded up when not in use, to reduce drag. Finish work on the yacht would be expedited so her commissioning would be in time for the New York Yacht Club cruise in August. The New York Yacht Club's archives do not, alas, include a list of the yachts participating in that cruise.

One thing the *Times* piece did not include was the confusion over *Aloha*'s figurehead. Arthur had told Clinton Crane that he wanted his yacht to have a figurehead, and he had decided to surprise Harriet by having it carved in her likeness. He supplied Crane with portraits of Harriet. Crane gave the photographs to the sculptor and forgot about it amid the more essential details of construction. Finally, when it was approaching the time for the figurehead to be installed, Crane went to see the sculptor. "When I went to inspect it," Crane wrote, "I found it had been modeled in the nude. The sculptor said that was the way figureheads should be, but I persuaded him to put on some Greek drapery."

In fact it was Arthur who had jogged Crane's memory about the figurehead. Arthur had stopped by the sculptor's studio to check the work in progress, and had been greatly amused by what he saw. He couldn't disagree that the figurehead tradition had been dutifully followed with the topless rendering of his wife's likeness. But he knew a bit of draping would have to be done.

Arthur had arranged for the sculptor to leave him the key to his studio so he could privately show Harriet what would be more of a surprise than he had planned. Anyone passing by the studio that evening would have heard gales of laughter coming from the young married couple, followed by a titillated female voice saying, "But Arthur, you know that's not me!"

Through their yacht club and design associations, Arthur and Clinton Crane became close. "He was such a loyal friend," Crane wrote, "that he always forgave me my mistakes and stood by me through thick and thin. He loved the sea, was never seasick, and especially loved long ocean voyages where the square rigs were really at their best."

There was nothing Arthur wanted to do more than jump aboard his new *Aloha* with Harriet and a bunch of their friends and go cruising. But business reared its head in the form of another struggle for railroad expansion. This time it would take more than a midnight raid on a rival railroad's crossing to settle the issue. And this time, James J. Hill's Great Northern was involved. Having committed himself to Hill's transcontinental dream years before, this was not a fight Arthur could ignore, even if he were only playing a supporting role.

The Hill interest also included the Northern Pacific railroad, in which Hill was a major stockholder. The Northern Pacific had preceded Hill's Great Northern, and covered a similar, but more southerly route. The competition between the two had always been friendly. But the Northern Pacific had not been well managed, and it had declared more than one bankruptcy. The Hill team had bought in, and Hill had J. P. Morgan, D. Willis James, and Arthur on his front line. Opposing them (once again) was E. H. Harriman, who now owned the Union Pacific Railroad. Both sides were bent on completing a northern, transcontinental route into California. To do so, both sides had determined they needed to acquire one of several feeder lines that would give them speedy access to Chicago. Both selected the Chicago, Burlington & Quincy system that had become a force in the Midwest under a brilliant financier named John Murray Forbes. It had been guided by a capable manager in Charles Perkins, who had been president of the Chicago, Burlington & Quincy for twenty years.

During Perkins's tenure, the CB&Q had tripled in size. In 1901, it connected Chicago with St. Louis, Kansas City, Omaha, Denver, St. Paul, Minneapolis, and Billings, Montana. It was an important, very strong system, "the" supply line for manufacturing and agriculture for the entire Midwest. But Forbes had died in 1898, after having overseen the finances of the company for forty-seven years. And in early 1901, Perkins would retire, but he remained a powerful influence on the board. Having failed to reach the West Coast with the CB&Q, Perkins had realized the line's best move was to make it part of another railroad's transcontinental plan. Perkins had been approached by E. H. Harriman, but felt Hill's Northern Pacific/Great Northern system was a better fit, perhaps because of the similar "personal" reputations of the two companies. Those who were associated with both lines, from customers to employees, felt that if all else failed, they could go to the top—to Hill, or even the famously irascible Charles Perkins—and get a fair hearing.

Perkins set the price of Burlington shares at $200. Harriman had balked, but Hill's team met the price and by 1900 was poised to take over the line that not only would provide the high-speed connection to Chicago it needed, but would, as Perkins said, "assure us of what we do not now possess—a permanent connection by the shortest line with the great Northwest."

With that midnight ambush on his Union Pacific still smarting, and the grating memory of the hefty payoff it had cost him to reestablish relations between Western Pacific and Phelps Dodge's El Paso & Southwestern Railroad, Harriman would not take this defeat sitting down. The Burlington was held half by the Great Northern and half by the Northern Pacific. In early 1901 Harriman began a stock raid on the Northern Pacific, his goal being to buy the controlling interest and use that to put friendly faces on the Burlington board of directors.

As B. H. Meyer reports it in *A History of the Northern Securities Case*, Harriman proceeded to buy $8 million to $9 million (or roughly 10 percent) of the Burlington stock. But he ran into a problem. "Much of the stock had been held for many years by people who had inherited it," Meyer writes, "and it was found impossible to secure control of the property through purchases in the open market."

Harriman then opened negotiations with the Burlington, asking that his Union Pacific be included in the purchase of the line. He asked for half interest. He was refused. The sale was final, with Hill's two railroads—the Northern Pacific and the Great Northern—sharing ownership of all the stock.

Refusing to quit, Harriman began a second raid on the

ESTABLISHING A "COMMUNITY OF INTEREST"
Cartoon by W. A. Rogers, *Harper's Weekly*, May 25, 1901

Northern Pacific, buying up a significant amount of the railroad's stock. Hill and his team responded by increasing their holdings in the line, especially in common stock. This would be key, because, as B. H. Meyer explains, "Harriman's . . . majority lay in preferred shares which could be retired on any first day of January prior to 1917—that is, before the present owners could get an opportunity of exercising the authority which was assumed to reside in them, and which would give them the coveted control." That had been a resolution of the board of directors.

A battle royal between Harriman and Hill interests began on Wall Street on May 1, 1901, when Harriman's raid on Northern Pacific stock became known. As Meyer tells it, "Short selling of Northern Pacific stock and the scramble to cover, when it was discovered that only a limited supply was to be had, drove the price of Northern Pacific common stock up to about $1000 per share. This was the climax of a series of events which culminated in the stock-exchange crisis of May 9, 1901, when the markets of the world were convulsed, the equilibrium of the financial world shaken."

Meyer ominously concluded: "Had this battle on Wall Street been fought to the last ditch and the Union Pacific interests had triumphed, the measure of the injury done to the Great Northern and Northern Pacific would have been destruction."

But it wasn't. The Hill team let it be known they were considering a postponement of the October 1901 board meeting until after January 1, 1902, at which time the preferred stock held by Union Pacific could be retired, eliminating the Union Pacific's sole weapon for taking control of the Northern Pacific and wreaking destruction. The failure of the Harriman team to exercise within the one-year period their right as preferred stockholders to convert the preferred stock to common stock remains a mystery. It left the Union Pacific a minority stockholder. "This potential power [of Hill's team to retire the preferred stock]," Meyer writes, "appears to have generated a conciliatory attitude on the part of Union Pacific interests." An understanding was reached between the embattled sides, under which membership of the Northern Pacific board of directors was left in the hands of J. P. Morgan—the banker, financier, and yachtsman who was a few years younger than D. Willis James.

With the idea of preventing future raids upon Northern Pacific and Great Northern stock, a holding company, the Northern Securities Company, was formed by the Hill interests in November 1901. Chartered in New Jersey, and capitalized at $400 million—roughly the combined total of the stock of the Great

Northern and Northern Pacific—a board of fifteen men represented those two railroads (six from each), and the Union Pacific (three). Less than a week after the Northern Securities charter had been granted, opposition to this "great railway trust" began in the form of a statement issued by the governor of Minnesota protesting a monopoly. Thus began the Northern Securities Case, which went on for years and helped mature the laws that regulate monopolies. It took two Supreme Court decisions to resolve it.

Having had a priceless education on the highly competitive financial front lines of the biggest business that existed at the time, Arthur Curtiss James wasted no time getting back to sea. Perhaps he felt the essential rhythm and awesome power of the sea, the overriding and calming focus it demands for the well-being of vessel and crew, and the constant resourcefulness it extracts from those who venture upon it would be the perfect antidote to the many stressful months of financial combat he had just endured. Problems taken to sea have a way of losing their bite under a boundless dome of sky and the striking immensity of nothing but water in every direction as far as the eye can see.

Arthur wanted to go sailing. His yacht had been waiting there at Tebo Basin in Brooklyn, virtually untested since it was launched in June 1899. The prolonged fight with Harriman over control of the Burlington line had come at just the wrong time. Put a new boat, large or small, at the dock of any serious sailor and that is the only thing he will be thinking about. The first moment he could, Arthur alerted his crew, rounded up a few friends, and set sail.

For his new yacht he had a new skipper, Captain Peleoman Bezanson. The same age as Arthur, Bezanson had been a boatbuilder in Nova Scotia before going to sea. In 1895 he had rescued the crew of a coasting vessel off Cape Cod, for which he was awarded a presidential gold medal. Now he was in command of perhaps America's finest sailing yacht.

It would be a busy and fun couple of years under sail on *Aloha*, beginning with a variation of the West Indies cruise Arthur had taken on *Coronet*, with ports of call in Barbados, Trinidad, the Windward Islands, Santa Cruz, Puerto Rico, Cuba, and Nassau. Once again, members of his party were selected to become scribes for the various journeys. Their journals indicate that Arthur was busier than ever on board, especially when Neptune had one of his querulous moments. Halfway to Bermuda on their first cruise they encountered a gale. "Captain Arthur was on deck all day," the scribe wrote, "and had also been taking the lion's share of the watches at night. We all turn in with a blissful sense of security in spite of the storm, knowing him to be in command and fully alive to every need of boat or crew."

Two days later, Neptune had a tantrum that would have put E. H. Harriman to shame. "The storm of the past Sunday melted into insignificance," the scribe wrote. "Arthur said it was the worst storm he had ever been in, though he had encountered a typhoon off the coast of Japan. The sea was lashed to a fury almost at once. The waves piled up higher than the yards, thirty-five feet above the deck. It seemed as if it must be impossible for any boat to live in such a sea.

"Arthur we only saw from time to time, as he ran in with hair and beard dripping and pools of water forming around his feet, to report all well and to answer anxious, if useless inquiries as to how soon under heaven did he think it would stop."

It did stop, of course. All storms do, eventually. What lingers is the damage they have wreaked. But *Aloha* and her crew proved up to handling this storm, with only minor damage here and there to the vessel, and nothing to crew and passengers that several hours in a bunk followed by a warm, drying day couldn't cure. Arthur, Harriet, and their friends cruised the West Indies as they had done previously on *Coronet*, playing shuffleboard on deck, sightseeing ashore "like a traveling circus," as one scribe joked, and dining with local authorities who were delighted by the visit from these important, wealthy dignitaries from America. In Trinidad they marveled at the women washing the clothes and linens from *Aloha* in the streams, and the lady scribe provided this description of the party crossing a stream in their wanderings around Trinidad, a sign of the times:

> *When it came to the ladies, it was very embarrassing. Two darky boys made "ladies chairs" by crossing their hands and grasping the wrists, and on these chairs we were obliged to sit, one arm around each boy's neck. My chair was of a decidedly reclining nature, so tilted back that I was mighty uncomfortable, and then, too, to find that Arthur was trying to take a picture! Fortunate for me that the light was poor.*

Five months later, the *Aloha* cruises continued into the Gulf of St. Lawrence and Quebec, where fishing and some bird hunting would be the amusements. It began with the yacht doing duty as a mother ship for three Seawanhaka Raceabouts, a class of small boats that Clinton Crane had designed in 1900. On the way north, *Aloha* towed the Raceabouts from Seawanhaka to Buzzard's Bay for a team race against the Beverly Yacht Club in Marion, Massachusetts. Today, small race boats start at 7 feet, 9 inches (the length of the Optimist pram for kids age fourteen and under), move on to the Olympic Laser class (13 feet), and more or less include anything under 22 feet overall. In the early 1900s, the 34-foot Raceabout was considered a "small" boat, but then that was yachting's gilded age.

The Raceabout was a gaff-rigged, centerboard sloop that was beamy as suited her day, low on the water with pretty lines ending in overhangs at both ends. Another handsome creation by Clinton Crane. A crew of four or five raced the boat from a roomy cockpit.

As a Seawanhaka regular whose term as commodore of the exclusive club ran from 1901 to 1905, Arthur was pleased to have *Aloha* cast in the mother-ship role. With convenient access to New York City provided by the Long Island Railroad, James was just one of many industrial titans who were drawn to Long Island's North Shore in the early twentieth century. The local telephone books read like a *Who's Who* in business and finance, with names like Sloan, Chrysler, Astor, Gould, Whitney, Gubelman, Roosevelt, Belmont, Morgan, and Pulitzer—among many others—affixed to palatial waterfront estates that often consumed 100 or more well-landscaped acres. The yacht clubs built to meet the increasing recreational and social needs, including the Knickerbocker, Manhasset Bay, Port Washington, Huntington, Sea Cliff, Hempstead Harbor, and Cold Spring Harbor clubs, would become homes to many of the fast, 65- to 80-foot commuter yachts that sped these captains of industry into New York City every morning.

Arthur never built on the North Shore, but good friends like William J. Matheson, whose dye works became Allied Chemical, and Arthur's cousin, Dr. Walter James, an acclaimed Manhattan physician who also ran the Trudeau tuberculosis clinic in Saranac, New York, welcomed him as a frequent visitor.

Arthur was attracted to the Corinthian culture of the Seawanhaka club. At a time when owners often stepped aboard yachts made ready to sail by professional crews and (possibly) take the helm, Seawanhaka sailors were known for their hands-on approach to sailing, for their joy in rigging, prepping, and sailing their own boats. Hence the term "Corinthian," or amateur. Center Island also happens to be a convenient port of call for yachts sailing between New York City and Newport, Rhode Island. Both of James's large sailing yachts had accommodations of such consummate comfort that building a house near the club would have been redundant.

Aloha arrived in Marion with the Raceabouts under tow early on the morning of race day. Things did not go well for the visitors from Seawanhaka. They lost convincingly to the Beverly sailors. As the ever-hopeful, designated scribe put it, "It is too bad to lose the Cup, which is a beauty, but there will be a chance to win it back next year."

Another race was about to take place, as it happened. Yachts from the New York Yacht Club cruise had descended upon Marion that night. The next morning the fleet began its race to Vineyard Haven. Arthur decided to cruise along with them, but not race, even though a brigantine in the fleet named *Mohican* would have provided good competition. As *Aloha* neared Vineyard Haven, *Aloha* caught up with *Mohican*, now towing a disabled yacht. *Aloha* signaled, asking if they needed help. *Mohican*, mistaking the signal for a challenge, signaled back to come within hailing distance. They did. "Will race you for $100 cup to Marblehead," was *Mohican*'s hail. *Aloha*'s scribe wrote: "'Gee, I'd rather do anything than that,' Arthur said to us. But through the megaphone he shouted like a man, 'Alright, when will you start?' and the answer is, 'Now!' Poor *Aloha* has a foul bottom and is minus her main stays'l, very much needed in this wind, but left behind by mistake, so Arthur did not feel we had much of a chance. We had a pretty start. During the next three hours the two boats were neck and neck. Toward dark, however, *Mohican* drew away."

The following summer found the Seawanhaka team once again traveling to Marion for a rematch of the team race they had lost. The America's Cup has always been known as "the" no-holds-barred competition between notable industrialists, with money being no object. In the gilded age of yachting, every meeting on the water between rival clubs bore that same kind of intensity. Captains of industry were involved, and losing was simply not acceptable to them. In response to the loss to Beverly, Seawanhaka had contacted Clinton Crane. "While I was in Scotland," Crane writes in *Yachting Memories*, "my friends at Seawanhaka had been having team races in the Raceabout class. One was between Seawanhaka and Beverly Yacht Club on Buzzards Bay, and the Seawanhaka team was pretty badly beaten. I had a letter from my Seawanhaka friends asking me to design for Mr. Arthur Curtiss James a boat to race in the team races the following year."

It's clear that while Arthur was the prime, or even the sole contributor to the design and building of a new Raceabout, his intention was to provide a boat for his club that would be sailed by a hot racing skipper who would be selected by consensus.

Crane got to work and produced *Lanai*, another Hawaiian

name offered by Arthur, that was 300 pounds lighter and was seldom beaten in its career. The next season, the Seawanhaka team trekked back to Marion with *Lanai*, its secret weapon, in tow. At the helm was Clinton Crane himself. He tells what happened in the next meeting with Beverly: "*Lanai* was the outstanding boat, and was able to save the day in one of the races, but in the final race, although *Lanai* won, the other members of the team were not well placed and the team lost."

That same summer, Arthur took the helm of "his" Raceabout in a team race against American Yacht Club, in Rye, New York. As James Parkinson noted in his book, *SCYC 1897–1940*, "Clinton Crane had designed a new wider, centerboard Raceabout named *Lanai* for Commodore James, which he sailed to victory that day over Stuyvesant Wainwright's *Howdy*, which was second."

* * *

Part three of *Aloha*'s first series of cruises was to Reykjavik, Iceland, that summer. If there was a common thread to Arthur's blue-water ventures, it was encounters with nasty weather. There was nary a voyage of any length where the assigned scribe did not haul out the adjectives to describe the furies of the deep, the deathly discomfort of the passengers, the heroics of the crew, the laudable behavior of the vessel, and the stalwart, confidence-inspiring leadership of Captain James. The approach to Reykjavik was no exception. "After two days of driving into the teeth of a northeasterly gale, we made harbor this morning at Reykjavik, glad enough to get in after our buffeting in the face of a gale, which brought with it the breath of Arctic ice fields. . . . The gale still continues with unabated fury. And all are glad to be riding quietly out of its reach, once more on an even keel after eighteen days at sea."

After a few weeks of sightseeing in Reykjavik, *Aloha* sailed on to the Shetland Islands, cruised the fjords of Norway, then visited Denmark, Stockholm, and Edinburgh, and finally making port in London, where the whole party went on a two-week tour of the countryside by horse-drawn coach. On October 1, 1903, they all boarded the SS *Cymric* of the White Star Line for the trip back across the Atlantic.

Not long after Arthur was back at work in his office at 99 John Street in New York, he received a letter from *Aloha*'s Captain Bezanson, reporting that the brigantine had been struck by a steamer. At the time, the yacht was 200 miles west of the Island of Ushant, off the western-most point of the French mainland.

"I am most sorry to have to write you that we have met with so serious an accident," Captain Bezanson wrote, "but more than thankful that our lives have been spared." Bezanson went on to say that *Aloha* had been hove to for three days in the teeth of a southwest gale blowing at times with hurricane force. The night of October 27 the gale moderated, with rain continuing. At midnight they proceeded on course (west-southwest) under shortened sail, reaching hard, "with seas running like mountains." At 3:30 a.m. they sighted a steamer's red light close by, an indication that the steamer was running a parallel course off to their right. The steamer suddenly altered course to the left, which would put the large vessel on collision course with *Aloha*. The mate was on deck, and shouted to the helmsman to steer hard to port (left). At best, the response time on a sailing vessel the size of *Aloha* is close to thirty or forty seconds in ideal conditions. That night, prior to sighting the steamer, the wind had come ahead. *Aloha* was making all of two knots into a lumpy head sea. The helmsman put the helm hard over with all his might (that would have been fifteen to twenty turns), and watched the steamer come at *Aloha* while he waited helplessly for the big sailboat to respond.

"He struck on the starboard bow," Captain Bezanson wrote, "carrying away all headgear, figurehead, starboard buffalo and forechannels; we swung around broadside to him and both seemed to be coming together when on a huge wave we rolled apart, he forging ahead passed clear of us; this I wish to state was all that saved our ship and lives. If we had met in the trough of the sea the *Aloha* and all hands would have been at the bottom of the ocean."

Captain Bezanson went on to report that the steamer, the SS *Zoroaster*—a 3,800-ton cargo ship that would be sunk by a German mine in 1916—stood by until dawn, making sure *Aloha* was seaworthy before it went on its way to Port Said, Egypt. *Aloha* had been surveyed, and *Zoroaster's* company had been notified they were responsible for all damages. The captain wrote:

We had bad luck after you left us. For a month the wind has been blowing a gale . . . the varnish has washed off the deck and houses, but we have tested her seagoing qualities and find her a fine sea-boat; not afraid to go anywhere in her. Well, Mr. James, it was the nearest call I have seen yet. If the Aloha *had gone, there was no chance for us . . . the sea was running the highest I ever saw it, and combing so bad I consider us very fortunate. Feel bad to lose so much time and expense, but very glad we were spared to get into port safely again. I expect some of the crew will leave, as they were pretty near frightened to death.*

At 99 John Street, Arthur's secretary heard an exclamation of distress from her boss's office. Concerned, she stopped what she was doing and warily opened his door. Arthur was seated at his desk, his head in his hands, a letter on the desk before him. She asked if he were all right. He looked up, stared blankly at her for a moment, then said: "We must commission a new figurehead."

* * *

Upon recrossing the Atlantic, *Aloha* went into the yard for a total overall. A few new crewmen were hired, and within months Arthur and friends were off again on trips to Germany and Great Britain. Perhaps no one understood how captivated by the sea people can become better than novelist Joseph Conrad. Like divers with decompression sickness who find temporary relief by returning to the depth where they were struck, many of Conrad's sailors felt comfortable only when they were at sea. Ashore, they were out of sorts, drinking to excess, getting in fights, and often ending up in jail. Only by returning to the sea was their sense of calm and well-being restored.

Arthur, as we have seen, was not at all derailed by life ashore. In fact he seemed a master of both worlds, as comfortable in the throes of copper-mine problems and railroad finance as he was at the helm of his mighty yachts. In either case, he appeared to take it as it came by being prepared, and maintaining balance. That letter Arthur wrote to Mabel Todd in Japan is a good example. There he was, cruising Japan's Inland Sea on a steamer he'd chartered, manned by a drunken, unruly crew that was threatening his party. And he wrote: "For two nights we had to keep watch with our revolvers in our hands to prevent their robbing us." That's it. No string of colorful adjectives, no frantic calls to the coast guard for help. Just the facts. Take it as it comes. If the crew gets drunk and unruly, keep watch with your revolver drawn. Next?

The word "cool" comes to mind. It's an old word, a much used and abused adjective that has long since broken free of the dictionary to run amok on the streets. Writing in the *New York Times* (July 25, 2017), columnist David Brooks perhaps defined it best: "The cool person is stoical, emotionally controlled, never eager or needy, but instead mysterious, detached and self-possessed. The cool person is gracefully competent at something, but doesn't need the world's applause to know his worth. That's because the cool person has found his or her own unique and authentic way of living with nonchalant intensity."

Arthur seemed able to put life's constant annoyances to one side and focus on the satisfactions. Nonchalant intensity. As he once wrote, "We made many voyages to England and back simply for the sake of glorious days at sea which, after all, is the chief charm of yachting." It's safe to say that no one has ever sailed transatlantic without a couple of difficult days of one sort or another. But for Arthur, it seems all days at sea were glorious.

Milestones

Arthur had been off sailing during much of the protracted legal battle involving the Northern Securities Case, a battle that progressed from local state courts to circuit courts and finally the Supreme Court. Briefs issued by both sides were in the 400- to 800-page range. But it is safe to say Arthur did not miss any of the essential opinions that were delivered, decisions that helped shape, and reinforce his philosophy about the railroad business.

The initial grievance expressed by the governor of Minnesota, urging his fellow governors of nearby states to "fight the great railway trust," was quickly followed by the categorization of Northern Securities—the holding company created by James J. Hill, J. P. Morgan, and D. Willis James for the protection of Great Northern and Northern Pacific Railroad stock—as a monopoly. That allowed the Sherman Antitrust Act of 1890 to be invoked, the language of which prohibits interference with trade, and addresses the reduction of economic competition. Despite the entreaties of J. P. Morgan, President Theodore Roosevelt considered it a trust and ordered the Justice Department to file suit in 1902.

It took almost three years before the case got to the Supreme Court at the end of 1903. In March 1904 the Court ruled 55 to 4 that Northern Securities was a monopoly and should be broken up. That body of ultimate judgement declared the disassembling of a monopoly was not under their jurisdiction, and returned it to the state court. Despite its dismissal, the language of the Supreme Court's decision made it clear that the Sherman Antitrust Act against monopolies should prevail. James J. Hill immediately sent out a circular to his stockholders: "Your directors, at a meeting held this day, have, under advice of counsel, decided that in order to fully and promptly comply with the decree in this suit, it is necessary to reduce the capital stock of the company and distribute to its shareholders the shares of stock of said railway companies now held by it."

That aspect of the case, the reduction (by 1,000 percent) and distribution of stock, would start phase two in the battle: still another attack by Harriman involving the stock Union Pacific had purchased on its raid on the Northern Pacific. At the Northern Securities stockholders' meeting in March 1904, all the shareholders present voted to accept the plan presented by Hill. A month later, Harriman's legal team argued that the plan was illegal and in violation of their rights. The Harriman arguments would be advanced for another year before they were resolved by the Supreme Court in Hill's favor. In his *History of the Northern Securities Case*, B. H. Meyer quoted from the Supreme Court's decision, which was unanimous:

It became the duty of the Securities company to end a situation that had been adjudged unlawful, and this could be effected by the sale and distribution in cash, or by distribution in kind, and the latter method was adopted, and wisely adopted, as we think, for the forced sale of several hundred millions of stock would have manifestly involved disastrous results. The title to those stocks having intentionally been passed, the former owners or part of them cannot reclaim the specific shares and must be content with their ratable proportion of the corporate assets.

There was certainly much for Arthur to learn from the financial resolution Hill and his team engineered for the stock of Northern Securities, but overriding that was the issue of monopoly as it applied to railroads. The Northern Securities case fostered a noteworthy legal debate that had covered nearly four years, produced hundreds of witnesses and many thousands of pages of testimony and briefs, and had not been resolved to the liking of economist and historian B. H. Meyer, for one. Meyer was also a railroad expert who wrote the history of the case. As for the application of the Sherman Antitrust Act, Meyer wrote:

It was assumed that competition had been stifled without first asking the question whether competition had actually existed; and whether, if competition could be perpetuated, the public would profit by it. Opposition to the Securities company rested chiefly upon the same ground that opposition to agreements among railway companies, pools, and all cooperative movements among carriers has generally rested. This undiscriminating opposition to all forms of open concerted action on the part of the railways is in my mind the greatest single blunder in our public policy toward railways. [Meyer wrote that in 1972.]

In 1932, Arthur Curtiss James had written an article titled "A Plea for Our Railroads" in the *Saturday Evening Post* magazine. He had warned:

The railroads of the United States face a most serious crisis… the result of archaic legislation involving the railroads in endless red tape; or direct and hidden Government subsidies to competitive carrier systems; of public meddling in railroad business and the resulting hindrance to expedient changes of policies. Actuating these causes is the popular misconception that railways constitute a monopoly, and the lack of public understanding of the true relation railroads bring to national prosperity, to the progress and success of the commonwealth, and to industry in general.

Many years, and many miles of track of his making would be behind Arthur before he wrote that, but his words reflected basic principles that had guided him since he was in the student club at Amherst College that backed Grover Cleveland, the presidential candidate who ran on an anti-tariff platform in 1888.

* * *

In 1904—the same year Northern Securities was dissolved—Arthur succeeded his father as a trustee of Amherst College. D. Willis James had been on Amherst's board since 1891, and had become one of the college's largest benefactors. He had given Amherst $200,000 while his son was a student, and before he joined the board. His gifts were often earmarked for professors' salaries. He felt that paying professors salaries commensurate with their talents would "always secure and retain the very best men for the several chairs," according to *A History of the Endowment of Amherst College*, by Stanley King, who was president of Amherst from 1932 to 1946. As a trustee, Arthur would go on to exceed even his father's generosity, working hard on committees, chairing the board in his later years, and being called by King in *"The Consecrated Eminence"* (his second book on Amherst), "one of the most generous benefactors of the College."

But he would still find time—make time—for sailing. Many of the same names pop up on the list of guests who accompanied Arthur and Harriet on their voyages. Arthur helped set more than one of them up in small businesses so they would be able to answer his call to the sea. In 1904, *Aloha*'s cruising was held to ports along the East Coast. But in 1905, off they went again across the Atlantic. The little vest-pocket logbooks Arthur kept are of minor interest unless one is fascinated by repetitive listings of course, speed, wind direction and velocity, and amount of fuel oil consumed. But when Arthur filled in the logbooks from 1903 through 1912 from memory, twenty years later, he provided occasional glimpses of the grand, whirlwind nature of these many voyages.

On the first cruise in 1905, for instance, they were exploring the lochs of northwest Scotland. "At a bad turn at 9am we ran on a smooth rock, but did no damage," Arthur writes. "As the glass was falling and the weather threatening, decided to start around the northern coast for Inverness." That is an ambitious sail of several hundred miles, touching on latitude 60 degrees north. But they made it to Inverness in two days, there to anchor and batten down under the thrashing of still another gale.

They left the yacht in Inverness, took a train to Edinburgh to visit a relative ("Uncle Willie" it says in the log, Arthur's infamous half-uncle), then took an overnight train to London. The next day they took a ferry to Ostend, Belgium, from whence they took a train 600 miles to the Carlsbad Medical Spa in what is now the Czech Republic, "where Harriet was to take the cure," Arthur writes. "The cure," at Carlsbad, was built around twelve thermal springs, waters that contained varying degrees of carbon dioxide. The waters were taken externally and internally, for both specific ailments and generally to promote good health.

Spas like Carlsbad were quite the health-craze from the 1870s until World War I. "Taking the cure" was a popular, upper-class thing to do. It involved a mix of medical, recreational, and light-hearted connotations. Taking the cure was certainly restful. No doubt it relieved stress, and it was good for those convalescing from an illness. The fact that Harriet took it for three weeks suggests it involved a bit more than recreation on her part. There was no illness noted that she was recovering from. One has to wonder if she might have hoped that taking a serious approach to "the cure" might promote her ability to conceive a child, something she and Arthur had not been able to accomplish. Such things were not discussed beyond the privacy of a doctor's office in 1905. Conception does require two fertile people, but Arthur, for his part, showed no interest in taking the cure. They arrived at the spa on September 2. Arthur wrote:

We remained [in Carlsbad] until September 23 and the monotony for those of us who were not taking the cure was relieved by a motor trip to Dresden via Prague and the Hartz Mountains. The condition of automobiling in 1905 is illustrated by the fact that in going up a hill we had to back up the car in order for the gasoline to feed the carburetor. We did not average over ten miles an hour on the trip and on the way back from Dresden broke down completely and had to go back by train.

They went on to Vienna for a few days, and then to Paris for a week. "The women of the party are doing what they are expected to do in Paris," Arthur wrote in the log, "and the men are killing time and eating too much." Finally they arrived in London, where after a week they sailed home on the SS *Kronprinz Wilhelm*. After he got back home, once again Arthur would receive a letter from his beleaguered Captain Bezanson, this time reporting the loss of a sailor overboard followed by his recovery. The captain's report, as Arthur noted, was "thrilling":

At eight bells, the wind started to blow, and in five minutes was blowing hard and the sea came all of a sudden. I felt her dive quite deep, but no water came over. All at once she lifted her bow and plunged head first, seemed as though she struck a wall of water.... There were three men furling the flying jib at the time. Andrew Anderson was washed overboard while the other two held on and crawled in with only a few scratches. Anderson caught the bob chains, but could not hold on, and when he let go the vessel passed partially over him.

They threw the lot of floatation gear at Anderson, including the log line, but it parted. Bezanson tried to stop the vessel with the engine full astern, but the sails prevailed. The dinghy crew sprang into action, while the rest took in sail.

I don't think the man was in the water five minutes before the dinghy crew was after him. . . . They threw a life ring to him, came around and hauled him in almost exhausted, and rowed up alongside, got him on board, and hoisted the life boat up without even scratching it. I never saw a boat handled better, or braver men.... The night was very dark and I never expected to see him again, but thought the chance worth trying. The first time I ever heard of a man being washed off the jib boom at night and saved. I think, Mr. James, our boat drill saved that man's life; and good courage. He said he lost sight of Aloha *and thought he may as well give up, then all at once he saw us coming right for him. He cried out for us. His cries were getting very low when we got to him.*

Thrilling for Arthur, and certainly reassuring. Such a laudable report from his captain would make any owner—any skipper—proud.

Arthur's pattern with *Aloha* was evident. At the advent of summer cruising season, he and Harriet and their guests would frequently cross the Atlantic with the prospect of touring on the other side. They would often sail home on a steamer in order for him to return to his office in a more timely manner. And usually, the guests had experienced their fill of being pitched about on the sea. Whether *Aloha*'s ports of call would be in the north—Iceland, Scotland—or further south, depended as much on the weather as on whim. For Arthur, it didn't really matter where they went. For him, the sailing was always more important than the destination. Those who love sailing will understand. The ordinary person who is obsessed with sailing will be out on the lake, river, or bay in his small boat to enjoy "glorious" days on the water with such regularity that his neighbors will be shaking their heads. Arthur was doing the same thing, only on a very grand scale. His boat just happened to be a 160-footer with a full-time crew of fifteen (including a cook and a captain) managing 20,000 square feet of sail. His lakes were the seven seas.

In 1906, the beat went on. Off they went to Europe again, without incident this time until they anchored off the ancient-storied Eddystone Light, 13 miles southwest of Plymouth on the English Channel, a light that has been well-celebrated in a song sung with gusto at many a sailors' bar.

Oh me father was the keeper of the Eddystone light, and he slept with a mermaid one fine night.

There they found the Channel enveloped in a thick fog. "Hove to for the night," Arthur wrote in the log, "within sound of the Light's gun and passed a very uncomfortable one due to the large number of steamers passing us in every direction."

This time, Amsterdam was their initial destination. They took the yacht's motor launch for a trip through the canals, went to museums where they admired the Rembrandts, then motored on to Rotterdam in *Aloha*. "There was a strong breeze against the current in the Channel making the sea very rough," Arthur noted, "and our party again had the pleasures of seasickness."

They went on to Paris again, where they were pleased to find the usual suite awaiting them at the Hotel du Rhin, but there was trouble. *Aloha*'s steward had placed quantities of cigars and cigarettes in all their trunks without saying anything. "They were immediately noticed," Arthur wrote. There was a French tobacco monopoly at the time. Quantities of unpackaged (and thus un-stamped) smoking materials were in violation. "Soon the whole French government was on our backs," Arthur wrote. "We were fined 200 Francs and glad to get off without going to jail."

There followed a "hectic" motor trip through the country-side of Brittany and Normandy. Arthur's rendition has a curious-ly twenty-first-century ring to it: "In the early days of motoring, one's whole ambition seemed to be to cover as many miles as possible in 24 hours, and we rushed madly from place to place having no distinct idea of anything and becoming thoroughly tired and our usual placid dispositions much ruffled."

Their last foray was a car trip to Liverpool, where Arthur and Harriet paid a call on Mrs. Daniel James—Sophia, Daniel's second wife—from the British side of the family, at Beaconsfield House. "She seemed very ill," Arthur wrote in *Aloha*'s log. "The whole place had an aspect of sadness, as all the servants who had been in the family for years were in the last stages of decrepitude."

Again they took a steamer home—the *Oceanic*—but this time they crossed paths with *Aloha*, being delivered home by Captain Bezanson and the crew. "As this was before the days of wireless," Arthur recalled some fifteen years later, "it was a good guess on Capt. Bezanson's part to figure out where the *Oceanic* would be at a given time and try to be in her path, and he succeeded admirably." It was so typical of Arthur not to wax ecstatic about what must have been the great thrill of seeing his yacht from an ocean liner in mid-ocean.

* * *

The cruise of 1907 turned out to be life-changing for Arthur. It started out routinely enough. Arthur had been made vice commodore of the New York Yacht Club that year. It made sense for *Aloha*'s transatlantic passage to begin by joining the club's annual cruise in July. The destination for each summer cruise of the New York Yacht Club is determined by the commodore. In 1907 that was Cornelius Vanderbilt, who had planned three point-to-point races that would take the fleet to Newport, Rhode Island, for day races around the buoys. *Aloha* accompanied the fleet to Newport, then sailed north.

Arthur's plan was to visit some remote areas of Labrador, including one of the centers established by the medical missionary, Sir Wilfred Grenfell, in 1892. The Grenfell Missions provided medical and social services to Labrador's remote rural communities.

Chased by bad weather, a few days later *Aloha* made for a tiny inlet called Narrow Tickle, about mid-point on the south coast of Nova Scotia.

"We anchored in one of the most desolate spots I have ever seen, in a howling gale," Arthur wrote. "We were storm bound in this God-forsaken place four days without a vestige of anything of interest, nor a blade of grass, nor human habitation in sight." The hiatus wasn't a total loss. During those four days, Arthur discussed with Captain Bezanson the elements of an ideal new yacht and sketched out the plans of a vessel he had been dreaming about: a 216-foot bark that would also be called *Aloha*. Given pad and pencil, and locked in by bad weather—or plagued by a sleepless night—sketching dream boats is not an unusual exercise for sailors. But in a few years, the 216-foot *Aloha* would be built. Having such a grand dream become a reality is most unusual.

Meanwhile, far up the coast, *Aloha* called at an Inuit mission at Nain run by German Moravian missionaries. *Aloha* arrived there in the midst of a food crisis. The mission's supply vessel that came to them once a year was overdue. Arthur immediately opened *Aloha*'s stores to the mission, tiding them over until the ship arrived. Arthur would keep up a correspondence with the head of that mission for nineteen years. "I must certainly take my hat off," he wrote, "to their disinterested and consistent missionary spirit in the face of fearful hardships and constant discouragement in ministering to a dying race."

With that, *Aloha* turned east, setting course for England. No sooner had they dropped anchor in Dartmouth, 50 miles east of Plymouth on the southwest coast of England, than a cable arrived: while on vacation at the grand hotel in Bretton Woods, New Hampshire, seventy-five-year-old D. Willis James had fallen severely ill with heart disease. Arthur and Harriet caught a train to London. Midway, a guard handed a second telegram to Arthur with the news that D. Willis had passed away.

Arthur was devastated. He wrote in his log: "[This] was the turning buoy in my life's race.... I lost my pilot, my best friend, my revered father. The carefree days of youth ended on

September 13, 1907, and from that time the responsibilities of life had to be met without his steady, guiding hand and wise, loving counsel."

He also expressed his gratitude for the train guard who had the unpleasant job of handing him the telegram about his father. "He very gently and kindly told me I must be prepared for bad news," Arthur wrote. "Although I only saw him for a minute as the train stopped at a station, his thoughtfulness and sympathy to me, a perfect stranger, can never be forgotten. In the time of sorrow, human sympathy and little acts of courtesy mean much and I have ever since remembered with gratitude and affection the kindness of the Cunard Line officials... they did everything in their power to assist us." Arthur and Harriet sailed back across the Atlantic on the Cunard steamer *Umbria*, the following day.

D. Willis was said to have died as one of the hundred wealthiest Americans, leaving an estate of $26 million ($660 million today). James had made the most of his immigration to America, taking Phelps Dodge into productive ventures that radically changed, and enriched, the company. Phyllis B. Dodge, who wrote *Tales of the Phelps Dodge Family*, wrote this about D. Willis's influence: "When Willis James and Will Dodge turned the focus of Phelps, Dodge & Company toward mining in the American West, Phelps, James & Company in Liverpool lost its raison d'être, and thereafter slid quietly toward its eventual dissolution."

Phyllis Dodge went on to make sure the reader knew how little inconvenienced the Dodge relatives associated with the company in Liverpool had been by that dissolution. "They lived handsomely on their inherited wealth," Mrs. Dodge reported, "buying lavish country estates, enjoying yachting and shooting and breeding racehorses... with no need to spend wearisome hours in offices, mines, or factories."

In addition to all his corporate titles and seats on various boards associated with Phelps Dodge, D. Willis was a member of the Metropolitan Museum of Art, the American Geographical

D. Willis James

Society, the Society of Natural History, and the National Academy of Design, among other esteemed organizations. He also belonged to a clutch of clubs, including the New York Yacht Club, the Metropolitan, the Century, the Riding, the Downtown, and the National Arts Clubs.

D. Willis James was also among the most respected Americans, a man who practiced his oft-repeated belief, that "the wealthy should give until they feel it." One of his major gifts included a gift of land in Morningside Heights on the Upper West Side of Manhattan to the Union Theological Seminary upon which that institution built its present home. He also gave a library to his adopted "home town" of Madison, New Jersey, where he had also built a thirty-five-room Tudor mansion on 240 acres of land.

One of D. Willis's many lesser gifts, an elaborate drinking fountain in Union Square, Manhattan, exemplifies the nature of the man. It should be noted that drinking fountains were popular in New York after 1842, to celebrate the completion of the Croton Reservoir that provided a consistent supply of fresh water to the city. The James fountain was a sculpture in bronze of a larger-than-life grouping of a mother with two infants standing on an ornamental pedestal, towering 20 feet above four lion-head drinking fountains. James said the piece was intended for the comfort of the people, to teach a lesson of religion, and to cultivate an appreciation for art. It was dedicated in 1881. The fountain continues to carry out its various missions in Union Square to this day.

Among his many, ongoing charitable projects was the Children's Aid Society, of which he was president for many years, and a long-time trustee. A few years before his death, James received this letter: "There has never been a day that my heart has not nurtured a grateful remembrance for the fostering care extended to me and noble incentives imparted at the threshold of my life by the Children's Aid Society." The letter was from ex-governor Andrew H. Burke of North Carolina, who, as a waif, was picked off the streets of New York and given a new start in life.

His father's philosophy and countless acts of generosity were as essential a part of Arthur's inheritance as the money he received, and the corporate positions he would assume. One of the first things Arthur and his mother did after D. Willis's death was to donate a chapel to the Union Theological Seminary. This message was carved into the interior limestone wall of the chapel in manuscript calligraphy font, and gold-leafed:

In the Glory of God this chapel is erected in the loving memory of Daniel Willis James by his wife. As a director for forty years of Union Theological Seminary and vice president of the board from 1898 to 1907 he gave constantly of his best thought toward its spiritual life and in unstinted measure of his means for its material welfare, the site of this Seminary being one of his gifts.

Born April 15, 1832 and entered into rest September 13, 1907

Not slothful in business • Fervent in spirit • Serving the lord
Romans XII-II

Feathering 5 the Nest

Upon his father's death, Arthur, an only child, inherited some $23 million ($560 million today) after D. Willis's bequests had been deducted. He became a director and vice president of Phelps Dodge, and took over his father's significant interests in the Great Northern, the Northern Pacific, and the Chicago, Burlington & Quincy railroads.

Arthur took his business responsibilities seriously, as he did his trustee duties at both Hampton Institute and Amherst College, which began in 1904 and would last through 1938. On the business side, his duties were supervisory in the broadest sense. It was customary for extremely wealthy men of the time to organize their lives so that prolonged absences, often for world travel, were common. Arthur's seemingly unfailing judgment of people served him well in this regard. Without the instant global communication we have today, loyalty and honesty from lieutenants and workers were as important as their capabilities. Throughout his career, Arthur's ability to identify smart, reliable, fiercely loyal associates—self-starters who didn't need much direction—and give them all the credit and praise while remaining in the background, was what allowed him to succeed in business while living the life he wanted.

But for a year and a half after his father died, trips were restricted to essential business. Settling the estate and getting a grasp on what lay in store for him was all-consuming. Until the death of D. Willis, Arthur had enjoyed the relatively carefree life of an only child of great wealth. As we have seen, his father was both very comfortable and also proficient at running the business. Arthur had been a conscientious student of the Phelps Dodge Company, but he had also taken advantage of the situation. He knew his freedom would come to an end, and he was prepared for that. And while he had taken advantage, he had not fallen into the excesses of wine, women, and song that ensnare so many young men of elevated fortune, a circumstance that requires little or no effort to survive in this world. It's a situation that all too often sabotages one's inner resolve. But Arthur was stable, energetic, a most capable and highly respected skipper of two yachts over 100 feet. He was caring by all accounts, generous, and very aware of the responsibilities that come with great wealth. Those values had been instilled at his father's knee.

While he was busy finalizing the estate and evaluating the corporate duties he had inherited, he was also starting to contemplate his personal future. He was approaching his fortieth year. It was about time to move out of the confines of his Manhattan residence at 92 Park Avenue (between 39th and 40th Streets) and establish a more attractive, livelier homestead. And maybe a new boat, something a bit larger and more comfortable. His notebooks were full of sketches that had begun when he had been battened down by weather at Narrow Tickle.

It was boats that first brought him out of his brown study. In 1909 Arthur had risen to commodore of the New York Yacht Club, an office that required the planning and organization of the club's annual summer cruise. Arthur selected Bar Harbor, Maine, as the destination, with the usual day races from port to port along the way. The pattern of stormy weather plaguing Arthur's voyages continued when the fleet sailed into a severe northeast gale off Boston. "[The gale] was historic," Arthur wrote in his log, "and brought out all the qualities of seamanship of the amateur sailors in the club." Arthur was praised for the way he handled the situation, personally checking in with skippers of the damaged yachts, offering assistance and support.

Newport

That same year, Arthur bought an estate in Newport Rhode Island. According to Rockwell Stensrud, in his book *Newport: A Lively Experiment 1639–1969*, "Newport's second Golden Age was in full flower by 1880." Newport's spacious, deep-water harbor had historically been an attraction for military and commercial interests. By the 1880s, yachtsmen had been taking advantage of Newport's harbor connected as it is by broad water to Narragansett and Mount Hope Bays to the north, and just a brief sail down a lovely passage to the Atlantic Ocean to the south. Beginning in the late 1800s, a collection of mansions—"cottages," in the caustically dismissive parlance of the owners—the likes of which had never been seen in America, had been built on Newport's Bellevue Avenue and Ocean Drive. Because it was the Gilded Age, a similar outcropping of super-estates had begun appearing about the same time on Long Island's North Shore.

While the Long Island mansions were elaborate country homes on properties measured in hundreds of acres, Newport's "cottages" were more monumental, more enormous palatial creations of granite and marble, constructions looking more like fortresses than houses. They were built on more modest sites, given Newport's small land mass. But their settings were more dramatic, thanks to the breadth of the Atlantic Ocean breaking on their rock-bound front yards. The carving and installation of their marble interiors often required a score (or more) of craftsmen imported from Europe for several years. As the late cultural historian Brendan Gill wrote in his introduction to *Long Island*

Country Houses and Their Architects, "the simple act of build-ing is the surest means of announcing that one has made good. A man who puts up a bigger house than his neighbor... is a better man than his neighbor: the set of values that most of us live by is, I fear, as simple and undiscriminating as that."

As Rockwell Stensrud wrote, "from 1880... life in New-port for the well-heeled was an uninterrupted holiday, a time for building 'cottages' and yachts, bathing at Bailey's Beach, and be-ing seen at the Casino, at parties.... For those who had 'arrived,' the era was positively dreamlike, drenched in vivid colors and a seemingly unending series of entertainments."

Dreamlike indeed, with a disturbing dose of nightmare thrown in. Authors Mark Twain and Charles Dudley Warner coined the term "Gilded Age" in their 1873 book *The Gilded Age: A Tale of Today*. Economist Thorstein Veblen came up with "conspicuous consumption" to summarize what he observed to be high society running amok in Newport in the 1890s. It was a taste crisis *le nec plus ultra*. As Archibald Lyall, known for his pithy, written commentary about the South of France, once commented, "Taste is a merciless betrayer of social and cultural attitudes." Stephen Bayley, who wrote the definitive book on the subject—*Taste*—provided the stinger: "More is worse."

It had begun in 1892 with the building of Marble House by Alva and William K. Vanderbilt, and Ochre Court by Ogden Goelet, followed by the Breakers in 1895 (Cornelius Vanderbilt), the Elms in 1901 (Edward Berwind), Rosecliff in 1902 (Theresa Fair Oelrichs), and several other behemoths that line Newport's tree-shaded Bellevue Avenue, and that have become major tour-ist attractions today. The outlandish creations themselves, cost-ing upwards of $250 million each in today's dollars, and what went on inside them, were unparalleled societal (and financial) extravaganzas. Headline-hungry hostesses would sprinkle hand-fuls of diamonds into the sugar bowls on their dinner tables. The flowers for one party given by Alva Vanderbilt at Marble House cost $11,000 ($200,000 today).

Many were the private clubs created to protect the super rich from the influx of celebrity stalkers drawn to the gaudy display of wealth. Massive quantities of alcohol were consumed during each summer season, and according to Deborah Davis, who has entertainingly chronicled the era in her book, *Gilded: How Newport Became America's Richest Resort*, "adultery was so widespread in Newport circles that there was a sliding scale of misbehavior."

Newport mansions (*clockwise from top left*)—Marble House, interior of the Elms, the Breakers, and the heart-shaped staircase of Rosecliff

While the men were busy keeping the money rolling in to cover the enormous expense of gilding all the various lilies, the women were in charge of the lifestyle. There was an ongoing power struggle among the likes of Caroline (Mrs. William Backhouse) Astor; Alva Vanderbilt; and Marion "Mamie" Fish, for social queen of the Big Party in which no punches were pulled, in which every perceived lapse of taste or behavior was held up for public ridicule (the *Newport Mercury* was the first newspaper in the country to have a society page). Failing to make the list of who was "in" could lead to nervous breakdowns. Bets were hedged.

Alva Vanderbilt once brought the entire cast of a Broadway show to Newport to do a single performance for her guests.

The immensity of the wardrobe these belles of the balls needed for a summer day's activities in Newport was daunting. Changes were required for the beach, tennis, yachting, motoring, and for each meal. As Davis wrote, "one Newport hostess boasted she set aside $10,000 each season [$250,000 today] for her wardrobe mistakes." Another hostess calculated she needed eighty or ninety outfits a season, which would be worn once or twice and put aside. It reached an amusing apogee in 1898, when three pretenders to the crown that had been worn for some time by the aging Caroline Astor formed a group they unashamedly named the Newport Social Strategy Board. Its goal was to break with traditional standards for entertaining. As Deborah Davis concluded, "these women lived in a world where social achievement was the definitive unit of measure."

Arthur was no stranger to Newport. When one is cruising around on a sailing vessel of more than 100 feet, large deepwater ports like Newport have a gold star of welcome beside their names. The Jameses had visited Newport many times in *Aloha*. They had friends there. Among them was the esteemed Dutch painter Hubert Vos, and his wife, Eleanor Kaikilani Coney, who was named after her maternal great-grandmother, High Chiefess Kaikilanialiiwahineopuna, a descendent of the Kamehameha line and the last high chiefess of the Puna district of the island of Hawaii. Hubert Vos traveled extensively for his work, which had included a commission to paint a portrait of the Empress Dowager Cixi of China (1905), for which the grateful empress made him a "Commander of the Double Dragon." Vos had also painted a portrait of D. Willis James.

But one might have thought that while the Newport anchorage was perhaps the best available anywhere on the East Coast, the uncouth behavior of their wealthy contemporaries would have dampened the Jameses' long-term interest. Celebrated novelist Henry James's family had moved to Newport on the eve of the Civil War, when James was a teenager. Henry James (no relation to Arthur) had returned to Newport in 1906, when he was sixty-three years old, and had written an article for *Harper's Magazine* about the change that had taken place in the town he "knew too well and loved too much for description or definition." Despite that declaration, James went on to depict the unspoiled Newport of his youth as a "little bare, white, open hand with slightly parted fingers . . . a small virtual promontory, of which, superficially, nothing could be predicated but its sky and its sea and its sunsets." On his return he had seen that the new arrivals had put a few things into that white, open hand:

> . . . *things of their own, and of all sorts, and of many ugly, and of more and more expensive sorts; to fill it substantially, that is, with gold, the gold that they have ended by heaping up there to an amount so oddly out of proportion to the scale of nature and space. . . . This process of injection and elaboration, of creating the palpable pile, had been going on for years to such a tune that the face of nature was now as much obliterated as possible, and the original shy sweetness as much as possible bedizened and bedeviled. . . . The little white hand had always been so full of treasures of its own as to discredit, from the point of view of taste, any attempt, from without, to stuff it fuller.*
>
> *There remained always a sense, of course, in which the superimpositions, the multiplied excrescences, were a tribute to the value of the place. . . . And that has been, thanks to the "pilers-on" of gold, the fortune, the history of its beauty: that it now bristles with the villas and palaces into which the cottages have all turned, and that these monuments of pecuniary power rise thick and close.*

Long Island's North Shore "Gold Coast" would seem to have been a viable alternative for the Jameses to consider. The way of life on Long Island was certainly more reserved, more traditionally formal, and more suited, one would have thought, to Arthur and Harriet's sensibilities. Arthur had been visiting and sailing there since his days as a young man growing up in and near Manhattan. He'd served four years as Commodore of Seawanhaka. He and Harriet had many friends there. They had often stopped in Oyster Bay on the first *Aloha*. And land was plentiful on the North Shore. No doubt his lack of interest in settling there had to do with the typical calms and swift currents of Long Island Sound—a small inland sea one-seventeenth the size of Lake Michigan—versus the energizing experience of living alongside the more robust nature of the Atlantic Ocean; of feeling its stinging salty breath, of being lulled to sleep by its crashing surf, and of relishing the might of its occasional thrashings. The closer any blue-water sailor of his great passion can be to the source of his joy, the more content he will be. [In the late 1920s, Arthur was quoted as saying he had lived in Newport "as a boy," but no indication of a family residence there can be found.]

Another discouraging detail about Newport would have been that E. H. Harriman, the railroad baron who had caused no end of problems for James J. Hill, D. Willis James, Arthur, Wall Street, and Phelps Dodge, had moved to Newport in 1906. Harriman's penchant for being troublesome had not diminished. According to Deborah Davis, after Harriman had been shunned by a prominent Newport hostess, he had arranged to have her husband fired from a long-standing post at a major railroad. Newport was a fair-sized town in 1908 (population 27,000), but certainly Harriman would be traveling in the same elevated circles as Arthur, no doubt eating and drinking at the same private clubs, attending the same social gatherings. That could be uncomfortable. The town might not be big enough for the two of them.

And while Harriet James enjoyed being socially active, the conservative style of this parochial woman from the sedate New England country town of Northampton, Massachusetts, was far removed from the manipulative, fiercely combative scale upon which "society" was being practiced in Newport. Harriet's most noteworthy social accomplishment in Northampton had been to support George Washington Cable's Home Culture Clubs, a prime example at the time of Christianity practically applied. The goal of the Home Culture Clubs was to gather together people from different walks of life to share opinions, air differences, and communicate through common enjoyments like games, cooking, sewing, or gardening. The real agenda, of course, was to promote Christianity. Harriet, along with Smith College's president, was on the Home Culture Clubs board in 1896, and the James family gave generously to the organization. The house in Northampton purchased for the Home Culture Clubs offices was named the "Harriet James House."

As it happened, the same year Arthur and Harriet made their initial excursions into Newport, a certain amount of reform was seeping into the colony. Those women who had taken pleasure stirring the social pot ("fire burn and cauldron bubble") were getting old. Mrs. Astor had died that year. As Deborah Davis wrote, "a concerned group of cottagers... embraced a healthier life style, advocating plenty of outdoor exercise and early curfews, replacing the showy affairs... with simple picnics and sedate dinners." The consumption of alcohol in Newport in 1908 was the lowest ever recorded.

Arthur and Harriet had done what any couple might have done before settling in a new town. They rented a house in Newport for the summer of 1908. Shortly thereafter they purchased Belvoir, a 28-acre estate on Beacon Hill (aka Telegraph Hill), the highest point of land in Newport. It came complete with an elegant stone house built in 1880 that had been designed by the prominent New York firm of McKim, Mead & White, known for its creation of Manhattan's Pennsylvania Station (which would open in 1910) among other notable landmarks. The Jameses are said to have paid $125,000 ($3,230,000 today) for the property, which also included a stable.

It would be a mistake to assume that Arthur was at all seduced by the "bigger house—better person" competition observed by Brendan Gill. In Newport, the wretched excess of

"Bigger House" had eclipsed all previous American standards, and had more or less been played out before the turn of the century. If Arthur had wanted to compete with "the Joneses"—a silliness that will always be with us—he could have built another showplace on the Bellevue Avenue main line, where it would have been noticed. Making that sort of social statement wouldn't have appealed to Arthur. Instead, he opted for land he could populate with flowers, vegetables, and animals. And a tennis court, of course. As always with Arthur, privacy was of prime importance.

Next to boats, houses held the strongest appeal for him. In 1900, he had built a thirteen-room, 7,500-square-foot brick house on 1.4 acres in Northampton, presumably for his and Harriet's use when they were visiting her family or attending events at nearby Amherst College. The house had been designed by Isaac Newton Phelps Stokes, the son of Arthur's cousin, and was complete with servants' quarters and a double master bedroom suite. Arthur addressed real estate with the same degree of detail he brought to his yachts.

Sitting atop Telegraph Hill, Newport's highest point, Belvoir was an imposing three-story rectangular structure of pudding stone, a gray, cement-like stone often infused with colorful pebbles. Pudding stone is abundant on Aquidneck Island, upon which Newport is located. Stanford White was the first architect to use it. Belvoir was no beauty, but its robust façade was a good match for the rugged, Atlantic coastal environs. Had it not been found to be full of structural cracks, possibly the effect of dynamiting for the building of nearby roads, the Jameses might have re-done Belvoir's interior and called it home. Instead, according to Elizabeth Toombs, (who wrote about the building of Beacon Hill House in *Town & Country*, August 10, 1912, "Stone by stone [Belvoir] the mansion of 30 rooms was taken down, new cellars blasted from the rocks, new foundations laid, and stone by stone Beacon Hill House was carefully reconstructed on the exact lines of the house as it was designed by Stanford White

more than a dozen years ago." Stanford White was no longer available to design the successor house, even if Arthur would have wanted him. In 1906, he had been killed by a jealous husband who believed (correctly) that the profligate architect had forced himself on his wife when she was a teenager. Called the "crime of the century," the murder of White played into the image of the debauchery of New York's excessively privileged.

While there are gross similarities, photographs of the two rectangular, multi-dormered buildings dispute Toombs's claim of the house being reconstructed on the exact lines of the White specifications, most obviously at the ends, which are rounded, not square, with extended, matching patios. Certainly architects John Mead Howells and I. N. Phelps Stokes, who are credited with the design for what Arthur named Beacon Hill House, would have taken umbrage at Toombs's description. [The only clue as to where the name Beacon Hill House might have come from is the European side of the family's Beaconsfield House in Liverpool.]

The talented I. N. Phelps Stokes had opened an architectural firm in New York with Howells in 1897. He and his partners compiled an enviable portfolio of work that included the Baltimore Stock Exchange (1905); the American Geographical Society Building in New York, and the Turks Head Building in Providence, R.I. Stokes's private housing commissions included a New York State country house for a cousin, as well as Beacon Hill House for Arthur and Harriet. His family wealth permitted Stokes to be both architect and volunteer public servant. He would become known as a pioneer in the amelioration of conditions in New York tenements and the development of public housing projects. He was the lead author of the six-volume *Iconography of Manhattan Island*, an ambitious compilation of the physical development of the city. Stokes and his wife, Edith Minturn Stokes, are the subject of a painting by John Singer Sargent that was a wedding gift from a friend. Stokes was known to be as committed a philanthropist as was his uncle Arthur.

To accommodate plans for entry roads to Beacon Hill House, Arthur purchased an additional seven acres (the estate would eventually contain 125 acres). Work on the property commenced under the overall direction of the Olmsted Brothers from Boston, the most influential landscape architectural firm at the time. As much attention was paid to details like the friendliness and beauty of the entry roads (there were four, including the service entrance), and the nature and location of the many gardens, as to the construction of the new dwelling.

(*Above*) The Beacon Hill estate of Arthur Curtiss James. (*Previous page*) Aerial photograph of the estate; note *Aloha* anchored in Newport Harbor.

The Olmsteds had done work on the estate under the previous owner. The firm produced some 470 drawings for the various gardens, an area of particular interest for Harriet James. There were specific plants she wanted, and she had firm ideas about the floral color scheme. According to Arleyn A. Levee, who wrote *The Blue Garden*, a book about the Jameses' most famous planting at the Newport estate, James Dawson, who taught painting at University of Pennsylvania—the brother of a partner at Olmsted—"prepared rendered illustrations of the proposed garden scenery as indicated by the plans." Arthur produced a list of vegetables and fruits he wanted grown on the estate. (Arleyn Levee is an historian and preservation consultant who specializes in research concerning the Olmsted firm.)

The fact that money was no object didn't mean that Arthur didn't keep a discerning eye on his contractors' whims. Arlyne Levee recounts a tale of an Olmsted horticulturist named Koehler visiting other Newport estates to examine how location was affecting the success of various plantings. Based on his predictable finding that most flora was no match for open exposure to Newport's blustery, oceanic weather, Koehler recommended "plant material for spring-summer planting that would 'give a somewhat finished and matured effect at once.'" The cost for this "plant material" was $16,000 ($400,000 today).

"James balked at the expense," Levee writes. The Koehler recommendation, no doubt significantly modified, became part of Olmsted's General Plan for the Estate, a plan that included landscaping the grounds to properly withstand the prevailing southwesterly winds with their heavy salt content; the placement of tennis courts; the design and placement of a tea house; and the addition of a "Telescope House" so Arthur could watch races in the harbor with his collection of telescopes.

An interesting aside was the appearance of a man named John Greatorex, who was hired by Olmsted Brothers to be "inspector and head gardener," according to Levee. Greatorex was hired "to supervise the soil preparation, seeding and planting and any other work that might 'influence the appearance of the final result.'" It should be noted that it was Arthur who discovered John Greatorex. On one of his trips to Europe on *Aloha*, Arthur had gone shopping for wine at one of the Rothschild vineyards in the Médoc region near Bordeaux, France. There he had encountered Greatorex, who was working at the vineyard. Always on alert for talented, reliable people, Arthur had been impressed by the man's knowledge and presence, and had contacted him as soon as he became serious about buying the estate on Telegraph Hill. Greatorex answered the call, came to Newport, and turned out to be a valuable asset. "As the clients' and the firm's appreciation of his wide-ranging skills grew," Levee wrote, "[Greatorex's] duties were increased to include construction supervision for wall and road building, utility installation, and development of the vegetable garden complex."

Greatorex had a big job. Details like the proper curvature of the driveways approaching the house, and the view of the estate from those driveways, and the nature of walls and planting that would enhance the beauty of the approach without blocking the view, were critical. And since Aquidneck Island is essentially one very large rock, the dynamiting required to shape the driveways had to be done with finesse in order to preserve existing vegetation. Greatorex managed it well. He would become one of Arthur's favorite employees.

During the construction, the Jameses again rented a cottage in Newport for the summer.

* * *

All-consuming as it might have seemed, construction at Telegraph Hill wasn't the only thing going on in Arthur's life at the time. There were the usual small bits of day-to-day business that had to be dealt with. While still serving his term as commodore of the New York Yacht Club, Arthur, a well-known contributor to the YMCA—thanks to his wife's and stepfather's early interest—was approached by one Dr. Frederick Knowles, a director of the physical department of the Harlem branch of the New York YMCA. Knowles had gotten wind of a 108-foot schooner called *Amazon* that was for sale. After confirming *Amazon*'s seaworthiness, Knowles saw it as just the right vessel for taking members of the YMCA cruising, to show them the benefits of yachting without them having to be millionaires. As F. M. McClintic wrote in *The Rudder* magazine, "Dr. Knowles approached Commodore James and placed his plan before that gentleman, with the request that a check be drawn for the purchase amount. 'You wish me to furnish all the money?' inquired the astonished Commodore. 'That's it,' was the brief reply. Commodore James admires nerve in its most refrigerated form, and after regaining his breath he complied with the request." McClintoc went on to report that $1,000 ($25,000 today) had to be added to the purchase price (not stated) to refit the yacht for its new duties. He then wrote about *Amazon*'s initial cruises, the enthusiasm with which the young men approached their training, and their pleasure under sail.

Aloha the bark

At the same time Beacon Hill House was being built, *Aloha* the bark was under construction at Fore River Shipbuilding Company, in Quincy, Massachusetts. Given the attention being lavished upon the dwelling on Telegraph Hill, the influential companies and many experts involved, it is difficult to comprehend that *Aloha* the bark was an even more demanding operation. But it was. Either project would have been considered an ultimate expenditure of time, energy, and money for most capable, dynamic men of means. But Arthur Curtiss James handled them both with aplomb. And not from his easy chair. He was fully involved in both.

James initiated the original sketches for the yacht, as we know, and the multi-talented Captain Bezanson built a large, detailed model of the vessel as imagined during *Aloha*'s winter layup at New London in 1908 to '09. While Clinton Crane was again the lead designer of the vessel, both Crane's design firm, Tams, Lemoine & Crane, and the firm of A. Carey Smith & Ferris were involved. Nearly three years were spent planning before the building contract was placed, during which time six sets of plans were drawn (all by hand in those days), and six models were built. James was on top of the project the whole way.

Built of steel, *Aloha* would be the new flagship of the New York Yacht Club. Rigged as a bark (a sailing ship, typically with three masts, in which the foremast and mainmast are square-rigged and the mizzenmast is rigged fore-and-aft), the yacht was

216 feet overall, 167 feet on the waterline, with a beam of 35 feet, 6 inches, and a draught of 17 feet, 6 inches. Fully rigged, *Aloha* would weigh in at 659 tons. Her mainmast would just make it under the Brooklyn Bridge at mean high water (276.5 feet). Her lines were elegant. Her freeboard (distance from waterline to deck) was on the shallow side, giving a yacht of such size and tonnage an unusually racy look. The sweep of her sheer was subtle. Her overhangs fore and aft—40 feet in total—were finely tapered. Her decks were teak, which was heavier, but longer-lasting, than the traditional pine. Noncorrosive white metal was used for deck gear and fittings instead of brass, which would have required constant polishing. Her service boats included steam launches of 30 and 21 feet, three lifeboats housed on a boat deck and launched by steam power, and a dinghy. *Aloha* would carry 20,000 square feet of sail, and make ten knots under the power of a 400-horsepower, triple-expansion steam engine driving a feathering propeller (diesel power would replace steam in 1926).

Below were six large staterooms for owner and guests in addition to accommodations for maids, and a doctor. The owner's stateroom spanned the full width of the vessel. The spacious fo'c's'le housed the crew of thirty-eight men. The main salon measured 32 by 17 feet. A sickroom afforded isolation if need be. A laundry room was outfitted with the latest machinery, and there was hot and cold running water throughout the vessel. Below the berth deck was the hold, a cavernous space with seven feet of headroom, housing the main refrigerators, and storerooms for wet and dry goods.

One detail in particular is an example of the amount of care and thought that went into every aspect of the yacht. It was the shape of a hatch opening on the overhead of the dining saloon that Arthur wanted to stimulate his guests' sense of beauty. According to the man who built the hatch at the Fore River yard, whose name has been lost, "Commodore James stipulated that the hatch opening, as viewed by diners seated in the saloon, had to be shaped as a perfect ellipse. It was my

job," the builder wrote, "to arrange for this thing of beauty. Sole dimensions given to me comprised the major and minor axes. Shaping of the metal was not permitted until after the naval architect came to Quincy from New York and checked the layout for accuracy of ellipse."

The décor below deck was just as carefully considered by Arthur and Harriet. On a stop at Iceland on *Coronet* some years before, they had marveled at scenes from Norse literature in which the various Icelandic sagas are set. When it came time to decorate *Aloha*, replicating these scenes seemed most appropriate. Not just with murals, but with hand-carved teak panels. They called upon acclaimed artist and teacher Karl von Rydingsvärd, who carved three large panels illustrating Viking sagas of hunting and fishing, and—largest of all—a panel showing the saga of Sigurd wresting the sword from the Brandstock tree. Von Rydingsvärd also carved a series of smaller panels representing the evolution of vessels through history, including a Chinese junk and Cleopatra's barge. Von Rydingsvärd carved furniture of his own design for the cabins, pieces that bore the heavy, strong characteristics of Scandinavian antiques.

That Arthur would have a fascination for depictions of the Viking sagas makes sense. At about the same time he was commissioning Von Rydingsvärd, he had become involved with the American Museum of Natural History in New York, and with the artist, Frank Wilbert Stokes. After a more or less traditional education both in the United States (the Pennsylvania Academy of Fine Arts under Thomas Eakins) and abroad, Stokes had packed off to Greenland with explorer Robert Peary in the late 1880s and '90s. He would join a Swedish expedition to Antarctica in 1902. The work he produced in those challenging climates was dramatic, evocative enough to give viewers a chill.

Chances are Arthur became interested in Stokes through his relationship with Robert Curtis Ogden, his fellow board member at Hampton Institute in Virginia. An associate of the

John Wanamaker dry-goods empire in Philadelphia, Robert Ogden was known as a reformer who promoted education for both blacks and whites in the South. As a trustee of Union Theological Seminary beginning in 1897, Ogden had enjoyed a close working relationship with D. Willis James, whose generosity to the Seminary was unparalleled. Ogden was also an elder of the same Presbyterian Church in New York that Arthur attended. An interesting aside that illustrates the dimensions of the small aristocracy of the day: Thomas Eakins would paint a portrait of Robert Curtis Ogden.

A large collection of Stokes paintings at the Smithsonian Institution are in the "Arthur Curtiss James and Robert Curtis Ogden Memorial Collection." At the American Museum of Natural History, the Stokes paintings representing the Greenland Eskimo—the mural decorations of Eskimo Hall, completed in 1909 to '10—were given by Arthur Curtiss James. It's evident that Arthur not only appreciated art that depicted historic adventure and exploration on a grand scale, but, as a blue-water sailor himself, admired the artist who participated, who traveled to the ends of the Earth to bring back the essence of dramatic scenes.

John Matheson, whose dye company would eventually help create Allied Chemical Corporation, and who was a close friend and frequent shipmate of Arthur's from Cold Spring Harbor, Long Island (Matheson had been vice commodore of Seawanhaka Corinthian Yacht Club when Arthur was commodore), wrote this in the foreword to one of the new *Aloha*'s first logbooks:

The Commodore, with his industry and infinite capacity for taking pains, which someone has aptly called genius, has produced a yacht that no naval architect, however skilled, could have designed without his long and painstaking observation and experience. The Commodore takes nothing for granted, and finds the ship's position independently every day, projecting his plans far into the future. So constitutional is this with him that is it carried out not only on the yacht, but on shore, where everything is thought out in advance, and every provision made for the comfort and convenience of his guests and the best disposition of their time.

Aloha Landing

And yet another project simultaneously underway was Aloha Landing, a boathouse and service dock for *Aloha*. The new yacht's size made it impossible to bring her in to any docks that were relatively close to Telegraph Hill. This was not a detail that had escaped Arthur's plan. Before the yacht was even launched, he purchased a little sliver of land on Brenton Cove, a very brief car ride down the hill from his newly acquired estate. There, he built a handsome stone boathouse for keeping sails and gear, and with ample docks where he could keep his launches. From the Landing it would be a short trip by oar or engine to *Aloha*, moored in the harbor. The 500-foot lane sloping down to the boathouse was very narrow. With the 10-foot walls and the roadway handsomely paved with stone, it looked even narrower. There was not enough space at the end to turn a vehicle. A true railroad man, Arthur solved the problem by having his crew build a hand-cranked turntable. It too was paved with cobblestones to match the roadway.

Mabel

No matter how many projects he was monitoring, Arthur always made time for his trustee duties at Amherst, and for maintaining his frequent correspondence and visits with Mabel Todd. Conveniently, the duties and visits were both in Amherst. Their correspondence had started with the long note Arthur had sent to Mabel after their transpacific crossing on *Coronet* about the nature of the Japanese people, and the unruly crew on the steamer he had chartered while in Japan for the eclipse. Yale University's Sterling Library harbors several boxes of letters from Arthur to Mabel, scores of letters all filed under "Mabel Loomis Todd" that represent a fraction of their correspondence. Sadly, there are only a few letters from Mabel to Arthur. While there is nothing to match the steamy quality of the exchanges between Austin Dickinson and Mabel that are contained in Polly Longsworth's book about their affair, Arthur's interest in this talented, seductive woman is plainly evident. Given that it is difficult not to fall for Mabel Todd just from reading about her, looking at photographs of her, and being exposed to her work, one could safely surmise that a man of Arthur's keen intellect and appreciation of people would have been quite taken by this talented, intelligent, engaging woman. The letters confirm his interest.

All of Arthur's letters to Mabel are beyond reproach. Formality and etiquette are always carefully observed. But there is a subtle progression from letters about specific business, to those with a more personal tone. A few months after arriving home from the eclipse trip, Arthur wrote by hand on his office letterhead, "My Dear Mrs. Todd, I am sending you today, by mail, a copy of Mrs. James's journal of the trip." Then he adds this little quip alluding to Mabel's own book on the same subject, a sure-fire attention getter: "I trust that the immense sale which this book will undoubtedly have will not injure the revenue expected to be derived from *Corona and Coronet*. Very Truly Yours, Arthur Curtiss James." Alas, we don't have Mabel's reply.

A few months later, Arthur wrote to tell Mabel that Harriet was confined to her bed with typhoid fever. He added, "When you come [to New York] I shall hope to see you, although with two nurses in the house I'm afraid we have no room to take you in at [92 Park Avenue]."

In early 1898, one senses a bit of longing coming from Arthur's pen: "My Dear Learned Lady," he begins. "Where are you? It has been many moons since our doorway has been brightened by your presence. Do not women's clubs flourish in Gotham? At any rate my literary taste pines for a treat from your work. I leave for the West on Thursday." It is signed, "Changelessly, Arthur Curtiss James."

Changelessly? Changelessly.

A year or so later, in May 1899, Arthur wrote Mabel about her offer to send him the photographic plates from *Corona and Coronet* for use in Harriet's book, *Coronet Memories*. As usual, the letter was addressed to "My Dear Mrs. Todd," and continues: "In looking over the pictures in *Corona and Coronet* we have thought things that make it <u>very</u> desirable for me to be there for a day or so, but it seems impossible as I am practically alone at the office. I wish you were planning to be in this neighborhood between now and commencement." The underline is Arthur's.

Then in 1904, the year Arthur accepted his trusteeship at Amherst, he wrote "My Dear Mrs. Todd, Many thanks again for your kind invitation which reached me on my return from the West. I find that I have been appointed on the Grounds and Building Committee at Amherst, which will necessitate going there even more often than heretofore. This is a pleasure, and on my next visit, I will be only too glad to accept your hospitality, if you still want me."

There's another unfortunate gap. But two years later, in June 1906, the beat went on. Arthur accepted Mabel's invitation to stay with her over Commencement, adding this incidental fact: "I am sorry Harriet has decided not to come this year." That fall, Arthur wrote (on a typewriter): "I am certainly having bad luck getting to Amherst this year and was very much disappointed at having to return after the trustees' meeting instead of spending the night at your house; but an imperative engagement arose, which made it necessary for me to get back. I will do my best to come up in the near future, and as I am on the committee for alteration of the Barrett gymnasium, expect to have to go there before long."

Arthur kept up his correspondence with Mabel Todd. He occasionally wrote to David Todd as well, although unfortunately those letters cannot be found. In letters to Mabel, several times he referred to David as "Henpecked," evidently a private joke between him and Mabel. On June 18, 1912, Arthur wrote: "Looking forward to seeing you then, and thanking you for again taking me out of the cold, cold world." Just ten days later, he wrote: "Just as I was about to write you a "bread and butter' letter your additional invitation for next October arrived, so I will combine the two and thank you for the last good time you gave me and tell you how much I anticipate the next one on the 15th of October."

ARTHUR CURTISS JAMES,
99 JOHN STREET.

NEW YORK, **Feb. 28th,** 1900.

My Dear Mrs. Todd,

I was very sorry indeed not to see you when in Boston last week, as I went to the Parker House early Saturday morning and found that you had been there and gone. I left a note for you saying that I would return some time during the morning, and did so, but failed to find you.

A year later he wrote: "Many thanks for your kind note and I am looking forward to seeing you sometime on Monday next. Harriet and I are motoring over from Newport and I suppose she will stay with her sister, as usual, in Northampton, but if you will take care of me for a couple of days I will be delighted to accept."

Mabel would continue to travel with David as he photographed solar eclipses, making five trips to various corners of the world between 1900 and 1914. She would suffer a stroke in 1913, ending her lecture career. She and David would move to Florida in 1917, when he was retired from Amherst due to his erratic behavior, and he would be institutionalized in 1922.

Aloha launch

Commodore James and Harriet had logged 60,000 miles on *Aloha* the brigantine. In 1909, after her final season as the New York Yacht Club's flagship, the boat was sold and put in service as the steam trawler *Heroine*, fishing out of New York, working on the Grand Banks. It had turned out to be a brief tour of duty. In 1920 she sprang a leak and sank off Rhode Island. In one of his log books, Arthur states that "*Aloha* laid her bones off Point Judith whistling buoy, having foundered when returning from the Grand Banks." His eulogy is brief:

> *The little brigantine had a splendid record and was comfortable and seaworthy under all conditions of wind and weather, and even the increased comforts on present* Aloha *have not made any of us forget the good times covered by the ten years of cruising on her.*

But that was ten years after her successor took to the water on March 20, 1910. Harriet, looking cheerful in mink coat and matching pillbox hat, deftly demolished a bottle of bubbly against the stem of the yacht, and *Aloha* the bark rolled majestically down the ways at Fore River Shipyard in Quincy, Massachusetts. Just two months later she had been fitted out and made ready to sail. Her sea trial was the New York Yacht Club cruise of that year, on which she led the fleet and also served as the race committee boat for day races around the buoys. In early September that year, Arthur took the boat transatlantic for the first time.

By all accounts, she was a sight to see. In his book *Legendary Yachts*, the late William W. "Bill" Robinson wrote of encountering *Aloha* ghosting along on Long Island Sound one calm spring evening as the sun was setting. The boat Robinson was on overtook the bark. "Suddenly her black hull and rigging pattern firmed in the pale light... the ghostly white of her sails changed to sharp silhouettes. There, against the glow remaining in the northwest sky, was the starkly outlined tracery of the rigging and sails of

Harriet christening the bark *Aloha*

a graceful bark. She was one of the most romantic yachts ever built, a bridge between the age of square riggers and the luxurious floating palaces of the early twentieth century. No one who saw her will ever forget her."

Aloha's maiden voyage to Europe was unremarkable. The crossing was plagued by rain and light winds. Arthur and his party of six (including himself and Harriet), left the yacht in

Edinburgh, took a motor trip through France and Spain, and on October 5 left for home aboard the liner *Lusitania*.

Aloha departed for New York a week later. That's when both the new yacht and her crew were severely tested. As the *Boston Globe* headlined on December 10, 1910: "ENCOUNTERED FOUR HURRICANES—*Aloha*, II, America's Finest Pleasure Yacht Home After Being Blown 1794 Miles Off Course." Various newspaper accounts painted a grim picture of a voyage from hell. "The black gloss is gone from her steel hull and deckhouse. Her spars have been stripped of their shining varnish coats, with main topgallant mast and yard sent down.... 'It was uphill all the way,' said Capt. Bezanson. 'A gale off the Lizard drove her off course... we have had her so far over that the lifeboats in the davits were in the water."

The log of First Officer Melvin O'Brien provide the facts of an unusual, sustained beating: "Nov 6, moderate gale and confused seas, shipping large quantities of water all day; Nov 7, heavy gale; Nov 8, fresh gale, rain squalls and heavy hail (big stones fell); Nov 10, heavy rain squalls; Nov 11 heavy gale, heavy rain, hail squalls; Nov 13, wind backing to south and increasing to gale with heavy rain squalls; Nov 14, strong gale, heavy thunder squalls and hail; Nov 16 strong gale ranging to northwest, high confused sea—with more of the same through Nov 20; Nov 22 gales resuming with heavy cross sea, ship laboring heavily, smothered in seas. Barometer 29.06 in center of heavy revolving gale blowing with hurricane force." Sailors reading this will grimace at more than two straight weeks of gale-force conditions. During one four-day period, *Aloha* had managed to sail only 30 miles.

Aloha put into Bermuda on December 2, but as soon as they left for New York more gales and rainsqualls dogged the crew until they raised Montauk Light on the end of Long Island a week later. Captain Bezanson said it was the roughest trip he had ever made in all his years at sea. "But she has found herself," he said of the yacht, "her staunchness is proved."

Gifts

Shortly after Arthur and Harriet arrived home on the *Lusitania*, Arthur made page 7 in the newspaper in Madison, New Jersey, where his mother still lived, for his gift of $1 million ($25 million today) to the American Board of Commissioners of Foreign Missions (ABCFM). The *Madison Eagle* reported that Arthur's gift, targeted for colleges in foreign lands, was the largest ever made to the Missions by a living individual. The ABCFM had been founded in 1810, in London (following the Missionary Society founded in 1795), to export the Christian gospel to non-Christian countries. D. Willis James had long been a contributor. Arthur's gift was given in memory of his father.

Americans had begun venturing overseas in the early 1800s to spread the Christian gospel, first to India, Burma, and Hawaii, then to the Middle East. By the 1870s, the initial intention of encouraging "multiculturalism," by having missionaries preach and move on, allowing targeted cultures to integrate Christian beliefs into their own way of life, would be replaced by a more aggressive and sustained effort to establish a firm foothold for Christianity. As Daniel Bays, a modern China scholar, wrote in *The Foreign Missionary Movement in the 19th and Early 20th Centuries*, "late in the [nineteenth] Century there was a visible rise in national self-confidence and an assumption that American values and institutions were as valid as the Christian gospel. . . . In this context it was easy for American missionaries to conflate the Protestant responsibility to evangelize the world and the assumption that the United States was a special model of civic virtue and republican civilization."

Arthur's interest in promoting Christianity abroad was keen. Since the early 1900s he had been actively recruited by a group of American missionaries who had founded Canton Christian College, in Canton (now Guangzhou), China, in 1888. "To make China strong," the college prospectus read, "the anti-opium edict has the support of the people. To make China strong, the people themselves are abandoning the foot-binding torture. And to make China strong, the whole nation is seeking 'the useful learning' of the West, which has made Europe and America strong, and given Japan her place among the nations."

No doubt the story of Amherst alumnus Joseph Neesima's crusade to bring Christianity to Japan had helped provide more than a passing interest for Arthur in the Canton project. Every student at Amherst had learned about one of the college's legendary alumni, Joseph Hardy Neesima, who as a boy growing up in Japan had developed a consuming fascination for the West. Born in 1843 as Niijima Shimeta, as a young man he had converted to Christianity, and was ostracized for rejecting the worship of "dumb idols" then prevalent in his country. Neesima was convinced that Christianity, and a combination

Joseph Neesima

of religion, "civilization," and general education, had to be embraced in Japan to prepare his country for the future. An outcast who was beaten for his beliefs by his parents, Neesima stowed away on a schooner bound for Boston. After a harrowing voyage, he found work at a shipyard. His employer, a devout Christian and board member at Phillips Andover Academy, was so impressed by Neesima's story that he arranged a scholarship for him at Andover. Neesima had gone on to Amherst, graduating in 1870. After experience as a missionary and being ordained as a Christian minister, he would return to Japan in 1875. There he would found a school that became Doshisha University, a Christian college to which Arthur contributed.

Beginning in 1905, Arthur contributed regularly to Canton Christian College. In a report published by the school in 1908, "Arthur C. James" was listed as a principle contributor. But the large volume of letters between Arthur and various Canton officials, preserved in a collection at Yale University, generally indicates a somewhat reluctant supporter. And he became quite perturbed when college administrators informed him he had not only been elected to the board of trustees, but was seen as the logical candidate for president of the board. His reply was very stern, bordering on a rebuke. "I am very much surprised and greatly annoyed at the action taken by the board of trustees," he wrote. "I have repeatedly and definitely declined to consider for one instant going on the board of the Canton Christian College, and to be elected without consultation and without my consent is not the way I like to do business. I must decline absolutely and finally to consider it for a minute, and of course the Presidency of the board is entirely out of the question." Apparently his anger did not affect his financial support. In 1911, Arthur's mother sent $5,000 ($125,000 today) to Canton College. In 1913, Arthur sent Canton a check for $25,000 ($650,000 today).

About the time *Aloha* was rolling down the ways at Fore River Shipyard, Arthur was putting his signature on another large check in memory of his parents. The town of Williston, North Dakota, had grown up in the 1890s because of the arrival of James J. Hill's Great Northern Railroad. Hill had named the town for his great friend, D. Willis James. "He was one of the best men that ever lived," Hill had said of his friend during a speech he had given in Williston in 1909. "I knew him well, and it was for him that I called this place Williston. Willis James was one of the straightest men I ever knew." Hill also showed his cunning nature when he went on to make a suggestion to certain folks in Williston who had been trying to raise money for a library. "If you people want a library," Hill said, "the best thing you could do is write to Arthur Curtiss James, Willis James's son in New York, a mighty fine man. He is the kind of man who would be deeply interested in the place."

A Mrs. Whitehead, wife of Ben G. Whitehead, editor of the *Williston Weekly State* newspaper, had taken it upon herself to send an appeal to Arthur. She received his wholehearted assurance of help. And wholehearted it was. Arthur wrote a check for $25,000 ($625,000 today), an amount that covered the acquisition of the site, the design (Greek Revival), construction, and interior furnishings and equipment. The James Memorial Library (now Art Center) opened its doors in 1911. Arthur would make periodic donations to the library throughout his life. In 1951, the foundation created by his will contributed $15,000 to the library. The building itself was listed on the National Register of Historic Places in 1979.

Edgehill

In Newport, Arthur acquired several other properties that surrounded his Beacon Hill estate. The expansion included a house described in architectural terms as "a large, rambling two-and-a-half-story random-course-ashlar stone-and-shingle house with a stretched-rectangular-plan main block picturesquely intersected by curving conical-roof towers and projecting cross gables." In plain English, it was a sprawling, slightly imposing, mysterious-looking place measuring several hundred feet end-to-end. With its weathered masonry façade of rectangular pieces of thin, "ashlar" stone, and mossy, shingled roofs, it rose out of the rocky hillside as if it had grown there. Named "Edgehill," it had also been designed by McKim, Mead & White, and built in 1887 to '88.

In 1911, Edgehill became the summer home of Mr. and Mrs.

E. Hayward Ferry. The Ferry family's roots in Massachusetts can be traced to the 1640s. Hayward was a Harvard graduate who went into banking. By 1910 he was a first vice president of Hanover National Bank, in New York. More to the point, Ferry, who was five years older than Arthur, had married Harriet Parsons' sister, Amelia, a year before Arthur had married Harriet. The Ferrys had one daughter born in 1891 named Harriet, after Amelia's sister (Arthur's wife).

One's in-laws are not always one's friends, but as luck would have it, there had been an instant connection between Arthur and Hayward Ferry. Their business lives intertwined as much as their personal lives. Two of the boards Ferry served on were Phelps Dodge and the Northern Pacific Railroad. Like Arthur, Ferry was a committed philanthropist. He also had a global interest in promoting the early twentieth century's accepted idea of Christian values. In the 1890s he was secretary of the Ramabai Association in India, aimed at making women's lives better and, in particular, eliminating the practice of *sati*, or widow-burning (under *sati*, a woman is expected to fling herself on her husband's burning casket, or otherwise commit suicide "without undue delay"). Like Arthur, Ferry's philanthropy included medicine. For his part, Arthur James sat on the board of Hanover National Bank.

The Parsons sisters were close. More good luck. Both had attended Smith College (Amelia was a graduate). They enjoyed the same traditional brand of social life. They supported the same charities—chief among them being the YMCA—and they enjoyed vacationing together with their husbands. It made sense when Edgehill became part of the James estate that the Ferrys would become next-door neighbors each summer. Hayward would be available to go day-sailing with Arthur on one of the small boats he owned, and the sisters would continue to flourish in one another's company.

The Ferry family would grow and provide Arthur with more good neighbors. Robert DeForest Manice, a Newport resident now in his sixties, relates that after his grandmother Harriet Ferry married his grandfather William DeForest Manice, their children were raised at the Beacon Hill Estate. "My father and his brother and sister," Robert Manice says today, "felt as if they were Arthur's and Harriet's children. They lived at Edgehill, and had the run of the place."

Arthur built an additional house on the estate, called Vedimar, as a guesthouse. There are indications that he built it for his physician, Dr. Lewis Frissell. In any case, the Frissells made Vedimar their summer home for many years. Dr. Frissell's wife, Antoinette Montgomery, was the daughter of one of the contractors who had built the Great Northern Railway. The Frissell's son, Vareck, had gone to work for Sir Wilfred Grenfell, the Scotsman who had started the philanthropic missions in his name that provided medical and social services to rural communities in Newfoundland and Labrador. Vareck would be killed in the early 1930s when one of Grenfell's service ships exploded. Arthur, we recall, had visited and been impressed by a Grenfell mission during a cruise on the first *Aloha*.

Arthur also built "Zeerust," a delightful, ivy-covered cottage with a separate studio building for his painter friend, Hubert Vos. It was all part of James's grand plan to build a private little enclave for himself on Beacon Hill. But Arthur wouldn't exactly isolate himself from goings on in Newport. He joined a few clubs, including the Newport Reading Room, a gentlemen's club founded in 1854, and for many years he served on the board or on various committees of the Newport Casino. The Casino, a prime example of Victorian shingle-style (designed by Charles McKim), still resplendent today at the center of Bellevue Avenue, was built in 1880 by New York newspaperman and yachtsman James Gordon Bennett Jr. after the Reading Room had chastised his friend, Captain Candy, for riding a horse onto the porch of that establishment. Bennett had sponsored Candy to come to Newport to teach Americans how to play polo. The Reading Room had suspended Candy after the incident with the horse. Having had his feathers ruffled, Bennett decided to build a less stuffy club, as the name he chose implied. The Casino (best known as a tennis club today) became an important social center, and published a pored-over periodical that kept track of who was doing what, and with whom.

The Jameses attended parties, and more than held their own as entertainers, as we will see. But for Arthur, the acreage on Beacon Hill was his blank canvas. Like most only children, Arthur was adept at self-entertainment, comfortable in his own company. The comprehensive scene he was creating on the Hill would be immensely satisfying for him. Newport was there for the taking, but Arthur would always be quite happy at home tending his various projects. He began raising German shepherd dogs, for one thing, each of whom he named after characters in operas. (Here, Tristan! Sit, Isolde!)

In addition to arranging to have several friends and relatives as neighbors, he employed men and women he respected, and whom he enjoyed seeing, like John Greatorex, to help run the estate. He needed a captain and thirty-seven crew to run his 216-foot yacht. He would eventually need more than two hundred workers to run the 128-acre Beacon Hill estate.

Lanai

His endless curiosity, his sailor's penchant for getting things done in a timely manner, and a head full of ideas kept Arthur well engaged. In between all the construction on Beacon Hill, and the significant input he was having on the design and building of *Aloha*, he found time to come up with the basic concept for a 70-foot shallow-draft houseboat. The Norwegian-born yacht designer John Trumpy drew up the lines, and the boat was built by the Mathis Yacht Building Company in Camden, New Jersey. The idea of a houseboat wasn't exactly new, but what Arthur brought to the genre produced a marked improvement. As *Motor Boating* magazine concluded in its September 1912 issue, "*Lanai* is a boat and not a floating residence." (Another *Lanai*! The Jameses were stuck on Hawaiian names for their vessels.

When they finally sold this boat, Harriet made the buyer sign a legal document causing him to rename it. The name *Lanai*—in Hawaiian, an open-sided veranda, or porch, and the name of an Hawaiian island—belonged to the Jameses.)

The telling significance between *Lanai* and previous houseboats of the period was that while *Lanai* was roomy enough to live aboard for long periods, the boat had enough of the proper cruiser about her to make long, comfortable runs along the coast. The rake angle from chine to keel, for instance, was increased over

Lanai moored in front of Aloha Landing (*left of boat*)

previous boats of her type, and her keel width was increased from 16 inches to 27 inches—both to afford better stability. She cruised happily at 10.5 knots, a decent speed for the day. Locating the pilothouse forward, shaded by an eyebrow overhang, gave *Lanai* a workmanlike appearance and afforded an unobstructed view for the helmsman. The boat's plumb bow was raised and flared to protect the pilothouse from seas, and her waterline length was just three feet less than her 70-foot length. Her 17-foot beam was comfortably wide, and while her depth of hold was more than 8 feet, her draft was just 2 feet, 3 inches. She was powered by twin gas engines. There were two tunnels built into the hull at the stern to house and protect the wheels while maintaining the shallow draft. More light and ventilation was obtained inside the boat by the use of square windows instead of the standard round ports. Many of *Lanai*'s features would go on to be applied to the houseboat genre. Harriet was proud to be listed as the boat's owner.

Blue Garden

Meanwhile, the undisputed showpiece of the Jameses' estate was being built under the direction of John Greatorex. It was called the Blue Garden because all the flowers were shades of blue. Or white, for eye-pleasing relief, and, as the Impressionists discovered, as an effective counterpoint to make all those blue blooms sing. In her exhaustively researched work *The Blue Garden*, author Arleyn Levee was not able to discover why Harriet James wanted a blue-themed garden. "Whatever she read or saw," Levee concludes, "by September 1911, Harriet James had developed definite ideas of what she wanted her flower garden to be, 'blues and purples, no reds.'" Levee reports that a *New York-Tribune* article of July 1911 had described a garden belonging to a wealthy Long Island woman as "a riotous mass of blue," and surmises that Harriet had probably visited that garden.

"There is an austere elegance about a green garden," Harriet Phelps Jackson wrote in *Newport in Flower*, "pink or yellow or red are frivolous except as accents, but the garden that appeals to the romantic, universal soul is the blue garden."

The Jameses' Blue Garden was a large, formal layout in the overall shape of a cross. A square pool four feet deep was centered at the axis of the cross. A second, rectangular pool was centered on the long leg of the cross. This pool was only 2½-inches deep, with fine spray jets along the sides. At the top of the cross, a curved, elevated pergola provided a clear view of the entire garden. Another pergola was in place at the opposite end. The garden was contained by a low wall backed by an evergreen hedge. "A very stately garden it is," Harriet Phelps Jackson wrote, "with the iridescent quality which blue flowers that really are mauve and purple and grayish, rather than true blue, impart."

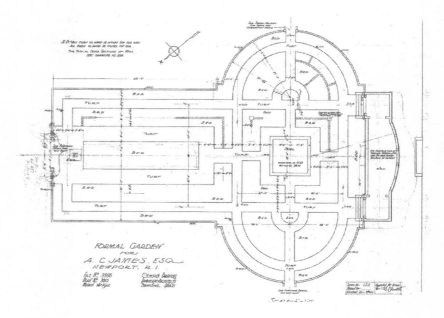

By the time plans for the Blue Garden were taking shape in the offices of the Olmsted Brothers, Arthur had spent around $2.5 million (in today's dollars) on other landscaping and planting. As previously noted, around 470 sets of plans for planting had been drawn by the Olmsted firm. Drafted by hand, many of the plans are works of art in themselves. There were many separate elements, including an enclosed orchid garden, and a tropical plant house that produced bananas. The vegetable garden was a tour de force that took up several acres. The rose garden was 1,000 feet long, having been blasted out of granite rock and planted with 5,000 roses of many varieties. There wasn't a plant, seed, tuber, or a bulb on the estate that wasn't given a number and represented by a scale drawing indicating its placement:

211. *Campanula rotundafolia*, 4126 plants, 1-inch apart, Scotch hairbell

215. *Myrica serifera*, 210 plants, 2½-inches apart, Bayberry

A.C. JAMES. ESQ.
NEWPORT, RHODE ISLAND.

SKETCH SHOWING LOTUS POOLS
AT NORTH EAST PERGOLA -50

File N° 3550
Plan N° 408

Olmsted Brothers
Landscape Architects

There were 40 sets of plans drawn for the Blue Garden alone. No detail was left to chance, from the selection of more than 80 varieties of plants to the specific composition of dirt and fertilizer each would need, to the nature of the columns supporting the pergola roofs, and to what shrubbery would be best for backing up the wall. The water and pumping system for the pools posed a creative engineering problem. Selecting the tiles for the floor of one pergola required weeks of thorough research and discussion. And Harriet's desire to install various art objects she had collected in the garden resulted in the usual, politically diplomatic arm wrestling between their client and the professionals at Olmsted that often resulted in frustrating compromises for the professionals. But when it came to using the antique gates, the folks at Olmsted bristled. As Levee recounts in *The Blue Garden*, "Mrs. James was also determined to use another prior purchase, antique gates, somewhere in the Blue Garden space, suggesting that these would close off the end of the walled garden." The reply from Olmsted: "It is distinctly our feeling that to introduce a gate at the northeast end of the garden, separating it from the plaisance and the pergola beyond would be a great mistake." Olmsted won that battle. Harriet's wrought-iron gate was replicated as a pair, and a bit smaller, so they would fit between columns at the two side entrances to the garden.

Having been most specific about their desires, having approved all the decisions about design and materials, and with the trusted John Greatorex in charge, Arthur and Harriet did what any group of contractors would appreciate owners doing during the construction phase: they went on a prolonged vacation. They sailed *Aloha* to Egypt and a trip on the White Nile, "where we hoped to at least see big game in their native haunts, and possibly have some good shooting," Arthur wrote in a log of the trip some years later. "The lure of the wild had seized us, and we wanted to see for ourselves the Central African country of which we had been told. 'The whole scene presents an aspect of desolation beyond the power of words to describe!' We were not disappointed."

They left on November 15, 1912. Two weeks later they sailed past Gibraltar. A further two weeks later they landed in Cairo, where Arthur's aunt and uncle—Mr. and Mrs Arthur James of England—joined them for the White Nile section of the trip. The log reads like a textbook of things to see: the tomb at Abydos; the tombs and mummies of Amenhotep III, Sety, and Ramesses III at Luxor Thebes; and Abu Simbel. By January 9, 1913, they were on a train from Hyksos to Khartoum, "absolute desert, slow time, but more comfortable than camels," Arthur wrote.

At Gebelein, south of Luxor on the West Bank of the Nile, they began to see game. Arthur shot a gazelle and an antelope, and had his "first view of the absolute African savage, whose only clothing is wood ashes." The trip continued for almost a month, with daily highlights alternating among the shooting of game, visiting tombs and historic sites, and visiting local leaders and politicians.

From Egypt they sailed on to Jaffa (now Tel Aviv, Israel), where weather prevented a stop in Jerusalem. They continued past the Albanian coast during the Balkan War: "in passing we could see the smoke of the battle then in progress." After a stop in Venice for a few days, they sailed west across the Mediterranean to Cannes, where they would leave the yacht and take a steamship back to New York, arriving in April. According to Arthur's log, they had sailed 10,617 miles on *Aloha*, and Arthur kept a very precise log.

When Arthur and Harriet returned to Newport, the Blue Garden was nearly complete. Three years in the making, at phenomenal expense, the Blue Garden would be declared finished sometime in the spring of 1913. Long before that, Arthur and Harriet had been discussing how they might dedicate this floral extravaganza that would, they expected with good reason, define their estate.

Beacon Hill House had been finished, and it was indeed a showplace. Everything about it was oversized, including the vases for holding masses of flowers. The paneling for the living and dining rooms, dating from the mid-1600s, had been brought from the South

Triptych of Harriet in the Blue Garden

of England. Jacobean design, from England's second Renaissance (early 1600s), recognizable for its busy, colorful patterns and full, three-dimensional (often bulbous) treatment of furniture, was a prevailing theme of the interior. Walnut paneling, and heavily carved cornices and ceilings adorned many rooms. A collection of tapestries, then valued at $300,000, hung in the two-story Great Hall. There was no ballroom, but a partition between the dining room (which itself could seat 40) and the living room could be removed for formal dances. One room was described by *Town & Country* magazine "as though a delightful flower garden had been caught between flowered walls. At one side is a quaint wall fountain of white marble. In the center of the room is a circular marble basin in which float lotus flowers and water lilies of dull rose and white."

Beacon Hill House could certainly have stood on its own as the focus of a celebration to formally announce the opening of the James estate. It was that grand. In addition to the exotic décor, there was also the greenhouse of orchids onto which many of the bedrooms opened. And Arthur's radio room housed the very latest in communications gear for contacting ships at sea. But with Marble House, the Elms, the Breakers, Chateau sur Mer, and half a dozen other larger and even more extravagant Newport palaces in place, celebrating "the house" had been done to the extreme.

For months, Harriet had been thinking about the garden as the centerpiece of a grand celebration. Despite the wretchedly excessive state the Newport social scene had attained, it was impossible for a woman of Harriet's station and sense of heartfelt social responsibility not to imagine herself orchestrating a gala event. Such an undertaking was not Arthur's cup of tea, but his support for Harriet in all things seems to have been unconditional. And while some of the more notable social queens of the wild and crazy days were still at work on Newport's creative party scene—Marion "Mamie" Fish being one—both the pace and the extravagance of entertaining had diminished to a level that was more in line with Harriet's more temperate social sensibilities. The Blue Garden could definitely be the vehicle, but what to do?

The Masque

The answer began taking shape when Arthur and Harriet met the American painter Joseph Lindon Smith. It is uncertain how the Jameses met Smith, but as we have seen, the Jamese embraced art in their daily lives, and were generous patrons as well. A significant contributor to the Metropolitan Museum of Art for years, Arthur would be elected to the museum's board in 1918.

Along with John Singer Sargent, Anders Zorn, and other artists of renown—including the writer Henry James and the poet Robert Browning—Joseph Lindon Smith had been an enthusiastic participant in Isabella Stewart Gardner's Venetian salon at Palazzo Barbaro, flourishing in the late 1800s. In fact, Smith had been a favorite of Isabella Gardner. A prominent patron of the arts from Boston, Gardner had some influence on Smith being commissioned to paint an homage to Venice in one of the new Boston Public Library's vestibules. This idea did not sit well with Charles McKim, who had designed the library, and the reverberations of the resulting tiff would not have escaped patrons like the Jameses, who paid attention to the art world's controversies.

Smith was primarily a painter. He started out doing portraits, but he once admitted that his frustration with the models moving too much had made him switch to inanimate objects. A trip to Egypt before the turn of the century sparked his interest in temples and sculptures, which he painted in profusion. Travel inspired him. According to a Smith biographer, Diana Wolfe Larkin, "cultural sights on [two European] and other trips early in his career inspired Smith to revisit historical styles through his own painted versions of works he admired from the past, especially from the Italian Renaissance and Classical Greece.... A passion for the distant past would drive him to spend much of his life recording, in oil on canvas, the artistic heritage of other cultures." Once again, the idea of an artist packing off to bring back riveting historical images from the far reaches of the world would have appealed to Arthur.

From his home in rural New Hampshire, Smith had also dabbled in writing pageants for friends. He had built two outdoor theaters in the process. But it was Smith's meeting with Percy MacKaye, in Europe, that launched his second career as a theatrical wizard. Percy MacKaye was the son of the great theatrical innovator, Steele MacKaye, who wrote thirty plays and initiated over one hundred items common to today's theaters, such as overhead lighting, folding seats, flame-proof curtains, and a machine for creating smoke onstage. Funding for the elder MacKaye's most ambitious project, a twelve-thousand-seat theater with twenty-five moving stages called the Spectatorium, proposed for the Chicago World's Fair in 1893, dried up because of the financial panic that year.

Smith joined with Percy MacKaye, who carried on his father's work, on a number of productions in Europe. Back home, Smith began producing pageants for private parties, civic occasions, and fundraising benefits. As Smith's wife, Corinna Putnam Smith, wrote in her biography, *Interesting People: Eighty Years with the Great and Near Great*, "...balls and masques and theatricals had been developed for social intercourse in eighteenth century England, but the higher reaches of American so-

UNSUNG TITAN OF THE GILDED AGE • PAGE 180

ciety were ready for these kinds of *divertissement* as the gay 90s spilled over into the first decade of the new century... Joe was appealed to by hostesses with imagination for something different in decoration and novel in the way of entertainment."

It seems likely that Harriet James was one of those hostesses who had been intrigued by Smith's talent with pageants, and like many who met the gregarious man, she had been charmed by his engaging manner and contagious enthusiasm. As Alan Chong, associate professor at the S. Rajaratnam School of International Studies in Singapore, wrote in *Gondola Days: Isabelle Stewart Gardner and the Palazzo Barbaro Circle*, "Smith certainly shows how a middle-class artist, possessed with some talent, but perhaps more importantly endowed with a sense of humor and great charm, could be quickly swept up into the upper reaches of society... with a client list that read 'like a page in Boston's *Blue Book*.'" Harriet asked Smith if he would write a "Masque"—an entertainment wherein masked players represent mythological or allegorical figures—to dedicate the Blue Garden. Smith took the commission, and the results would be spectacular.

According to Dennis O'Conner, a Chicagoan who is both a devoted collector of Smith's work and a determined potential biographer, Smith was fascinated by Steele MacKaye's innovations. What MacKaye had done with lighting was of special interest. Until MacKaye began experimenting, stage lighting was available in eight or nine colors. MacKaye upped it to seventy or more colors. While in Europe, Smith secured the plans for the Spectatorium and began his own experimentation with lights.

Smith used his own innovative lighting techniques in a pageant he did for the Tiffany Studio in New York, in 1912—imagine the shimmering effects of lighting all that glass! But what he brought to *The Masque of the Blue Garden* a year later was even more advanced. First, he illuminated the roof of the blue canopy that had been erected at the entrance to the garden, and that funneled guests to bleachers that had been built to accommodate the three hundred fifty invited guests.

But his major accomplishment was the stringing of miniature lights he had designed, in white and blue, that were scattered in profusion on all the bushes, trees, and plants. "The little lights faded on and off," Dennis O'Conner says, his voice rising with incredulity when he thinks about it. "No one had ever seen such a thing! These were the lights that turned into what we buy today, a hundred years later, for our Christmas trees!"

On the clear, moonlit night of August 15, 1913, guests arriving at Beacon Hill House parked their carriages and automobiles on the lawn. Their wraps were taken by attendants, who directed them under the lighted blue canopy, thence into the garden, where Arthur Curtiss James greeted them. His friends could only tell it was Arthur by the beard and the glasses. The rest of him had been elegantly transformed into Cosimo de Medici, the dominant force in Florence, Italy, for fifty years in the late 1300s and early 1400s. Arthur was draped in full-length robes and adorned with all the oversized accessories. He wore a large and intricately decorated hat of the period. Complexion-altering theatrical makeup completed the transformation.

Casting the host as de Medici was a brilliant concept that assuredly came from the mind of Joseph Lindon Smith, with Arthur's approval. The comparison was apt. Arthur and de Medici had much in common. Cosimo de Medici was born into wealth, and grew it, becoming the founder of the Florentine de Medici dynasty. He became perhaps the wealthiest man of his time through his prowess as a trader and banker. Cosimo de Medici was described as a "graceful schemer who gently corrupted his way to the top." The Rome branch of the bank he founded managed the finances of the Catholic Church and took care of its hierarchy's accounts as well. His wealth combined with his "popular" policies made him a prime target of other wealthy families. He was forced to flee Florence. He was incarcerated on a trumped-up charge. Thanks to bribes, he survived assassination attempts. A year later the Medici family regained power, and Cosimo triumphantly returned to Florence.

Cosimo de Medici supported the lesser guilds and the poor against the wealthy aristocrats who ran the city. During his time in public office, de Medici reformed taxation, instituting a graduated scale that put a heavier burden on the wealthy. He put tax money into projects for the public good, something he believed was the civic duty of the rich.

In the Blue Garden, an orchestra set the tone with selections from Wagner. Harriet appeared and welcomed the guests. "My friends," she said, "I am glad to have you with me tonight to witness the dedication of my Blue Garden." She was wearing "an Italian costume of old blue and mauve brocade, embroidered with sapphires and amethysts," according to the *New York Times*—no doubt another Joseph Lindon Smith design. "Her headdress was amethysts and sapphires held in place by strands of diamonds. . . . Mrs. James waved an electric wand, and two little wood sprites appeared." The wood sprites were the daughters of Joseph Lindon Smith, ages nine and

Arthur greeting guests as de Medici

eleven. They were two of the cast of fifty-four that included a score of *Aloha*'s crew, performing as extras.

The drama commenced. The wood sprites were scared away by Cosimo de Medici and his friends, who were partaking of wine and fruits. An old Italian song was sung, and then Joseph Lindon Smith appeared to announce the theme of the pageant, as summarized by Arleyn Levee in her book *The Blue*

Harriet, dressed entirely in blue, greets her guests in the Blue Garden.

Garden: "A fanciful tale of a vintage time when the goddess of the harvest (Ceres) and the goddess of the flowers (Flora) with the earth sprites make offerings to Zephyrus, the gentle West Wind, to celebrate 'the ecstasy of life.'"

Cosimo de Medici gave Smith permission to proceed. "Two mermaids were brought into the garden on the backs of tritons," the *Times* reported. "And two little sea nymphs tempted the mermaids from their shells with fruits." For nearly an hour there followed dances by Zephyrus, and others, including

Ceres, "a gleaming blue-white figure... contemplated the surface of the lily pool. It began to bubble, and from its disturbed surface arose Water, a dripping figure with strands of lily pads upon her shoulders and arms. She danced across the lawn and was lost in the gloom." The *Newport Daily News* coverage was detailed, albeit confusing:

Pomona, Thyris, and Cyria, appearing to float across the moonlit grass, joined Ceres. With graceful, languorous poses, they stood in the bluish glow, until Ceres summoned Flora. She could not be found. The goddess called upon the West Wind to find her, and his meager covering of a small leopard skin did not impede him in his swift obedience. Flora was found under a rose bush, dragged into view and made to dance, garlands of roses flying behind her in the night breeze as she darted in and out among the shadows. Zephyrus joined her and danced until he fell exhausted by the pool's edge.

Then darkness fell on the Blue Garden. Between the marble columns appeared Diana, a white draped figure. She espied Endymion and flew to him. He carried her to the lily pool and they watched their reflection on the surface. Slowly they walked away and the gnomes had the garden again to themselves. At the far end they found two large seashells. Within these hid the water nymphs. The dwarfs lured them to the water's edge where the nymphs tried to drag them under the surface. In terror the gnomes fled.

"Things got a little livelier when Florence Noyes made her entrance," Deborah Davis writes in *Gilded*. Florence Fleming Noyes was a well-known modern dancer of the time. A few months before her Blue Garden appearance, she had portrayed Liberty in a tableau vivant in support of women's suffrage in Washington, D.C. Now, as Amphitrite, goddess of the sea, Noyes was carried in, recumbent upon a large conch shell. She awoke, and entered the water in a revealing, diaphanous costume, dancing with "reckless

grace before disappearing into the depths of the lily pond," according to the *New York Sun*. Her thin, wet gown clung to her body, bringing the men in the audience to full attention. "This beats anything I've ever seen," Davis reported one young man muttering, "as he watched the scantily-clad Noyes writhing in the water."

Afterwards, following a "pied piper" with trumpet, all three hundred fifty guests adjourned to Beacon Hill House where they dined on medieval fare, some of which was served from boars' heads by waiters in period costume. Dancing followed. But the drama was not over. As the *Newport Daily News* reported:

Reclining on a huge seashell, borne by six Tritons, Florence Fleming Noyes was carried into the ballroom where, in the presence of society, she interpreted the Sea Goddess in a pageant. Neptune, following in her wake on a white horse, greeted the Sea Goddess and invited her to dance. Throwing off her robe, she entered a tank glistening with the colors of the rainbow as it fell over multicolored lights. Then, as a climax to her dance, the Sea Goddess disappeared like the mist that rose from the water.

The report is tantalizing for what is missing. "In the presence of society" implies a dance interpretation that was risqué, to say the least. And Noyes "throwing off her robe," after her provocative performance in the Blue Garden pool, makes one wonder exactly what, if anything, this lovely dancer was wearing under it. And don't forget that West Wind character with his "meager covering of a small leopard skin." In any case, *The Masque of the Blue Garden* was an enormous success, making Newport forget about the Mother Goose-themed extravaganza given by Mamie Fish a few weeks earlier. With a single, well-orchestrated event, Arthur and Harriet had secured their place in Newport's hall of social fame.

It was just a few months later when Joseph Lindon Smith produced another hit at the James estate. Smith had built an amphitheater that held three hundred people in the rose garden. For the show, he had selected a series of circus-type acts for the evening that would eventually be gathered under one "big top." It was a production complicated by the diverse nationalities of the acts, and the many languages involved. Ten of *Aloha*'s crew were again recruited as muscle. Things got slightly out of hand in the wee hours of the next morning, when several of the *Aloha* sailors were seen darting about the ballroom, eluding ushers who were trying to round them up. When Corinna Smith, who was working as her husband's production assistant, decided to help, she was restrained by Arthur. "They are having such a wonderful time," Arthur told her, "don't pitch them out."

Joseph Lindon Smith went on to create, with Percy MacKaye, perhaps his ultimate masque, for the City of St. Louis's 150th anniversary in May of 1914. A cast of 7,500 people played to an audience of 100,000 people, four nights running.

Second 7 Homes

Manhattan

If Smith wasn't through, neither was Arthur Curtiss James. The two men would continue to conspire, this time over a mansion. Arthur had set tongues wagging when, in the winter of 1914, it was announced he planned to build a residence at 39 East 69th Street in New York, a fashionable section of the city known as Lenox Hill. Other than the projected million-dollar price of the new residence—$25 million today—what stunned New Yorkers was the fact that only a few months prior to the announcement of the Lenox Hill house, Arthur had paid a million dollars for a palatial apartment building at Fifth Avenue and 81st Street. Perhaps he bought it as a place to live while East 69th Street was being built. One presumes he unloaded the apartment building after the new house was finished, but that is not clear.

If Joseph Lindon Smith had a hand in the concept and decoration of the new house, the Boston firm of Allen & Collens handled the design and architectural drawings. The same firm had recently designed the new Union Theological Seminary complex. Measuring 80 by 110 feet, the house at 39 East 69th would take up half the block between 69th and 70th streets on Park Avenue. Side yards of 40 and 15 feet on either end of the house—enough for several townhouses by modern standards—were left vacant for gardens.

The Jameses' Manhattan mansion was one of forty-three houses selected by residential architecture scholar Michael C. Kathrens for his book, *Great Houses of New York, 1880–1930*, an honor that didn't come without a certain stigma attached. In his introduction, Kathrens pointed out that the great houses of London are what gave birth to the New York mansions, and that the London houses were "more than just large; they were presentation stages for the spectacular trappings of the ruling class. A Great House in London embodied both the taste and prestige of the English aristocracy. Visiting Americans were impressed with the quality and scale of the English social events, and had visions of duplicating them at home. It was not lost on Americans that to entertain on a grand scale required a commensurate setting."

Kathrens went on to describe an example of an entertainment "on a grand scale" hosted by the owners of one of the first great houses of New York, built in 1882 by William K. and Alva Vanderbilt, at 660 Fifth Avenue. The scene was evidently quite regal. Sparkling carriages discharged elegantly costumed guests onto a plush red carpet spread across the sidewalk. The numbers were impressive: twelve hundred guests; $10,000 for orchids and roses; the cost of two orchestras; $65,000 for a catered midnight supper. If the occasion had a familiar ring to it, it was because thirty years later, when the Jameses moved to Newport, the very same Alva Vanderbilt would be living in Marble House, the palace she had helped create on Bellevue Avenue. Her approach to entertaining had escalated markedly from those dreary days in New York. Catered midnight supper? How quaint, darling.

But Arthur's venture into the Great House concept does beg the question if, after prioritizing the perfect landscaping and extensive gardens of his Newport estate, the lavish creation of the Manhattan house confirmed Brendan Gill's postulate that the simple act of building is the surest means of announcing that one has made good? Did Arthur cave to that perceived tenet of stature: bigger house, better man? Because the house on East 69th Street, which took two years to build, was a tour de force.

In the book she wrote about her family, Phyllis B. Dodge was openly disparaging of the Jameses, recalling in a belittling way how Arthur always referred to Harriet as "the Commodoress," and going on to note that "all the Dodges derived a certain wry amusement from the Jameses' high style of living." While one reads Phyllis Dodge's book with a certain wry amusement about the elevated plateau upon which she places all members of the Dodge family, and the not-so-subtle snobbery with which she regards others, one can't ignore the caustic impression Phyllis Dodge relates of one Dodge relative who visited the Jameses at home: "Arthur showed us his numerous half-million-dollar toys while his wife was being groomed for the horse show." And another, Cleveland H. Dodge (son of William Dodge, who ran Phelps Dodge with D. Willis James in the early days), and who once had dinner with the Jameses at East 69th Street, is quoted by Phyllis Dodge: "we dined off large, gold-plated plates for all the courses which was very elegant, although slightly vulgar . . . the 'Commodoress' was in her element." It is a measure of Mrs. Dodge's acrimonious stance that she includes this further comment attributed to Cleveland Dodge: "He once remarked with sympathetic insight that he was sure Harriet James would gladly have exchanged all her golden plates for just one of his daughter Julia's eight children."

The house Arthur built was a mammoth English Renaissance structure four stories tall, rectangular, with a flat roof, and with matching extensions on the front (Park Avenue) corners that formed small rooftop terraces framed by balustrades. The façade was Knoxville gray marble. The exterior was more formidable than handsome, and of bank-like impenetrability. It was the interior décor from which greatness arose. C. Owen Lubin's descriptive article about the house in the October 10, 1917, *Town & Country*, is worth quoting at some length.

Commenting on the entrance hall, Lubin wrote: "It is a plea-sure to find that in this baronial hall the architects have been unconventional enough to adopt a style which chronologically takes precedence of Elizabeth, but for which modern building nomenclature has provided no set title. It is reminiscent of the big monuments of English architecture of the late Fourteenth and early Fifteenth Centuries, and might be called indifferently Mediaeval, Gothic, or early Tudor."

The James house at 39 East 60th Street in New York City

Lubin praised how the flavor of the abbey and the con-vent had been captured. "The impression the visitor first receives upon entering through the grilled doors of massive bronze, is when he finds himself surrounded by what is probably as suc-cessful a reproduction of Romanesque and Byzantine ecclesias-tical architecture as has ever been adapted to the uses of a mod-ern, private dwelling."

Lubin saw the entrance hall as an example of what could be done with the assembling of marbles: "With the exception of the wooden ceiling, the entrance hall is wholly of marble, the walls of Botticini, with the columns, arches, and mezzanine floor of Languedoc, gray Sienna and Formosa; the staircase of gray Sienna; the floors, treads, and risers of Tennessee. The antique finish of this marble is unusually well-executed so that it has the appearance of being weathered out of doors for centuries."

The wooden ceiling of the entrance hall was just one area where the ubiquitous Joseph Lindon Smith got involved: "The

ceilings of the entrance hall and of the mezzanine and staircase hall are of oak which has been stained a weathered, dull bluish gray with carved ornamental designs on the rafters, picked out in soft color and faded gold, a very successful treatment which is due to Mr. Joseph Lindon Smith, the Boston artist who gave his personal attention to the work." The exquisite level of both materials and

Interior of 39 East 60th Street

craftsmanship involved was staggering, and the medieval look was definitely in vogue at the time. It was thought to invoke peace, induce tranquility, and add a comforting religious motif to one's surroundings. The wealthy were known to purchase rooms from homes or churches in Europe and have them shipped to the United States, where they would be assembled.

But Lubin's description sounds more like that of a cathedral than a home. Add the "flavor of abbey and convent" achieved by the muted, mediaeval colors selected, and the busy scenes and soft colors of Flemish tapestries hung on the walls, to the fact that the land on which the house was built was previously the site of the Union Theological Seminary. Recall that the Seminary had been moved to Morningside Heights, thanks to a gift of land by D. Willis James, with follow-up gifts by Arthur, and the ecclesiastical theme is better understood.

The house also included a musicians' gallery capable of seating twelve musicians, and a proper pipe organ built by the Ernest M. Skinner Organ Company of Boston upon which Arthur would attempt to play Bach on occasion. On the 69th Street side, there were nine stained glass windows to temper the light, and to ensure privacy from passersby. Their themes were the armorial bearings of the James and Parsons families. The artist remains unknown, but the rendering smacks of the English school. There was an enormous library on the Park Avenue side of the house. Off the library was Arthur's den, wherein a carved wood frieze traced the history of early American settlers. And Lubin noted this ultimate finish detail: the wainscoting had been made "of oak from a frame of one of Nelson's ships which had fought at the Battle of Trafalgar."

As involved as he was in the details of the 69th Street mansion, that project did not deter Arthur from making well-considered, and also strong, decisions on the business front. In the fall of 1914, when East 69th was in the finishing stages, men of his elevated corporate status were confronted with the Clayton Act, an amendment providing further clarification (and power) to the Sherman Antitrust Act, the amendment that had closed down his father's Northern Securities Company. Clayton addressed subjects like price discrimination, price-fixing, predatory pricing, and unfair business practices. Bids for any business involving more than $50,000 in any calendar year were required. Transactions prohibited included the sale of railroad securities to banks. As a result, many bankers and industrial chieftains retired from railroad boards. Not Arthur. A publicity piece from the Great Northern Railroad praised Arthur's decision to "continue as a railroad director, and resign from those directorates which were within the inhibition. It has rendered Mr. James almost unique among his associates," the piece continued, "earned him a most enviable distinction, and has made him a notable figure in railroad circles."

Arthur's philanthropic activity was not diminished in the least by his involvement with the Manhattan mansion. In 1914, he and his mother established a professorial fund at Yale University in the name of D. Willis James, with a gift of $100,000 ($2.5 million today). Today that gift is worth $3.5 million, and produces annual interest of $150,000.

Florida

The house at 39 East 69th Street was among New York City's grandest. But there was one nagging problem that Arthur could not solve: in the winter, New York is cold.

The Jameses had first spent time in Florida in 1911. Florida's attraction in the early 1900s was the same as it is today, only fewer people knew about it, and even fewer could take advantage of it. As Wilhelm Miller wrote in *Country Life in America* (February, 1911), "in short, that little 15-mile strip from Miami south to Cutler is the only spot outside southern California where we may enjoy the main pleasures of the tropics without their discomforts, and without leaving our own country … and you can get here by rail in 37 hours from New York." Miller went on to rave about the profusion of tropical flora, the 70-odd species of fruits that grow there, and the blessed relief to be had from northern blizzards. In the 1920s, the enthusiasm for Florida expressed by Miller and others would combine with the economic relief following World War I to create a full-scale land boom that would raise the state's population by one-third in just five years. Before that, Florida was the retreat of the wealthy.

William Matheson, Arthur's close friend from Long Island, had become familiar with Florida when he had sent one of his sons to the Adirondack-Florida School at Coconut Grove in

1902. Adirondack-Florida was an exclusive preparatory school, unique for having a northern and a southern campus. (It is now the Ransom School, and is minus the Adirondack campus.) Because of his son's enthusiasm for Coconut Grove, Matheson had initially spent some time there for health reasons. Worried about business back home, he had only stayed a few weeks. He went again for a month, and grew to like it. When it appeared that his dye business could survive for extended periods without his presence, in 1905 Matheson built a home in Coconut Grove called Fourway Lodge.

The house was named by Kirk Munroe, a cousin of Commodore Ralph M. Munroe, and a popular author of short stories and a world traveler with home base in Coconut Grove. Com-

Fourway Lodge in Coconut Grove, Florida

modore Monroe was the Grove's most illustrious resident, and is well-remembered today. He was a yacht designer, a good friend of Nathanael Herreshoff; a New Yorker who had moved to Coconut Grove in 1886. At that time, he had purchased 40 acres of waterfront on Biscayne Bay for $400, and a boat worth about as much. He had founded the Biscayne Bay Yacht Club in 1887. Because of Monroe's reputation as a yachtsman and designer, and his prominence as a founding citizen of the Grove, it was natural that Matheson, and later Arthur, would become good friends with "the Commodore." Social events at the nearby Biscayne Bay Yacht Club, like the annual chowder party, would help bring these sailors together. Kirk Monroe had named Matheson's home after a poem by Rudyard Kipling written in 1897 that, with Kipling's soulful cadence, celebrates adventurous spirit, and the rediscovery of earth's blessings of sustenance and care. It is called "The Feet of the Young Men." The first stanza reads:

> *Now the Four-Way Lodge is opened, now the Hunting Winds are loose—*
> *Now the Smokes of Spring go up to clear the brain;*
> *Now the Young Men's hearts are troubled for the whisper of the Trues,*
> *Now the Red Gods make their medicine again.*

A few years later, Matheson had bequeathed Fourway to one of his sons and built another house for himself on nearby property also fronting Biscayne Bay. Over the years, the Jameses certainly had heard all the exciting news from the Mathesons about their newfound paradise, about how they picked oranges, grapefruit, avocados, and mangoes from their front yard in January, but Arthur and Harriet were busy with so many projects it wasn't until the winter of 1911 they were able to test the Florida waters for themselves. They did it quietly, but activities of the wealthy were watched with care by the media, even in 1911. "Arthur Curtiss James is leasing one of the Matheson bungalows in Coconut Grove," headlined a story in the *New York Herald*.

An early indication the Jameses would get serious about establishing a home there was when *Lanai*, the houseboat, arrived in Florida with "Miami, FL" inscribed upon its transom. The yacht was also listed with Miami as home port in the 1912 *Lloyd's Register of American Yachts*. In 1913, Arthur bought the 35-acre Fourway property from William Matheson for $150,000 ($3.7 million today).

The fourteen-room Fourway Lodge was certainly comfortable, but some critical observers thought it fell short of what might have been expected in the way of a winter retreat for one of the country's wealthiest men. It was built of Miami limestone on a square plan that included a central courtyard. The house featured raised, two-story sections at each corner. And like so many Florida houses of the day, it was mostly hidden by a profusion of foliage. It was the six acres of stout young Royal Palm trees—one hundred of which lined the driveway like sentries—and jungle-like groupings of tropical shrubs and trees that made Fourway a showplace. There were orange and grapefruit "groves"; a vine-covered "slat-house," a sculptured tangle of tropical vegetation with a watercourse flowing through it; and a large flight-cage of gaily colored birds that included toucans.

Open verandahs upstairs and down looked out over a vast lawn that sloped gently to the waterfront. Best of all, a channel had been dredged halfway to the house from Biscayne Bay, ending in a basin harboring *Lanai* and Arthur's collection of small boats. A kiosk containing a beacon had been built on the house side of the basin as a range to help Arthur properly line up the channel when returning to Fourway from the bay.

Harry Anderson, now in his ninety-eighth year (2019), recalls having lunch on *Lanai* with his parents and Arthur when he was a teenage student at the Adirondack-Florida School. Fourway Lodge was just a short walk down the road from the school. "When Mother came down to visit us," Harry recalls, "she'd be co-opted by Arthur Curtiss James to play tennis. That was his next favorite sport to yachting."

Harry recalls lunch that day on Biscayne Bay was stone crabs, and white flannels were the attire. He remembers Arthur as friendly, but more involved with the adults than with a boy of thirteen. "But he was good with children," Harry says, "affable, even though he had no children of his own. You can sum it up with what one reporter said, that he always had a twinkle in his eye."

Anderson has an unusually long list of illustrious ancestors, including Aaron Burr. But Arthur Curtiss James is unquestionably his favorite. The life James led, both his humanitarian philosophy, his work ethic, and his love of the sea, set examples that Harry Anderson enthusiastically embraced. The research Harry has done on Arthur is extensive, and has been a lifelong project. That research provided the foundation for this book, and for *Of Rails & Sails*, the documentary film that preceded it.

The Farm

Arthur had one more project up his sleeve to complete his masterpiece on Beacon Hill back in Newport. That was the construction of a model village designed after farms he and Harriet had seen on visits to Switzerland. The concept of a farm had been triggered by a herd of Guernsey cows, a prize-winning herd that had belonged to Arthur's father, D. Willis, and that had been kept on his estate in Madison, New Jersey. The Guernseys had remained in Madison after D. Willis's death, but the property was being sold off, and the cows needed a home. Harriet had fond memories of the immaculate farm villages in Switzerland. It didn't take long for Arthur to conclude that a model Swiss farm would not only make a good home for the cows, but delight Harriet at the same time. It would also please Arthur. Having the German shepherds around was good fun. Having the cows and a diverse bunch of farm animals on the property would be even better.

Arthur chose Grosvenor Atterbury and his partner, Stowe Phelps, who was a distant relative, a neighbor, and a social friend in New York, to design the farm. Atterbury had designed a model housing community, Forest Hills Gardens, where he used precast concrete components in the houses, an accomplishment that could have influenced Arthur's decision.

It's been commonly surmised that one of the initial names of the new farm, "Surprise Valley," had to do with Arthur creating the farm as a surprise for Harriet. The fact that construction had begun in 1915, was suspended during World War I, and was not completed until 1917, would have ruined any element of surprise. A more logical explanation that has been offered for the name is the fact that there was no valley on the Beacon Hill property until crews began blasting one out of the natural granite landscape. As Anita Rafael explains in *The Newport Harbor Guide*, the architects "made a deep valley at Beacon Hill... by blasting out a craggy escarpment... using materials that James employed in his mining company." Hence the "surprise valley." The many farm buildings were built from the rocks that were the result of blasting for the farm that was first known as Rocky Farm, and later as Surprise Valley Farm and/or the Swiss Village.

Lida Rose McCabe, who wrote an article about the farm for *Town & Country* magazine, took issue with the "Swiss" reference. "The architecture," she wrote, "is Italian, and the topography is that of northern Italy rather than Switzerland." Origins aside, the farm village, as designed by Atterbury and Phelps, was a triumph in stone construction. The many towers and chimneys, the arched doors and windows, and the roofs of barrel mission tile lent a properly antiquated feel to the farm as a whole. The stones used for construction were of all shapes and sizes, having been randomly created by dynamite. It is this collection of stones that creates an impression at once rugged and hand-wrought. There's almost as much mortar used in the walls as stone. As Anita Rafael notes, "When dark green ivy began to climb the walls, and moss and lichen filled the crevices in the stonework, everything looked like it had been there for 500 years." The stout, rough-edged buildings have a robust solidarity about them.

McCabe's first impression of the farm was, "theatrical, so obviously is the stage set, the curtain up." The immaculate nature of the place would prompt such a response. The picturesque setting was, of course, intentional. The addition of art, mostly done by Joseph Lindon Smith, enhanced that feeling of a Williamsburg recreation, or even a Disneyland-like creation, circa 1916. The sign Smith painted at the entrance was decorated with a snail, a pig, and a milkmaid. A poetic instruction on the sign addressed the visitors

Arthur allowed to cruise slowly through the farm in their automobiles (they were not allowed to get out and wander around):

You enter here to see the farm—Please drive at snail pace lest you harm—The pigs, the motors, maids and men—A cow, a duck, a dog, a hen—All these and more you'll meet today—So slowly drive along the way.

Another artwork was hung on the slaughterhouse, this one a wooden bas-relief of an Elizabethan butcher leaning on a bloody knife with the inscription, *End of Ye Pig*. And another Joseph Lindon Smith sign was attached to the hennery of sixteen hundred fowl. A cock and hen were depicted pecking at letters that read *From Egghood Through Pullet Age to the Inevitable End*. And mounted on the rocky wall of a pergola, where a weathered table and chairs indicated a place to pause, was a wooden panel. "On its mosaic-like surface," McCabe wrote, "is a glowing dairy scene—Master and Mistress in Dutch costume, seated at table, confronting each other with steins of foaming milk. *The Milk Toast* it is labeled, and the profiles of the toasters are no mean likenesses of Mr. and Mrs. James."

The twenty-four cows were the queens of this model farm. The cow barn was first to go up, since the Guernseys were impatiently tapping their hooves, awaiting accommodation. The barn came complete with a maternity hospital and a bull pen. The cows produced an average of sixty pounds of milk a day. The dairy also produced cream, butter, and cheese. Chicken and eggs came from the hennery. The piggery produced pork, ham, bacon, and sausage. All of this delicious fare was consumed by the hundred or so farm workers, *Aloha*'s crew of thirty-five to forty, and Beacon Hill and Edgehill residents and caretakers.

The farm had an even more significant side, as McCabe insightfully points out. "The motive power of Surprise Valley Farm is the community spirit fostered by Mr. James," she wrote. "Superintendent Greatorex and his associates are encouraged to

study the Farm's interests, and to develop ideas." As one crafts-
man from the carpenter shop told McCabe, "One expresses himself here in the repairing or the making of the beautiful, the
useful. One may experiment, develop his ideas." Could a crafts-
man, or any worker worth his salt, ask for anything more from
an employer? There was, in fact, more. Each workman living on
the estate was given a plot of land and seeds to grow a vegetable
garden for his own personal use.

America's Cup

All the fuss with managing their various homes didn't keep
Arthur from lending a financial hand to the *Resolute* syndicate, a
group of wealthy yachtsmen intent on successfully defending the
America's Cup for the thirteenth straight time. The syndicate had
gotten underway in 1912, laying the groundwork for the design
and building of the yacht that would be ready for the Cup match
two years later. The *Resolute* syndicate membership list read like
a *Who's Who* of industrial captains: Henry Walter (head), J. P.
Morgan, Cornelius Vanderbilt, Frederick G. Bourne, George F.
Baker, Harold S. Vanderbilt, Richard T. Crane, Payne Whitney,
Robert W. Emmons II, and Arthur Curtiss James.

Resolute was a keel sloop also fitted with a centerboard.
Designed and built by Nathanael Herreshoff, at his Bristol,
Rhode Island, yard, the yacht was 75 feet on the waterline, and
107 feet overall. *Resolute* cost $3 million (today's dollars) to
build. She would be steered by Charles Francis Adams II, assisted by an afterguard of five, and her sails would be handled by a
crew of twenty-seven Scandinavian sailors.

Resolute won the right to defend the Cup in 1914, but the
Cup match was postponed when the war broke out. The subsequent match against Sir Thomas Lipton's challenger, *Shamrock
IV*, would wait to be sailed in 1920. *Resolute* won easily. This was
the only time Arthur would get involved in the America's Cup.

Part Two

The 8ision

It wasn't always Arthur's primary focus, but his commitment to fulfill James J. Hill's vision of a transcontinental railroad never strayed from the front of his mind. Given all the houses, all the yachts, the number of philanthropies he was undertaking, and his vast range of active, intellectual interests, "primary focus" had to have been an elusive concept for Arthur. Or at least one that had afforded projects only a brief moment on center stage. To say that Arthur's plate was usually overflowing would be a colossal understatement. That might have been the reason he so often sought refuge on the sea. As he himself recognized, being at sea has a way of eclipsing all other earthly cares. Being at sea reduces one's life to basic essentials.

The multitude of projects Arthur had going were enough to weaken the knees of ordinary, high-energy mortals. One mustn't forget the man was also working full time at Phelps Dodge, where he was a director (1892–1941) and a vice president (1904–17), and also a director of Copper Queen Consolidated Mining Company (1891–1917). "Full time," when he wasn't putting 270,000 miles under the keels of his yachts. He also had three separate companies of his own: Curtiss Securities Company, Curtiss Southwestern Corporation, and A. C. James Company, all of which were used for managing finances.

Arthur's portfolio had gotten off to an enviable start when his father had left him significant ownership in the Great Northern, the Union Pacific, and the Chicago, Burlington & Quincy Railroads, the companies that had been involved in the evolution of James J. Hill's railroad empire. The Chicago, Burlington & Quincy holdings were of particular importance. If it had not been for D. Willis's large holdings in the Burlington, Arthur's father would not have become a major affiliate of James J. Hill, Arthur would not have been introduced to him, nor would Arthur have been afforded the golden opportunity to learn the fundamentals of efficient railway operation—including the value of efficient terminals—from that legendary pioneer. Nor would Arthur have become quite so captivated by Hill's transcontinental dream.

In 1889 the St. Paul, Minneapolis & Manitoba and the Minneapolis & St. Cloud Railroads had provided the key building blocks in the creation of Hill's Great Northern. "D. Willis James and financier John Stewart Kennedy were in direct management of the former," Henry Anderson writes in *James Railway System*, "and held major stock positions along with associates like Marshall Field. The conversion of Manitoba stock to Great Northern stock had given D. Willis a major position in Great Northern." One of Arthur's initial railroad jobs was being his father's eyes and ears at the Manitoba, after being made a director during his senior year at Amherst. Anderson also notes that D. Willis James, J. S. Kennedy, and James J. Hill were members of both the Jekyll Island Club in Georgia and New York's Union League Club, exclusive sanctums where the men who ran America conspired over brandy and cigars. For example, the Federal Reserve was created at Jekyll Island in 1910.

At the time of D. Willis's death, friends and advisors had encouraged Arthur to diversify his holdings, but he had gone his own way, not only retaining his railroad-heavy portfolio, but increasing it at every opportunity. By the 1930s, James was said to be the largest holder of railroad stock in the country.

In the mid-1910s, as he began seriously contemplating a plan to complete Hill's Great Northern route into California, Arthur's focus was on the Western Pacific Railroad. That bone-bruising ride he and Harriet and their party had endured on the Southern Pacific, while traveling from Seattle to San Francisco to meet *Coronet* in 1896, was one of those forever unpleasant memories. Since then, Arthur had been a student of railroad developments in that section of the country, mountainous terrain through which a route into San Francisco from the north would have to be built. Arthur knew the history of that area. It read like a novel by Joseph Conrad.

In the 1860s, a young engineer named Arthur Keddie had surveyed an old Indian track called Beckwourth Pass, a crossing of the Sierra Nevada Range near the California–Nevada border, the country's highest range. Beckwourth is some 2,000 feet lower than the infamous 7,000-foot Donner Pass. The crossing was near the north fork of the turbulent Feather River in a spectacular canyon of the same name, a 60-mile-long gorge with sheer walls as high as 100 feet, having been scoured over eons by the deep, fast-moving river. Unlike those who viewed the canyon as unconquerable, Keddie saw it as "the" answer to a transcontinental railroad route.

Arthur Keddie was one of thousands of engineers, entrepreneurs, and hustlers looking to make hay in what was America's biggest growth industry. And even though the pioneering had been done—the exploring, the engineering challenges of scaling mountain barriers and spanning rivers, and the often-deadly confrontations with Native Americans who sought to protect their land—building railroads still reeked of romance. At the time, a railroad was a business with unlimited financial potential, and with an even greater chance of commensurate financial ruin attached to it. The cost of building railroads was off the charts, but so were the rewards if a person got it right.

Browsing Stuart Daggett's monograph *Railroad Consolidation West of the Mississippi River*, written in 1933, one is surprised by the hundreds of names of railroad companies, several of them little feeder lines less than 10 miles long, all of them aiming to negotiate a payday through acquisition by one of the dozen major lines. In 1932, there were 1,566 different railroads operating in the United States. It was very much like the profusion of Internet start-ups in the twenty-first century. Keddie's vision, while it made a certain amount of sense, was very grand. It took many years for him to convince others that his concept was at all practical.

Keddie formed the Oroville & Virginia City Railroad Company, a line he envisioned would run 180 miles from Oroville, at the mouth of the Feather River, up the north fork through the canyon, and over the Sierra Nevadas to Virginia City, Nevada, 26 miles south of Reno. Virginia City had become a boomtown in 1859 with the discovery of the first major silver mine in the United States. After the Southern Pacific Railroad leased the Central Pacific in 1885, Keddie tried to induce the Union Pacific Railroad to take over the Oroville & Virginia City when the going got tough. But Jay Gould, who had gotten control of the Union Pacific, had scrubbed plans for a westward line into San Francisco that could have included the canyon route. He could have done it, Anderson points out in his monograph, "but after the death of Jay Gould and E. H. Harriman, their sons (George and W. Averell) lacked the perseverance, perspicacity, or the professionalism to complete what their fathers had started."

The Central Pacific, with a track to Virginia City through Donner Pass, a route that was often shut down by snow in the winter, did everything it could to forestall competition. Even though CP's route included difficult grades of 4 percent, requiring several locomotives hooked up in tandem huffing to push the cars over the top, the railroad had a monopoly in the area. Central Pacific management was doing very well by adjusting freight rates to the maximum it figured customers could afford and still

E. H. Harriman   **Jay Gould**

stay in business. According to G. H. Kneiss, who wrote an article about the Western Pacific on its fiftieth anniversary ("Fifty
Candles for Western Pacific" *Western Pacific Company Magazine*,
1953), C. P. Huntington of the Central Pacific had told Arthur
Keddie: "No man will ever be fool enough to build a railroad
through the Feather River Canyon." As the man with the monopoly, Huntingon was surely firing for effect. But just one look at the
canyon's sheer granite cliff faces and broad, fast-moving waters
was enough to give credence to Huntington's pronouncement.

A number of other railroad companies were attempting to
raise the big money needed for what promised to be a very lucrative
route from Denver through Salt Lake City to San Francisco. The
logic was that if it could be built, the Feather River route would be
very cost-effective. Keddie's biggest selling points were his calculation that the grade through the canyon would not exceed 1.3 percent, and at an altitude reduced by 2,000 feet, weather would not

be as disruptive to service. But the big money was not forthcoming.

In 1900, when C. P. Huntington died, E. H. Harriman got involved. Harriman had acquired the Union Pacific, and after Huntington's death had gotten control of the Southern Pacific. George Gould, Jay's oldest son, who was planning to extend his Denver & Rio Grande to California, suddenly found himself stymied by Harriman, who had effectively blocked Gould's path. Kneiss wrote: "It was Gould's ambition to have his own rails from coast to coast. They already stretched from Buffalo to Ogden, Utah, he had definite plans to reach Baltimore, and he had hoped to acquire the Central Pacific himself. Now, bottled up in Utah by Harriman, he decided to build a new road to San Francisco."

George Gould. (*Opposite*) Laying track through Feather River Canyon

To secure the land he needed, Gould's chief engineer suggested he form a mining company and blanket the entire route across the mountains with claims. That clever deed was done, with the emphasis on secrecy. But Arthur Keddie, whose eagle eye never left "his" canyon, got wind of it. Through an elegantly simple manipulation of previously filed routes, Keddie and his group won a rock-solid, five-year franchise for the route through Feather River Canyon. That led to the Western Pacific being formed in 1903, over Harriman's objections. Two years later, it was discovered that George Gould was the money behind the new venture.

Working in the canyon proved to be as difficult as predicted. Kneiss wrote:

Some [construction camps] were accessible by rail, and most of the others by wagon road. But for much of the distance through Feather River Canyon, not even a foot path was handy to the route. Indeed, the surveyors often hung suspended by cables from cliffs in order to set their line stakes.... At Cromberg (100 miles up the north fork from Oroville) it was necessary to cross the swirling river on a jittery rope bridge, and here 11 men were lost working on the cliffs or trying to cross the stream. They were tough men, too, mostly lumberjacks and hard rock miners. Where Grizzly Creek drops into the Feather, the field parties were forced to resort to rafts in order to bypass the sheer granite cliffs. Over at the Utah end, crossing the salt beds was a nightmare due to excessive temperature extremes and the killing glare which often blinded men after a few hours' work.

That was just the surveying phase. The actual construction is one of those tales that evoke wonder, that elevate men to super-human status given their extraordinary accomplishments without today's advanced equipment and technology. The 730-mile railroad track from Salt Lake to San Francisco was built from 1905 to 1909; just four years to construct 730 miles of track across the mighty Sierras. The 60-mile Feather River Canyon section involving the north and middle forks of the river, was beyond challenging, given all the steel, timber, and crushed rock that had to be brought in. On the entire route, 41 steel bridges and 44 tunnels were required. The project was so difficult that the highway (Route 70), which more or less parallels the railroad, wasn't built until 40 years later. The finished railroad was spectacular for its spine-tingling views of the sheer cliffs, and the stomach-turning elevations hundreds of feet above the raging waters.

The building of the Feather River route provided a fine case study for Arthur. Many were the lessons to be assimilated. There was the unexpected havoc Mother Nature could produce, as evidenced by the worst storm in California's history, which struck in 1907. The resulting floods temporarily halted construction, but they caused little damage to the work in progress, a testament to the thoughtful planning of the route's location. Among the lessons learned was the inestimable value of the excellent terminal that had been built in Oakland. That was not lost on Arthur, nor was what proved to be the smart choice of newer and heavier locomotives that were purchased.

Many lessons were economic. There was the preparation of traffic estimates. Diagrams were prepared for expected tonnage in both directions that confirmed the initial conclusions of James J. Hill fifty years before, who had demanded a maximum grade  of 1 percent, and no greater than a 10-degree curve for his tracks. And there was a telling little detail about the selection of a water stop. By considering the nature of the flat terrain where it was located, the town of Wendover, Utah, had been selected as the first stopping point west of Salt Lake City, although it was without easily accessible water. There were other options, towns with plenty of water and more resources in general. But it was all about location. Eastbound from Wendover, there were 130 miles of flat track into Salt Lake that would allow for maximum payloads of freight. The railroad was said to have saved $100,000 annually ($2.5 million today) by selecting Wendover. By comparison, having to drill for water required pocket change.

Freight service for the Western Pacific began at the end of 1909, with passenger service commencing on August 22, 1910. The day passenger service began, the largest celebration in Oakland's history took place. But business was slow at first, which was to be expected. And the winter of 1910 was a brutal one that forced slowdowns and exhausted maintenance crews. The truth was that the Western Pacific spent more and earned less than was anticipated. The first sign of impending bankruptcy came when it was discovered that George Gould had placed the financial responsibility for building the Western Pacific solely on his Denver & Rio Grande Railroad. The Rio Grande had underwritten $50 million in bonds ($1.25 billion today). Building and equipping Western Pacific had come in at twice the estimated $39 million, or nearly $80 million ($2 billion today). Excellent managers were in place, including a man named T. M. Schumacher, who was traffic manager for both Western Pacific and the Denver & Rio Grande. Schumacher had been the general traffic manager for the El Paso & Southwestern, which had been built as the Arizona & Southeastern Railroad by Phelps Dodge. Initially the A&SE was a 30-mile feeder line for the shipment of ore between Bisbee and the Sante Fe and Southern Pacific railhead at Fairbank. The A&SE became part of the El Paso and Southwestern—also created by Phelps Dodge—when the company expanded its railroad business. Arthur had been made vice president of the El Paso & Southwestern at an early age, so he knew Schumacher and respected his abilities.

Exactly when Arthur began quietly buying Western Pacific stock is not known, but all things considered it could have been as early as 1914, when the writing, for those who knew the language, was on the wall. At that time, neither the Western Pacific's nor the Rio Grande's earnings were meeting expectations, a situation that was causing distress in the offices of the Rio Grande, where the buck stopped. As Kneiss noted, in 1911 the Rio Grande had to suspend dividends on preferred stock to meet the interest coupons on the Western Pacific's first mortgage bonds. By 1914 it was trying to get the terms of the mortgage altered to eliminate the huge financial burden it was suffering. Those efforts were not successful. As a result, on March 1, 1915,

the directors of the Rio Grande defaulted on the interest coupons, plunging the Western Pacific into receivership.

The Gould empire was on thin ice. Hit hard by the economic
Panic of 1907, Gould's Wabash Tunnel project back east in Pitts-
burgh had bankrupted the Wabash Railroad in much the same
way Feather River had crippled the Rio Grande. George Gould
would be forced out of control of his 11,000-mile railway system.

Despite a spurt of growth caused by a six-month closing of
the new Panama Canal due to landslides, and America's growing
involvement in the war in Europe, the Western Pacific was sold
at auction on the steps of the Oakland station in June 1916.
Stuart Daggett's analysis of the company was not all negative.
"It suffers from inadequate industrial connections, and from the
absence of feeder mileage at its western end," he wrote. "On the
other hand, its position as a bridge between Salt Lake and San
Francisco Bay may be of great importance to a properly placed
connecting system." Daggett concluded there was reason for
buyers to have an interest in the company, mainly "because the
company, although weak, occupies one of the best of the limited
number of Sierra passes and has a foothold in productive territory in California." That had to have pleased Arthur Keddie, and
the value of a "properly placed connecting system" helped confirm what Arthur Curtiss James was thinking: a feeder line from
the north, namely a southern extension of the Great Northern,
would be a boon for the Western Pacific.

Conflict

James J. Hill died on May 29, 1916, in St. Paul, Minnesota. He was 77. Arthur attended the funeral of his mentor, his father's good friend and business partner, making the 22-hour ride from New York to Chicago on the fastest train at the time, the 20th Century Limited. The cost of a ticket was $40 ($786 today), with an extra $10 ($196 today) for a sleeping berth. The Limited made few, if any, stops.

The funeral was a private affair, with only the immediate family and Hill's associates and close employees in attendance. As reported in the *New York Times*, "following the simplicity which the family knows would be the desire of Mr. Hill, the request is made that no flowers or floral offerings be sent to the house." However, on the day of Hill's interment, all traffic on the rail and steamship lines Hill owned came to a respectful stop for five minutes. In the many obituaries about Hill published locally and nationally, Hill's accomplishments were praised, his genius extolled. The obituaries spoke of the fact that the Great Northern Railroad had not used one dollar of government subsidy or the grant of one acre of land to build its line from Chicago to Seattle; that Hill's crews normally laid track westward at the rate of a mile a day; that his railroad line left a trail of seminal farms and homesteads in its wake that would grow a robust series of villages and towns; and recalled how Hill and his partners had fought E. H. Harriman and won.

What must have struck the grieving Arthur, as he watched Hill's coffin being lowered into the ground at the private interment ceremony at St. Paul's Resurrection Cemetery, was true

James J. Hill, legendary railroad man

sadness that James J. Hill had died before he could witness the Great Northern's connection from Seattle to San Francisco. When Hill had finished the Great Northern in 1892, the economics of extending the line south to the City by the Bay were prohibitive. The alternative steamship service Hill had instituted from Portland to San Francisco had proved to be successful. In 1916, the numbers still weren't right. But there in St. Paul, witnessing the end of a friend's and brilliant mentor's storied life as a railroad pioneer, Arthur had to feel good about the progress he was making toward providing that missing link. The celebration of Hill's life on all sides had to have strengthened his resolve.

World War I had begun two years earlier in Europe. President Wilson had been determined to maintain neutrality for America. But then German U-boats had begun attacking ships bound for England, sinking American ships in the North Atlantic, and torpedoing the Cunard liner *Lusitania*, with the loss of 1,198 lives (124 Americans). Added to a score of other atrocities, the loss of *Lusitania* helped make America's entry into the war a foregone conclusion. (Much later it was revealed that *Lusitania* was carrying thousands of cases of shells, boxes of cartridges, and small arms ammunition. The ship's manifests had been falsified. *Lusitania* was thus a fair target.) In his petition to Congress, President Wilson had said, "Vessels of every kind, whatever their flag, their character, their cargo, their destination, their errand, have been ruthlessly sent to the bottom without warning, and without thought or help of mercy for those on board." Wilson urged Congress to join "a war to end all wars... to make the world safe from Democracy." It was a noble ambition. Congress complied. America entered the war in April 1917.

Shortly thereafter, Arthur, along with hundreds of other noted American yachtsmen, responded to the US Navy's efforts to procure sizable, seagoing yachts for immediate war duty. Turning *Aloha* over to the US Navy was not Arthur's first contribution to the war effort. In 1915, Arthur had become part of the "Preparedness Movement," championed by ex-president Teddy Roosevelt and supported by a large cadre of prominent industrialists, attorneys, bankers, and the like. Their aim was to build up the country's naval and land forces for defense purposes, the assumption being that America would be joining the war sooner or later. Arthur's contributions to the summer naval training camp at Plattsburgh, New York, were significant.

But turning *Aloha* over to the navy was another matter altogether. This was about much more than money. *Aloha* was Arthur's prized possession, the love of his life. Letting the navy have its way with the gorgeous yacht into which he had poured heart and soul had to have been immensely traumatic. The navy stripped *Aloha* of her massive spars and mighty tangle of rigging, and bolted guns into her pristine teak decks. Gray paint was applied to every inch of her hull, varnished wood, and gear. One has to wonder how Arthur could have endured it.

An incident the previous year might have provided the essential motivation required for Arthur to allow the US Navy to lay hands on his treasured yacht. According to the *Newport Daily News*, in October 1916, a German U-boat (U-53) was spotted heading toward Newport, Rhode Island. The German skipper, Hans Rose, casually radioed Newport and, thanks to the United States' neutrality at the time, was given permission to enter the harbor. Rose anchored his impressive, 212-foot *U-53* near the flagship of the Atlantic Destroyer Flotilla, and proceeded to make calls to high-ranking US Navy officers. Soon *U-53*'s crew appeared on deck in full uniform. Rose went ashore, according to historian Brian Wallin, paid a courtesy call on the commander of the Newport Naval Station, and invited high-ranking officials and their friends to visit his proud command.

Among those who went aboard *U-53* that day was Arthur Curtiss James. When offered a cookie, it is said Arthur pocketed one to see if perchance it could be traced to a purchase at a US port, a possible way of tracking the sub's movements.

Kapitänleutnant Rose's audacious public relations stunt would have been shrugged off if *U-53* hadn't departed that same afternoon and motored up the Massachusetts coast where Rose and crew captured and sank five British ships, a Dutch steamer, and a Norwegian ship. As Brian Wallin wrote, it demonstrated to Americans the destructive power of German U-boats and served as a warning of what would come if the United States entered the war on the side of the Allies. The challenge was not lost on Arthur.

Aloha's navy designation was *SP-317*, the SP being short for Section Patrol. *SP-317* served as flagship for Rear Admiral Cameron McRae Winslow, who was Inspector for Naval Districts, East Coast. Over the following two years, *Aloha* called at

Aloha **stripped down and painted grey to serve as the navy's** *SP-317*

many ports, venturing as far afield as New Orleans, while Admiral Winslow conducted his inspections. The yacht spent time in Chesapeake Bay, and on patrol between Boston and Maine before the war ended in 1918. *Aloha* entered the Brooklyn Navy Yard in January 1919 for decommissioning. A month later, the navy had cleaned up the yacht to its satisfaction, including polishing the brass and reapplying varnish. In a brief ceremony at the yard, the admiral's flag was struck and James's personal burgee was hoisted. Arthur did not attend the ceremony. It would take several months of hard work before *Aloha* would be restored to Arthur's prewar standard of splendor.

Arthur and Harriet had also given the navy Harriet's prized 53-foot runabout, *Mauna Loa*. As the USS *Mauna Loa* (*SP-28*), she served as a section patrol boat with a crew of seven and one machine gun. She patrolled the waters north of Boston until the end of the war.

At about the same time Arthur loaned *Aloha* and *Mauna Loa* to the US Navy, it was assumed he was responsible for a sizable gift ($5 million in today's dollars) to those European innocents whose lives were being torn apart by the war. Said to be from an anonymous donor, the check was received by J. P. Morgan & Company. The *New York Times* published the message that accompanied it: "Enclosed please find my check for $200,000 which I would thank you to hand to our country's distinguished guest, the Right Hon. Arthur James Balfour, with the request that the money be invested for the benefit of poor widows and orphans of England and Scotland, caused by the present war with Germany. This contribution is given by me in loving memory of the late Mr. and Mrs. D. Willis James of this city."

Arthur James Balfour had long been a Member of Parliament in Great Britain and, subsequently, twice Lord of the Treasury. In 1917, he was visiting America as Great Britain's Foreign Secretary. In November of that year, he would author the "Balfour Declaration," advocating the creation of a Jewish homeland in Palestine. Lord Balfour reportedly expressed great satisfaction at the generous action on the part of an American citizen.

Arthur and Harriet were also doing their part in the war effort stateside. Through the YMCA, Harriet headed women's teams of the United War Work Campaign, a consolidated effort to raise $170 million to provide entertainment for US troops abroad. The Jameses entertained hundreds of military personnel at their homes in Newport, Coconut Grove, and Tarrytown. In the fall of 1917, 1,000 troops stationed at Ft. Adams, in Newport marched to Beacon Hill House to present a cup to Harriet in appreciation offor her efforts on their behalf.

Bisbee

Just three months after America entered the war, and *Aloha* had been enlisted, war-related problems arose at Phelps Dodge's Copper Queen Mine in Bisbee, Arizona. The growing labor union movement in the form of the Western Federation of Miners (WFM) had sought to make inroads in Bisbee since 1903. At that time, a local organizer had taken stock of the harmonious situation in place at the Copper Queen and reported it would be a waste of the Western Federation's time and effort to try and organize there. Three years later the union returned, this time as a more evolved, comprehensive group called the Industrial Workers of the World (IWW). The Copper Queen initiated the formation of the Bisbee Merchants Association to rebuff the union. Once again, the union was dispatched, with some 400 mine workers having been fired along the way for choosing to support the union.

In 1917, the union's approach was more aggressive and more organized. The demands were similar, with safety and improved working conditions atop the list. But as Lynn R. Bailey pointed out in his book, *Bisbee: Queen of the Copper Camp*s, the union's tactics of threats and intimidation were more emotionally charged by the national crisis the war had caused. Virtually the moment the war had started in 1914, the price of copper had gone up, reflecting the increased demand for copper in wiring and munitions. The 14 to 15 cents a pound that copper had been selling for doubled in a matter of weeks. After a price dip caused by a temporary placement of copper on the contraband list by England—a move meant to keep it out of German hands—it continued upwards. By 1917 it had soared to 37 cents a pound. Bisbee was humming day and night, with three different mines employing 5,000 miners working three shifts. The miners' wages were good. In 1916, Phelps Dodge had announced a voluntary wage increase. But inflation caused by the war raised living expenses, virtually negating any gains for the miners. From 1913 to 1917, consumer prices rose almost 40 percent, while wages rose on the national average about 14 percent. And despite the tireless efforts of James Douglas, working conditions remained frightfully unsafe. Douglas had been promoted from head of Copper Queen to president of Phelps Dodge in 1908, but as the man who had successfully guided the mine through its formative years, James Douglas maintained a paternal affinity for the place.

Mining accidents, many of them fatal, were frequent in the

early 1900s, even at Copper Queen. What Douglas couldn't alter was the miners' casual approach to safety. The men's behavior would improve slightly right after an accident, but all too quickly the miners would return to the practice of dangerous habits. As a 1909 article titled "Prevention of Accidents in Metal Mines" in *Engineering and Mining Journal* concluded, "the men would lapse into an appalling indifference for human life." Their own included.

Over the years, Bisbee had become a company town. While there were other mining companies in Bisbee, Phelps Dodge had bought the existing store, then built a new one in 1891. In 1902, Phelps Dodge had built Bisbee's Copper Queen Hotel. A visible statement of corporate power, the hotel was a grand establishment, from its California redwood paneling to the monogrammed china and flatware used in the large, handsome dining room that seated 80 people.

Copper Queen also owned the newspaper, the *Bisbee Daily Review*, had introduced municipal utilities, and even ran the local ice-making plant. The ice plant was a part of the Bisbee Improvement Company run by Walter Douglas, son of Dr. James Douglas. Walter Douglas was also head of the Copper Queen Mining Company at the time. The first bank in Bisbee was a Copper Queen venture, headed by James S. Douglas, Walter's older brother. In its annual report, Phelps Dodge could have legitimately listed the town of Bisbee as a wholly owned subsidiary.

Combining insufficient wages and dangerous working conditions with the enormous profits being enjoyed by ownership that was primarily responsible to stockholders back east, and the total control Phelps Dodge maintained over the entire town, gave the union a solid agenda. The fact that ownership was more interested in getting the copper out of the ground than in the men who did the job was indisputable.

Significant change never occurs without a fight. Prior to their campaign to organize mine workers in Bisbee in 1917, the IWW had been cutting its teeth and fine-tuning its techniques of sabotage and work slow-down in various western locations. The culmination of that stage of unionism had happened in Everett, Washington, in the fall of 1916, when an IWW group had traveled by boat to Everett to lend support to shingle-weavers who were on strike. A posse of armed, deputized men would not allow the IWW representatives to land in Everett. Shots were fired and a gun battle ensued. Five IWW members and two deputies were killed. Galvanized by this spilling of blood, shortly thereafter the IWW would focus on recruiting the 5,000 miners

working in Bisbee. The IWW was encouraged in its efforts by a successful strike among the copper miners of Morenci in the winter of 1915 to '16.

The IWW's organizing efforts in Bisbee produced a classic confrontation. Demands were made by the IWW for higher pay and safer and less restrictive work requirements. Ownership's response was total rejection. The usual ad hoc groups were formed on both sides. Angry meetings were held. The miners took sides. Threats were made. The situation quickly became ugly. According to Lynn Bailey, neither Copper Queen nor the other two mining companies in Bisbee would recognize the IWW or its demands: "They would close their mines before submitting to what they considered extortion."

With the country having entered World War I only three months before, the general state of anxiety was high and easily manipulated. Rumors the strikers had been infiltrated by pro-German extremists bent on sabotage found fertile ground. The June 29, 1917, issue of the *New York Times* fanned the flames by suggesting the Bisbee strike had been instigated by German agents.

On June 26, 1917, half the miners in the three Bisbee companies had indeed gone out on strike. Soon 3,000 men, or 85 percent of the district's miners, were striking. A standoff occurred between ownership and the IWW. When compromise was suggested, Phelps Dodge President Walter Douglas lashed out from his office at 99 John Street in Manhattan: "There will be no compromise, because you cannot compromise with a rattlesnake."

Walter Douglas had inherited the office of the presidency from his father a scant month before the strike. One will never know how the elder Douglas would have responded to the escalating crisis in Bisbee, but from what we do know about his strong sense of fair play, and his commitment to providing better lives for his miners, his response would have been markedly different from his son's in both word and deed. According to James W. Byrkit, in his book *Forging the Copper Collar*, Walter Douglas had drawn a line in the sand about unions as early as 1907, when he was Copper Queen's general manager. At that time he had said the (then) Western Federation of Miners should never organize in Bisbee. Byrkit wrote: "Rather than see such a calamity occur, said Douglas, the mines would shut down. In so saying, he laid down a personal vow which became almost an obsession with him."

Ten years later, with Walter Douglas's backing, and (it was said) his tactical collaboration, the strike was "broken" in the most literal sense of the word.

Stirred by those rumors of German agents having infiltrated the ranks—rumors that were never proved or disproved—Bisbee's corporate collective martialed its forces, including miners loyal to the companies, in the form of vigilante groups. Paranoia ran deep, feeding hysteria. As Robert Cleland writes in the official Phelps Dodge history, "patriotism" ran amok: "the non-striking employees organized a Workman's Loyalty League of some 2,000 members who pledged to support the government of the United States and to defend each other, their homes, and their lives against the IWW." Secret meetings of the vigilante groups were held. When the local sheriff, Harry Wheeler, was unable to solicit a militia from the governor of Arizona, he deputized and armed a posse of between 900 and 2,000 men, some from many miles distant. Meanwhile, the IWW continued to issue provocative statements.

Earlier in July, the IWW had struck a Phelps Dodge copper mine at Jerome in north-central Arizona. More than 100 striking miners were rounded up by the authorities. Sixty-seven of them were put on a train and "deported" to California. That established a plan for what could happen on a much larger scale in Bisbee.

At midnight on July 12, 1917, the huge posse quietly assembled in groups at strategic locations throughout Bisbee. At 6:30 a.m., Sheriff Wheeler issued a proclamation of his intention to arrest, "on charges of vagrancy, treason, and being disturbers of the peace . . . all these strange men who have congregated here from other parts and sections for the purpose of harassing and intimidating all men who desire to pursue their daily toils. . . . This is no labor trouble—we are sure of that—but a direct attempt to embarrass and injure the government of the United States."

"All these strange men" included miners who had been living in Bisbee for years with their families, and who were on strike.

More than 1,000 men were rousted from their beds in a predawn raid. It was ugly. There were beatings. Women were abused. Two men—an irate striking miner and the deputy who attempted to round him up—were shot and killed. Around 1,200 men were corralled by the posse and marched through town to an El Paso & Southwestern freight train that had previously hauled a load of cattle. Manure in the cars was several inches deep. Under the watchful eyes of 180 armed guards, the striking miners were locked in box cars that had machine guns mounted on their rooftops. Under a broiling July sun, the train took the men on a four-hour ride to Columbus, New Mexico, where local authorities would not let them unload. The train backtracked forty minutes to Tres Hermanas, New Mexico, a struggling settlement of 100 or so people subsisting on run-down cattle farms in the middle of a parched landscape. In Tres Hermanas, the men were unloaded and abandoned. An El Paso

Striking miners being marched out of Bisbee and loaded into cattle cars

& Southwestern train brought food and water the next day, but the men were without shelter for two days.

At 99 John Street in New York, Arthur was distraught. He was vice president of Phelps Dodge at the time, a director of the company. But Walter Douglas was president, a job that had never appealed to Arthur, who preferred his role as a behind-the-scenes operative. That had been a perfect role for him during the many years he had worked in close harmony with Dr. James Douglas. For

Walter Douglas

those two, titles had little meaning. They simply put their heads together to get the jobs done and solve problems. But now Walter was running things, and in quite a different way. In particular, he was attacking the Bisbee situation with what Arthur thought was an unfortunate degree of emotion. The John Street offices were compact. In the days leading to the "deportation," Arthur could plainly have heard the righteous anger in Walter Douglas's voice coming from behind his closed door as he had shouted epithets and issued instructions to his lieutenants in Bisbee.

When Arthur heard that line about not compromising with a rattlesnake, he did something very unlike him. He barged into Walter Douglas's office, just as Douglas was slamming down the telephone receiver.

The two men stared at each other for a long moment. Then in a voice slightly hoarse with forced calm, Arthur asked Walter what he thought he was doing. With an equal amount of calm, Douglas replied that he was taking charge of the situation. Arthur said nothing, and again the two men locked eyes. Then Arthur turned, and walked toward the door. Before he reached it, Walter Douglas curtly asked him what he would do. Arthur left Douglas's office without responding. Because he honestly didn't have an answer.

That was the rub. Arthur's and Harriet's inability to have children had been a great sadness, but he'd been able to resolve that disappointment as part of the mystery of the Lord's work. There had to be a reason they were denied children that was beyond human comprehension. He could accept that. And truly one of the hardest days of his life had been knowing that his beloved *Aloha* was being stripped of her rigging, all that extraordinary beauty and craftsmanship disappearing under a thick coat of gray paint, his lovely lady of the sea being reduced to a number. But this, this Bisbee debacle, was different. Human lives were at stake. The fortunes of all those many families were dependent on this stupid struggle, families that had been so carefully nourished for so many years by James Douglas, who cared as much about his miners as he cared about the product—maybe more!—and yet he had somehow managed to keep both miners and stockholders happy.

Everyone had known it would be a different situation under Walter Douglas. Walter was impulsive, abrupt, a man devoted to the bottom line with little regard for how it was reached. For Walter, the miners were simply names on a list that could be replaced, like any other tools. His father had put faces and stories with those names, done his best to improve their lives. But it was a different time. The fears James Douglas had expressed about the powerful corporations interfering with relationships between workers and management had come to pass. Ironically, his son was among those leading the interference.

ARTHUR CURTISS JAMES

One assumes that, in his desperation, Arthur had tried to call his old friend, but without success. James Douglas was away, probably fly-fishing somewhere, a passion of his. Arthur surely struggled with the problem, going over the details again and again in a terribly frustrating, repetitive cycle that led nowhere. Yes, the working conditions were frightful. Yes, the union demands made some sense. Yes, ownership needed to maintain control . . . but with an armed posse of a thousand or more men mistreating miners and their families? And with the president of Phelps Dodge soiling the dignity of his position by hurling rattlesnake comments at the union?

And there was the *New York Times* constantly suggesting that German agents were responsible for the strike, fanning the wartime paranoia. Maybe the *Times* was right! One could not discount that possibility. It was a very dangerous subject. Just weeks before the Bisbee Deportation, Congress had passed and President Wilson had signed the Espionage Act, which was essentially used to silence (imprison) any Americans who spoke out against, or who wrote against, the war. Speaking at the Harvard Club, an aging Teddy Roosevelt had compromised his own dignity by coming down on Socialists, IWW members, and other antiwar groups as "a whole raft of sexless creatures." With units in more than 600 cities and towns, the American Protective League, formed by the Justice Department, did not hesitate to break into offices and read personal mail in its search for disloyal Americans. In the summer of 1917, a *New York Times* editorial preached: "It is the duty of every good citizen to communicate to proper authorities any evidence of sedition that comes to his notice."

So Arthur did nothing, an embarrassment of inaction that would accompany him the rest of his life. Because for him, the Bisbee Deportation had to be not only a personal failure; it was an indelible stain on the record of Phelps Dodge.

The Mediation Commission that had been formed by President Woodrow Wilson to investigate the deportation found the action to be "without justification, either in fact or in law." But it was one of those decrees that carried little weight. It was one thing, as Lynn Bailey pointed out in *Bisbee*, that the Commission "shifted the burden of responsibility for the deportation and attendant acts of violence to copper management." But it was another that "the august body was powerless to effect a legal remedy."

Many were the lawsuits filed. All but one were either settled out of court, shuttled between the state of Arizona and federal courts until it was worn out, or never tried. The one that went to court was a test case filed against Sheriff Harry Wheeler. The Law of Necessity, by which a community has the right to defend itself "when threatened with overwhelming peril," was invoked to pronounce Wheeler not guilty.

A prolonged search for any statement about the Bisbee Deportation from the Phelps Dodge Corporation resulted in this lone snippet from an interview with Dr. Alice Hamilton, a specialist in occupational health and a pioneer in industrial toxicology, who was traveling in Arizona in 1919, the same year she became the first woman appointed to the Harvard Medical School faculty. James Byrkit writes: "A 'mining official' in Ajo, Arizona [200 miles west of Bisbee] told Hamilton: 'But then the Phelps Dodge people never meant to deport so many—the thing got away from them.' Getting rid of fifteen or twenty agitators, he explained, would have sufficed, but the outsiders Phelps Dodge brought in and deputized were too aggressive."

Nationalization

War was also the reason President Woodrow Wilson nationalized the railroads in December of 1917. "Efficient operation" was the goal advanced by the president, the idea being to bring all parties—management, labor, investors, and shippers—together "in a harmonious whole working on behalf of the national interest." The railroads were admittedly in trouble at the time. One-sixth of the track in the United States belonged to railroad companies that were in receivership. There was a dearth of terminals, track, and rolling stock.

The problem had started in 1906, when in response to an unpopular rate hike decreed by the railroad companies to counter inflation, the Hepburn Act had been passed. Hepburn gave the Interstate Commerce Commission the power to set maximum railroad rates, and extended other ICC jurisdictions. The railroad union "brotherhoods" were strong, agitating for shorter workdays and better pay. Strikes had been frequent, and often ugly. In 1916, to avoid another strike, Wilson had gotten the Adamson Act passed, setting an eight-hour workday as the industry standard. Adamson was subsequently ruled constitutional by the Supreme Court. But in 1917, the war suddenly put pressure for goods and services on the railroads that they struggled to deliver.

Under the United States Railroad Administration, a result of the Railroad Control Act, competitive (duplicate) passenger services were eliminated, sleeping car services were cut way back by pricing them out of reach for most people, terminals and facilities were shared. Government traffic became a priority. It wasn't all bad. The government got the better and faster service it needed. The government also played Santa Claus, purchasing 100,000 railroad cars and 1,930 locomotives—the best money could buy—to replace outdated equipment, at a cost of around $9.5 billion in today's dollars. And the takeover didn't last long. As promised, shortly after the war was terminated in 1919, the railroads were returned to their former owners.

The effect of nationalization on Phelps Dodge was minimal. The company's railroad ownership was small by comparison, and while Phelps Dodge depended on rail to move its product, copper was the company's stock in trade. And copper, as mentioned, was doing quite well. But the nationalization process, beginning with the unsteady financial state of the railroad business, provided Arthur Curtiss James with a very useful case study that would serve him well. Many years later, in that *Saturday Evening Post* article he would write in January, 1932, Arthur summarized his thoughts about the economics of railroads, positions that had taken shape during nationalization, and had only been strengthened in his mind over the years:

The current [financial] crisis is the result of archaic legis-lation involving the railroads in endless red tape; of direct and hidden government subsidies to competitive carrier systems; of public meddling in railroad business and the resulting hinder-ance to expedient changes of policies. Actuating these causes is the popular misconception that railways constitute a monopoly, and a lack of public understanding of the true relation the rail-roads bear to national prosperity, to the progress and success of the commonwealth, and to industry in general.

What the railroads need is not a last-minute relief measure, but a comprehensive forward-looking plan. They must be al-lowed to make a fair profit, to pay their interest and dividends, and to build up a surplus during good times so that they are not faced with bankruptcy when conditions cause uncontrollable losses of revenue. It is essential to national prosperity that our railways earn a fair annual profit.

At Home

Arthur bought another house. There was some logic to the purchase in that the house, a 22-room Gothic/Italianate stone mansion in North Tarrytown (renamed Sleepy Hollow in 1996), New York, was already in the family. Standing on a 65-acre rise of land with a commanding view of the Hudson River, the house had been built in 1851 for Anson G. Phelps Jr., whose father had founded Phelps Dodge, and whose sister Elizabeth had married Daniel James, Arthur's grandfather. That made Anson Phelps Arthur's great-uncle. Anson Jr. had died in 1858. In 1909, when Anson's wife, Jane, had died at age 88, the North Tarrytown house, known as Phelps Place, had been willed to Jane's unmarried sister Helen, who died in 1918. It was then bequeathed to the Presbyterian Mission Board. In 1921, Arthur bought it back from the board and named it the James House.

Designed by John Butler Snook, the North Tarrytown house was an example of pre-Civil War grandeur, built of cut stone in the Palladian style, with marble fireplaces and columns, stained-glass windows, and crystal chandeliers throughout. The grand hall had 15-foot ceilings, with polished white-

and-gray marble floors perfect for dancing. The wrap-around verandah measured nearly 300 feet.

Today, the James House belongs to the Phelps Memorial Hospital. It rents out for weddings and other events, seating 170 people for dinners. Viewing the house today, with the hospital complex on the inland side, and full development all around, it's difficult to envision the unspoiled rural setting of a hundred years ago. Back then, the house emerged from the midst of trees and natural undergrowth. That was part of the appeal for Arthur. With Beacon Hill's acreage having been exhaustively sculpted, here was another blank canvas awaiting paint. Part of the creative process was not only what to do with the acreage, but who should be employed to get it done.

When one begins looking into who staffed the James houses, it becomes clear that for his multiple home fronts, from Coconut Grove to Newport, including Manhattan, and Northampton, Arthur created more an extended family than just the usual hierarchy of employers and workers. Formality was still observed. Workers and their families were not invited to dinner at the big house, but they were always warmly welcomed. Arthur made it a point to hire talented people he respected, people he liked. A priority for private people, only children like Arthur, is making their homes into places where they love to be. Because when they are not working, home is where you will find them. When the homes—and the yachts in Arthur's case—are grand enough to require large crews of workers to run and maintain them, it's important those crews consist of people the owner enjoys seeing every day. The old adage about only children being both willing and able—and lucky—to pick their brothers and sisters, is true.

The person Arthur chose to manage the grounds at James House was a man named Charles Waters, who had been working as a gardener at the Beacon Hill estate in Newport. Waters's friend, co-worker, and boss, was John Greatorex. When Greatorex's wife, Robina, was about to give birth, her sister Helen

Tarrytown house in 1921, and today, part of Phelps Memorial Hospital

arrived from Scotland to lend a hand. During that visit, Helen met Charles Waters. They fell in love and married.

When Arthur bought Fourway Lodge in 1914, he had asked Charles and Helen Waters to manage it. After a few months of living in Florida, they were miserable. Reluctantly, they told Arthur the hot, humid climate was too much for their Northern blood. Arthur brought them back to Beacon Hill until the North Tarrytown house was added to Arthur's real estate holdings, at which time he asked Charles Waters take on the superintendent's job. Waters did, and he and his wife found the Hudson River Valley climate much more agreeable. Waters hired a crew of local men to start clearing the James House property, plant flower and vegetable gardens, build a variety of outbuildings for the gardens, and erect a barn and install fencing for a herd of cows. A truck would pick the workers up in the morning, and drop them home after work.

Sybil Waters Guthrie, who in 2018 was living in Narragansett, Rhode Island, is one of Charles and Helen Waters's nine children. She turned a perky ninety in September of 2017. "We had the cows, a flock of chickens, a flock of turkeys, and wonderful flower gardens," Sybil Waters recalls. "It was so colorful in the spring, with primroses, tulips, roses imported from all over the world—all the spring flowers. It was such a wonderful place to grow up. It felt like my place. I thought everyone lived that way! When Mr. James was there he would drive around and stop if he saw me. He was very friendly, easy to talk with. I was seven or eight. I was a little nervous, him being the owner, but I didn't need to be."

Sybil says that Arthur and Harriet did not spend a lot of time at James House, perhaps a few weeks each summer, and maybe a week in the fall before they left for Florida. "He would often arrive in *Aloha*," Sybil says. "He'd anchor the boat in the Hudson, off the house, and come in by launch. He had a boat house and a dock down on the river. When Mr. and Mrs. James were there I didn't have the full run of the place, she and the other children on the estate were driven to and from school every day.

"Home" for Sybil and her family was an apartment over a three-car garage. When the family increased to four, the apartment became too small, so Arthur built a house for the Waterses on the property. "It was a lovely home, and big enough for what turned out to be my eight brothers and sisters." Sybil laughs. "When the Phelps hospital got built after the Jameses passed away, the house we lived in became the Planned Parenthood headquarters. I used to work there. My mother had to laugh at that. She said in her day, parenthood wasn't 'planned.'"

The freedom, and the warm family feeling expressed by Sybil Guthrie, was reflected by others who either lived on the Jameses' properties, or had relatives who did. It appears those who worked for Arthur Curtiss James considered themselves lucky. If they were high enough up in the pecking order to live on one of his estates, they were openly envied. Douglas Shewring, who was Arthur's butler for twenty years, lived at Beacon Hill with his wife and their daughter Joan. Joan Shewring Malkovich, who still resided in Newport in 2018, has only the happiest memories of growing up at Beacon Hill. Joan says at age three she rode her tricycle everywhere, climbed trees, and visited the farm anytime she pleased. "We were totally free," Joan says, echoing Sybil Guthrie, whom she remembers: "I felt quite like it was my place, felt completely at home, with no fear I shouldn't walk in certain places." The resident children at Beacon Hill were also driven to school every morning, picked up and driven home for lunch, and collected at end of day.

Douglas Shewring began as a footman, then took his butler's training in England. Joan says her father was a no-nonsense man who took his job seriously. Both qualities appealed to Arthur. In fact, Arthur regarded him so highly that Shewring not only ran the Beacon Hill House, but when the Jameses went to the Manhattan house, Douglas Shrewing went with them. "My father loved to take me to see Mr. James," Joan says. "He must

**Joan Malkovich as a child with her mother in the Blue Garden (*top*),
and with her father, Douglas Shewring, Arthur's butler**

BY ROGER VAUGHAN • PAGE 241

Estate children: Joan Malkovich riding her tricycle, Dorothy and John Greatorex feeding a baby pig at the farm, and waiting for a ride to school

have enjoyed it too or he wouldn't have accepted it. Mr. James was a very formal man, but also warm and sweet. I was never frightened of him. Dad was proud of me, so that's what we did. I don't think I ever met Mrs. James. It was always him."

The family associations thicken. Robin Anderson, who moved from Newport to Worland, Wyoming, in 2006, is John and Robina Greatorex's granddaughter, making her Sybil Guthrie's great-niece. Robin's mother, Dorothy, was raised in the gatehouse at Beacon Hill, where the Greatorexes lived, so she heard all the stories growing up. Robin said that John was plagued with a heart condition that would kill him when he was still in his thirties. Arthur was especially close to John. Robin said her mother told her that Arthur would frequently drop by their house to visit with John. When Arthur found out about John's heart condition, he sent him with his wife to a specialist in California to be treated. According to Robin, the Greatorexes stayed with friends of the Jameses in Beverly Hills, but the details of that connection are lost.

"When John died," Robin says, "Mr. James offered to deed the gate house to Robina. But she said it was too far from town, shopping, and school. So Arthur bought her a house she liked on Rhode Island Avenue in downtown Newport. She was a wonderful baker. Arthur would go visit her on Sunday mornings to eat scones. He wanted to set her up in a bakery, but she declined. He even bought her a car. When she wrecked it, he bought her another. My brother Donald and I joke about that relationship. We look in the mirror, look at each other, and say, 'you think we look like him?'" Robin laughs.

Arthur's strong commitment to Harriet, his unconditional loyalty to his wife, is well documented. He built the Blue Garden and the model farm both with and for her. He supported her lifelong interest in the YMCA, and other charities she embraced. It appears Harriet's opinions were always duly considered in the various projects the couple undertook. And unlike many men who sail on blue water, Arthur did not use his yachts for matrimonial respites, or trysts. When *Coronet* or the *Aloha*s made sail, it was always with Harriet on board. But the keen eye he had for boats and houses also applied to women. He loved the ladies. His flirtatious nature was evident in social situations. Sometimes it inevitably led to more. As Joan Malkovich says, "He was a very formal man, but warm and sweet, a very proper and lovely man . . . but he needed affection too. He had a nurse-maid he was sweet on. I heard stories, little snide remarks... people rolling their eyes."

One can be sure that the rolling of eyes was confined to the staff of the various estates, and was done with extreme sur-reptitiousness. Unlike his more outgoing friend, Mabel Todd, who in a fit of grief-inspired reckless abandon had taken her affair with Austin Dickinson public, Arthur would don the cloak of privacy for much less risqué activities. Even his all-too-likely liaison with Mrs. Todd was draped with a formal veil of unimpeachable propriety.

Margaret Borman Harrigan was one of the seven children who lived at the Beacon Hill estate. Her father, Ray Borman, was in charge of the dairy herd, so she and her family lived at Surprise Valley Farm. Margaret, who was living in Florida in 2018, said that her father kept daily records of the amount of milk and percentage of butter fat content for each cow, and that a man from the Guernsey Association would come by every few months to run tests on production. Margaret kept good notes herself, which she put down in a document she wrote in February 1999. "When the herd came in from pasture," she wrote, "each cow was washed and brushed and they were given new hay and feed. Each stall had a name plate above it, with all the names starting with Beacon Hill, as in Beacon Hill Astor, Beacon Hill Daisy. They were all milked by hand. The dairy was spot-less, with white walls and floors.

"Dad made butter at the dairy. He cut it into one-pound blocks and stamped each block with a Beacon Hill Farm stamp. He wrapped each block in parchment that also had Beacon Hill

Farm printed on it. No salt was added because Mr. James liked sweet butter. No coloring was added. Mr. James had products delivered to friends, but never sold any of it."

Margaret remembers many people who worked at the farm, including Ashby Jenkins, "a large black man with a hearty laugh," who washed the pigs every day. "Every day Ashby Jenkins went to the hen house, broke a raw egg, and down it would go."

She wrote that despite being Newport's largest taxpayer, Arthur had his own public works department for surrounding roads. His men would plow them in winter, and trim them in summer. "We were so fortunate," Margaret says. "All the estate houses were given milk and cream daily, and fresh vegetables in season. Also fresh chicken, lamb, and cured ham. When my mother needed groceries, she called the local store and they were delivered to our door. Our coal, telephone, and electricity were all paid for by Mr. James. Everything was provided for our home from dishes to furnishings. During the depression, food baskets were delivered to people who weren't doing well. Mr. James had his trucks deliver coal to families that could not afford it. He endowed many beds at Newport Hospital."

Margaret Harrigan often saw Arthur enjoying a game of croquet after tea, or playing tennis. She remembers a visit to Beacon Hill by the Crown Prince of Sweden and his wife. And she observed Harriet James taking care of her correspondence in a small, "secret garden." But among her strongest memories are the many times she and the other children were invited aboard *Aloha*, the bark. "What I remember most about that beautiful yacht was the elevator," Margaret writes. "My brother and I loved to ride up and down in the elevator."

Those entertained by the Jameses included many European royals and fellow captains of industry. But some of the guests fell outside those predictable categories, reflecting Arthur's appreciation for accomplishment as well as his intellectual curiosity. One honored guest was US Navy Commander Albert C. Read, for whom Arthur held a reception at Beacon Hill in July

1919, just two months after Read had piloted the first transatlantic flight in a seaplane, the Curtiss (no relation) NC Flying Boat (*NC-4*). There was much about this aviation milestone that would have appealed to Arthur. To begin with, the hull of the *NC-4* had been built at the Herreshoff yard in nearby Bristol, Rhode Island. And the flight had been a marvelous collaboration of America's air and sea capabilities, with as many as thirty navy ships strung out along the flight path for visual aid as well as safety. Three NCs had begun the flight, which took nineteen days, given the need for several stops for repairs and rest for the crews.

Commander Albert Read

The adventure turned out to be a harrowing test of men and machines. After the longest leg of the trip, fifteen hours to fly the 1,200 miles from Newfoundland to the Azores, the planes had to land on open ocean because of the lack of visibility. One of them sank after the crew was recovered. A second one had to taxi many miles into the harbor, and was then deemed unfit to continue. Only Commander Read and his *NC-4* made it to Lisbon, Portugal, the transatlantic destination.

The reception included many friends of Commander Read, who had previously been stationed in Newport. The *New York Times* coverage told of the "full-size 'flier' " that had been built on the lawn, "representing the *NC-4*, with the wings forming an arbor on which were trained rambler roses." And the entertainment was stunning. "During the afternoon, seaplanes from the USS *Shawmut*, which was at anchor in Newport Harbor and within sight of Beacon Hill House, flew over the house while the guests watched with interest. The affair was declared one of the most delightful given this summer." Seaplanes taking off in Newport Harbor in 1919 and *buzzing Beacon Hill House*?! The guests watched *with interest*?! Holy Mackerel!

Buried in the understated *Times* coverage was the hint of another fascinating story: "A silver airplane about three feet long was presented to Commander Read on the lawn by young William DeForest Manice Jr. The young lad made a speech and raised the American flag. Commodore James also made an address."

Read's Flying Boat seaplane, *NC-4*

Commodore James also made an address? How perfect! No one could have been more delighted by this . . . this dismissive mention . . . than Arthur. Had Arthur and the *Times* writer been in collusion? It had surely been Arthur's idea, hatching the presentation plan with his grand-nephew, young William DeForest Manice Jr. It had to have been their secret. William Junior was the (then) six-year-old son of Harriet James's niece Harriet Ferry Manice and William DeForest Manice Sr.

Oliver Manice, who is the son of William DeForest Manice

Jr., says his father's hero was Charles Lindbergh, and that William Jr. was known as an airplane buff even as a child. "I was told that he and his friends were always pretending their bicycles were airplanes," Oliver recalls. If indeed Arthur had suggested to young William that perhaps he should be the one presenting the airplane to the famous navy flier, the boy would not have given his uncle an argument. Arthur and William would have spent days secretly getting the speech right—meaning brief—and rehearsing it. Dressed smartly in shorts and a clean shirt, and with his hair neatly combed, much to everyone's total surprise the boy had taken the stage and pulled it off, much to Arthur's delight. Commander Read had known exactly what to do. As William had handed him the silver airplane, he had snapped to attention. Then he had bent down and shaken the boy's hand. After that, it didn't matter what Arthur had to say. With their "also," the *Times* got it right.

One of the more intriguing honored guests at the James mansion in New York was novelist Joseph Conrad. Intriguing, because while Conrad's celebrity status would have qualified him for the most desirable invitations—his likeness was on the cover of *Time* magazine the week he appeared at the Jameses'—the thematic nature of his work created the potential for him to be dismissed by the ruling social class. Born in Ukraine in 1857, when that country was ruled by Czarist Russia, and raised by Polish parents involved in the struggle for independence, Conrad often wrote about a capitalist system's tendency to dismantle societies. In his most famous work, *Heart of Darkness*, the character of Charles Marlow sees imperialism as a form of violent, aggravated murder on a grand scale.

That Joseph Conrad gave a talk, and a reading, at East 69th Street speaks volumes about the intrinsic value Arthur put on art in general, and on literature in particular.

During an extended global meander that led Józef Teodor Konrad Korzeniowski to evolve into Joseph Conrad, the English-speaking author, the fact that the writer spent many years indulging his passion for the sea had to have piqued Arthur's interest. Conrad had served on French merchant vessels for four years before joining a British ship as an apprentice. He had obtained British nationality and his master's certificate in the British merchant marine in 1886. Having retired from the sea in 1894, he published his first novel the next year. He finally gained a popular audience, and some financial success, in 1913.

Conrad's novel *Victory*, from which he read, had to have been fascinating for Arthur because the main character, Axel Heyst, combines traits so much like, and so unlike, those of Conrad's host.

In *Victory*, Heyst's father had taught him that man is essentially evil. So far, so good. John Calvin, under whose influence Arthur had been raised, had preached a similar view. But Heyst's father went on to admonish that one should never be a participant in life. One should only observe life from a safe distance. Calvin, in his turn, had urged God's chosen ones, who (for the most part) happened to also be the wealthy and powerful, to become very involved in both the leadership of and the responsibility for those less fortunate. That was a lesson Arthur had taken fully to heart. In *Victory*, Alex Heyst's undisciplined moments of compassion for his fellow man lead to nothing but trouble for him, including, in the end, his suicide. A series of such dire consequences resulting from good works had to be engaging for Arthur.

Conrad's talk at East 69th Street was one of only two he did in America. The fact that Conrad was a shy individual, whose lack of confidence as a speaker resulted from his foreign accent and weak voice, had something to do with that. Conrad's first appearance was before the staff at the plant of Doubleday, Page & Company, his publisher, in Garden City, New York. That was more rehearsal than anything, and did not include a reading. His reading at the James mansion five days later was therefore the only one he did in America. According to "Conrad's American Speeches and His Reading From *Victory*," by Arnold Schwab, which appeared in *Modern Philology* in May 1965, Conrad visited East 69th Street the day before his talk to check out the room. At the event the next day, he was introduced by his publisher, Frank N. Doubleday. According to Schwab, both publisher and writer were "exceedingly nervous" before the talk.

Mr. Doubleday's introduction would have done little to boost any speaker's confidence. "This is Mr. Conrad's first appearance in public," Doubleday told the assembled guests, "and please God, if I have anything to do with it, it will be his last." That introduction is so outrageous it begs the question of what could have possibly transpired between the two men, or how much spirits Mr. Doubleday might have consumed. But the quote comes from the pen of Mrs. Florence Doubleday, Frank Doubleday's wife, whom Schwab quotes from her book, *Episodes in the Life of a Publisher's Wife*. "Conrad smiled wearily and began," she wrote. "It seemed to take him a long time to collect himself.... After he finally began, his speech went quite smoothly until a female member of the audience started to leave the hall. Conrad stopped dead.... The next day, when I asked him why he had stopped, he said, 'Why I thought it was manners, if the lady wanted to go out, to stop and wait until she had left the room.' "

Conrad is said to have read from chapter 13 of *Victory*, recounting the death of Lena, the woman violinist from an all-female orchestra Heyst has rescued from being sold. He has taken Lena to Samburan, his island in the Java Sea. Whatever the problems were with his writer, that had caused Frank N. Doubleday to belittled Conrad in his introduction, they were swept away by the compelling tale that unfolded. Foreign accent and weak voice notwithstanding, the sobering flow of Conrad's words was, by all reports, captivating. In the hall at East 69th Street, draped with the somber Flemish tapestries, and hushed by the dark wood paneling, where 200 guests had gathered, one could have heard a pin drop as Conrad concluded:

With an amazing strength she asked loudly:
"What's the matter with me?"
"You have been shot, dear Lena," Heyst said in a steady voice, while Davidson, at the question, turned away and leaned his forehead against the post at the foot of the bed.
"Shot? I did think, too, that something had struck me."
Over Samburan the thunder had ceased to growl at last, and the world of material forms shuddered no more under the emerging stars. The spirit of the girl which was passing away from under them clung to her triumph, convinced of the reality of her victory over death...
Heyst bent low over her, cursing his fastidious soul, which even at that moment kept the true cry of love from his lips in its infernal mistrust of all life. He dared not touch her, and she no longer had the strength to throw her arms around his neck....
She tried to raise herself, but all she could do was raise her head a little from the pillow. With a terrified and gentle movement, Heyst hastened to slip his arm under her neck. She felt relieved at once of an intolerable weight, and was content to surrender to him the infinite weariness of her tremendous achievement. Exulting, she saw herself extended on the bed, in a black dress, and profoundly at peace; while, stooping over her with a kindly, playful smile, he was ready to lift her up in his firm arms and take her into the sanctuary of his innermost heart—forever! The flush of rapture flooding her whole being broke out in a smile of innocent, girlish happiness; and with that device radiant on her lips she breathed her last, triumphant, seeking for his glance in the shades of death.

Despite the apparent anxiety it caused him, it was said Conrad had enjoyed reading from his work. As he wrote to his wife after the talk at East 69th Street: "It was a most brilliant affair. I began at 9:45 and ended exactly at 11. There was a most attentive silence, some laughs, and at the end, when I read the chapter of Lena's death, audible snuffling. Then hand shaking with 200 people. It was a great experience."

Arnold Schwab duly reported that his exhaustive research did not unearth a guest list for the Conrad reading at East 69th Street, apart from the Doubledays and the noted journalist Christopher Morley, nor any record of written material about the event from Morley or anyone else. But if there is any victory in Conrad's story, it is Lena's. The defeat belongs to Alex Heyst, which must have given Arthur comfort.

* * *

From 1916 on, the Jameses spent the winter months at Fourway Lodge in Coconut Grove. Arthur and Harriet had an active social life there. As Laura Pincus and Arva Moore Parks wrote in *Crosslinked: A History of the Red Cross and South Florida*, "with its rare orchids and collection of other exotic flowers, Fourway Lodge was a gathering place for Miami's movers and shakers, and some of the elite who called Miami their winter home."

Those war years were a busy and stressful time for everyone, Arthur included. He was away on business much of the time. Left to her own devices, Harriet busied herself with the gardens, and with the various charities she and Arthur supported. Among them were helping organize and build the Plymouth Congregational Church in Coconut Grove, and continuing to support the YMCA and the local Community Chest. One of Harriet's more notable achievements came out of a meeting of community leaders and female activists that was held at Fourway Lodge on March 7, 1917. The goal set at that meeting was to form a chapter of the Red Cross Society. Harriet James is credited for taking the lead and staying solidly behind the effort to create a South

Florida Red Cross chapter. At the beginning of the war, there were Red Cross Chapters in 562 cities, with 500,000 members. By war's end, South Florida was one of 3,180 new chapters with a total of 31 million new members.

A glimpse of Harriet's life in Florida was provided by the late Constance J. Ely, who was related to the James by marriage.

Harriet James

Constance was the daughter of Walter Jennings, lifetime director and secretary of the Standard Oil companies. Jennings was also a president of the Jekyll Island Club, a famous retreat in Georgia for the power brokers of the day. The James and Jennings families knew one another socially, and were close. Here is an excerpt from a memoire Constance wrote in 1982 when she was in her eighties:

After I left Foxcroft School in Virginia in 1918, Mrs. Arthur Curtiss James invited me for long winter visits to her Florida home. I went down from New York in their beautiful private railway car. I was going to visit Harriet practically every year. Oh she was so lonely and such a delightful person really and had no occupation other than social life or bridge playing or the YMCA board.

Harriet, when she was in Florida, would never go near the water on the Bay or their pool because she had seen a dreadful accident when young and forever afterwards she was afraid the water would do the same to her, so she would never learn to swim. Well, the second year I was down there I said, Harriet you've got to learn to swim. This is ridiculous with this beautiful pool and lovely big bunch of bananas (a whole hand would be hanging at the end of the pool and when you came out of swimming you'd just go and break off a banana).

I finally persuaded Harriet to come into the pool with me. She had not put a foot in before. She came in and actually shook. I'd never seen anyone do that before, but she was actually shaking, head to foot. We stood in the water for quite a while until I said, come on, bend your knees at least. Eventually she got to laughing and at the end of two years she was actually walking into the pool by herself and standing, and bending her knees and sort of walking back and forth in the pool.

The "dreadful accident" Constance Ely refers to was surely Harriet's father's "suicide, drowning" according to the death records of Northampton, Massachusetts, that had happened when she was eight years old. Constance Ely's urgings could have just as easily triggered an emotional collapse. Just a few years later, Harriet would officiate at an annual swimming competition she started in Newport. The ad in the *New York Times* read: "All of the 'boys' of the summer colony from 30 to 90 who are eager for swimming honors will compete tomorrow at Bailey's Beach in a race held annually for a cup offered by Mrs. Arthur Curtiss James." As the host of the event, photographs show Harriet outfitted in proper 1920s "summer day at the beach" attire, complete with a jaunty hat that provided shade. She didn't go near the water, but there wasn't a soul on the beach—other than Arthur, who was being supportive of the event, resplendent in three-piece suit and fedora—who had a clue that the woman handing out the trophies couldn't swim a stroke.

Aweigh

August 10, 1921

Dear Mrs. Todd,
I know you would like to go on the trip, and I also know that there is no one in the world who has had more experience in parts of the world where we expect to be, than you and Henpecked [Arthur's pet name for David Todd]*, and I wish we could be together on this voyage. I am sending you herewith an itinerary, which, as far as dates are concerned, is not necessarily accurate, and places also, but it gives you an idea of where we are going. Naturally, we will go to the Philippines when in the Hong Kong district, and some of the other points of interest in the Straits Settlements. I wish you would drop a line some time, giving your advice of what ought to be seen.*

Very Truly Yours,
Arthur Curtiss James

It had long been Arthur's dream to sail around the world. As a young man he had read *A Voyage in the Sunbeam*, by Lady (Anna) Brassey, the story of how, in 1876, she and her husband and family—including servants and pets—had made an 11-month cruise around the world aboard *Sunbeam*, a 250-foot, three-masted, gaff-rigged schooner. From the moment he had first digested this tale, one that he would read many times, Arthur had vowed to do likewise. After he had commissioned *Aloha*, the bark, he had tried to plan the trip at least twice. But each time, something—like World War I—would get in the way. By 1921, he had made four transatlantic trips in *Aloha*, but those were just considered warm-ups for the circumnavigation. Finally, on the morning of September 15, 1921, *Aloha* had left her pier in New York City's East River, bound for . . . the world. In addition to Captain Bezanson and the crew, and Arthur and Harriet, the guests included regulars William Matheson and Andrew "Pete" Alford; a man named Karl M. Vogel, who was to write a book about the trip, *Aloha Around the World*; and an acquaintance of Mabel Todd's named Florence S. Sullivan who remains a mystery.

Vogel's book is more an extended log, a dutiful, day-by-day account of the weather, meals, amount of coal burned, bridge scores, games played, and exercises performed on deck, with frequent paragraphs of praise for Commodore James that seem slightly ingratiating. "In the evening," Vogel wrote, "Jake [Arthur] gave a concert on the pianola and finished off dripping but triumphant with the funeral march from *Götterdämmerung*." It's also a colorful travelogue of visits ashore. The ports of call, and the visits with celebrities, royals, and political leaders, many of which had been prearranged, read like an extended travel fantasy scribbled on the backs of envelopes during a long, alcohol-fueled evening with cosmopolitan friends.

They sailed south, turned west into the Gulf of Mexico, south into the Caribbean Sea and into the Panama Canal, which had opened in the late summer of 1914. They sailed west across the Pacific, with a stop in Honolulu, on to Japan, then on to

Peking, Shanghai, Hong Kong, and south through the Philippines to Borneo in the Malay Archipelago, with stops in Singapore and Rangoon, then to India, calling at Calcutta (Kolkata) and Madras (Chennai). They sailed around the tip of India and

Arthur's vest-pocket journal of the world cruise (*shown actual size*)

west to Aden, Yemen, before proceeding northwest up the Red Sea and through the Suez Canal, across the Mediterranean, and transatlantic back to Newport, Rhode Island. *Aloha* would put 28,827 miles under her keel in 160 days.

According to Karl Vogel, Arthur was his usual salty self during the trip, often starting his day at 4:00 a.m., taking noon sun sights, reassuring his friends in periods of bad weather, and always in the thick of whatever the yacht required. "The seas were very high and irregular," Vogel writes during one bouncy day on the Pacific, "and came aboard so constantly that rubber boots and oilers were a necessity for everyone except Jake, who still defies the elements in his accustomed garb, Quaker grey in color and Palm Beach in texture."

They were in no hurry. They spent many days in Hawaii, a favorite of the Jameses since stopping there on their trip to Japan in 1896. Like any eager group of tourists, they peered into the volcano Kilauea on the island of Hawaii. They were garlanded with leis, and thanks to Arthur's and Harriet's friendship with Hubert and Kaikilani Vos, who had notified Hawaii's royal family of the Jameses' arrival, they ate poi with Princess Kawānanakoa at a luau she gave for them.

The James party was hosted by notables at many of their stops, but perhaps the welcome Arthur and Harriet received in Japan was the most enthusiastic, and made the deepest impression upon them. In Kyoto, they visited Doshisha University, the Christian school founded by Amherst alumnus Joseph Neesima in 1875, and the Doshisha Girls' School across the street. At the main entrance to James Hall at the Girls' School, Vogel wrote, "two thousand boys and girls were gathered, and when President Ebina had introduced Arthur and Harriet there was tremendous cheering for those who had done so much to make Doshisha possible."

In 1911, in the interest of promoting Christianity abroad, and in recognition of Amherst's Neesima, Arthur and Harriet had donated $100,000 ($2.5 million today) to Doshisha Girls' School. Part of the donation (which was given under the name of Arthur's mother, Mrs. D. Willis James) was used to build James Hall, completed in 1914. In its annual report of 1922, the American Board of Commissioners for Foreign Missions reported: "The Mission has been greatly cheered by the visit of Mr. and Mrs. Arthur Curtiss James, who in their journey around the world, visited Japan. The Jameses have long been interested in the Girls' Department of Doshisha. On their visit, public meetings and private conferences were held with students and teachers, and all were deeply impressed by the spirit of honest Christian service which led Mr. and Mrs. James to make their generous gift."

The Japanese newspapers made much of the Jameses' visit. Several articles were "translated" in time-honored, fractured style, and presented to Arthur. One described "the graceful yacht of Mr. Arthur Curtiss James who has been lying her beautiful body on the sea just in front of Yokohama Yacht Club." Another attended to Arthur's status in America: "in addition to important positions as director in Phelps Dodge Corporation Mr. James is concerning widely into railways, banks and universities. Union Theological Seminary, New York Library, Orphan Asylum and many navigation clubs are owing their good development to Mr. James. A large sum of capital in organization of school for education of niggers and American Indians in Hampton, a girls' technical school in Turkey, Laborers' Hall in America are finding its resource entirely in the pocket of Mr. James."

The ethnic slur regarding Arthur's support of Hampton was unfortunate, if unintentional. Sad to say in the early 1920s, it was a slur being commonly used in Arthur's home country, which was even more unfortunate. But it was proper that the Japanese included Hampton in their short list of Arthur's interests. Hampton University's archives are thick with letters to Arthur, most of them thanking him for his large annual gifts as well as frequent larger donations for special projects and occasions. In the late 1930s, when James Hall (named for Arthur) was in need of rehabilitation, he wrote a check for the $77,000 required ($1 million today). But his

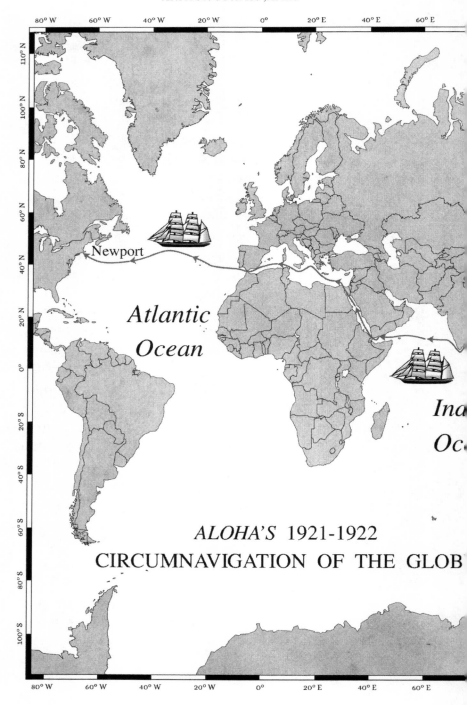

Newport

Atlantic

Ocean

Ina

Oc

ALOHA'S 1921-1922
CIRCUMNAVIGATION OF THE GLOB

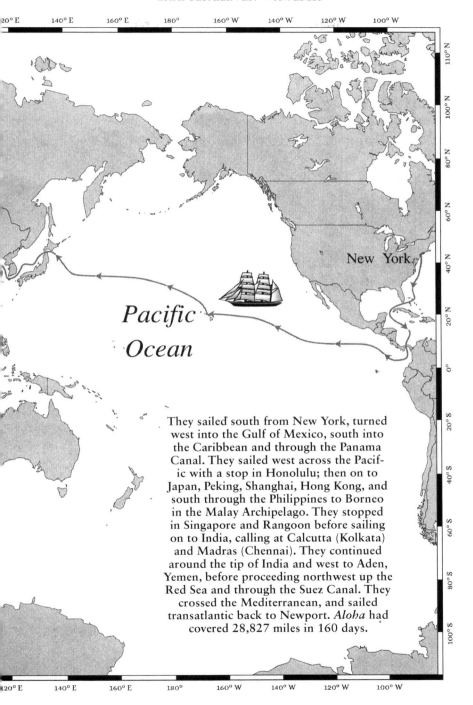

Pacific Ocean

New York

They sailed south from New York, turned west into the Gulf of Mexico, south into the Caribbean and through the Panama Canal. They sailed west across the Pacific with a stop in Honolulu; then on to Japan, Peking, Shanghai, Hong Kong, and south through the Philippines to Borneo in the Malay Archipelago. They stopped in Singapore and Rangoon before sailing on to India, calling at Calcutta (Kolkata) and Madras (Chennai). They continued around the tip of India and west to Aden, Yemen, before proceeding northwest up the Red Sea and through the Suez Canal. They crossed the Mediterranean, and sailed transatlantic back to Newport. *Aloha* had covered 28,827 miles in 160 days.

enthusiastic involvement in that community was even more noteworthy. When a long-time employee of the college retired, he bought the woman a car. When he thought a ranking administrator was being badly treated, he let the board know: "I was very glad to get a copy of the recent Minutes of the board," he wrote, "and am much pleased to see the changed resolution in regard to Billy Scoville's resignation, and the arrangement made for the family to continue to occupy the house. I must say that the first resolution passed by the board incited me to use language quite inappropriate for a Hampton Trustee." And in 1926 when the Massenberg Law was about to be signed by Virginia's governor—a law specifically designed to prevent interracial audiences in classrooms at Hampton—Arthur's letter to the college stated: "It is discouraging to have such ridiculous legislation passed."

Arthur was dubbed "a Monarch of Charity" by the Japanese press, and *Aloha* was called "an extremely luxurious boat accomplished with play rooms and bedrooms named after its color." Another paper noted, "Mr. James is very clever to earn money and equally clever to spend it."

In Beijing the James party found the Chinese attitude "essentially egoistic," and considered the Moros, the Muslim people of the Zamboanga Peninsula, Philippines, "a lawless lot." Vogel wrote this about the Moros: "they are subject to a peculiar psychical disturbance... in which the individual has hallucinations of the appearance of devils which he attempts to kill, is seized with an uncontrollable impulse to murder, and runs amuck." It is testament to the James party's adventurous spirit that they accepted an invitation to lunch with the superintendent of a penal farm in Zamboanga. "The luncheon was very good," Vogel wrote, "and was served on the cool veranda by five or six murderers beaming with smiles who proffered rice and chicken and waved long-handled fly disturbers over our heads with a courteous and kindly empressement that recalled the refrain of a song very popular in Casino days:"

We're an airy, fairy, cheery band of murderers,
and a nickel is our value of a life;
Any sanguinary job should be referred to us,
We'll relieve you of your money or your wife.

In Java, Arthur managed to arrange an audience with the local sultan, even though it was the man's day off. The esteemed gentleman was said to live "in pomp and pride" inside a 15-foot-high wall that was four miles in circumference. He oversaw a town of 15,000 devotees.

There is no record of Arthur's reaction to his visit with the sultan. But just being in Java, the setting of Joseph Conrad's novel *Victory*, which had been celebrated at Arthur's home in Manhattan, had to have been exhilarating. Cruising among the thousand little mysterious islands in the Java Sea would have helped bring Conrad's characters alive in a most vivid way: the reluctant Heyst, the woman-hating Mr. Jones and his murderous sidekicks, and the lovely, ill-fated Lena.

More noteworthy about the Java stop than meeting the sultan—even more exciting than lunch at the penal colony—was discovering the Jameses' artist friend Joseph Lindon Smith, the Blue Garden impresario, at Tjandi Boroboedoer (the shrine of many Buddhas), in Java. Smith had been at the shrine with his wife, Corinna, for three weeks, painting the extraordinary bas-reliefs of the galleries. Tjandi Boroboedoer was built in the ninth century around the partial remains of Buddha. The largest temple in the world, Tjandi is 150 feet tall, rising out of a level valley with majestic mountains on three sides, some of which are extinct volcanoes more than a mile high. There are nine galleries surrounding the temple, which covers three miles of ground. The galleries support seventy-two bell-shaped towers situated around the main temple. In each, a full-size Buddha is enthroned. One of the architectural wonders of the world, Tjando Boroboedoer was partially buried by eruptions over the years, and was cleaned up and restored in 1800.

There is no indication that Smith or the Jameses had planned to meet in Java. The slow, unreliable communication of the day, and the difficulty of coordinating their diverse and unpredictable means of transportation, suggests that such a plan would have been unlikely. One can only imagine the delight on both sides when they recognized one another in the otherworldly, overwhelming environment of the immense, ancient temple. The Smiths joined the James party, motoring around Java together. "Joe" Smith, according to Vogel's reporting, bought a collection of marionettes representing characters of Javanese folklore, little figures that had not

Aloha's crew (*opposite*) tidies up aloft during the round-the-world voyage. Joseph Lindon Smith (*above*) painting an Egyptian bas-relief.

been made for over fifty years. And four days after meeting Joseph and Corinna, Vogel wrote that "Arthur and Joe went to see the governor." When *Aloha* sailed for Singapore the next day, there was no mention of Joseph and Corinna being on board.

Yet a few days later, in Singapore, a Vogel log entry indicates Joseph and Corinna had indeed joined the yacht. "Harriet and Corinna went again to the YMCA [Harriet always made it a point to visit YMCAs whenever she could find one]. Jake was busy on affairs concerning the yacht, but the rest of us spent most of the morning looking for bargains in the Chinese pawn shops." And later, "Jake, Peter, and Joe departed by motor for a sixty-mile ride to Taiping on the mainland to see one of the famous tin mines." It was a long day, but Arthur was said to be fascinated by the primitive mining techniques being used.

Joe and Corinna would become part of the Jameses world cruise for two months, all the way to Colombo, Ceylon (now Sri Lanka). The Smiths joined the Jameses for a three-week tour of India by rail, went with Arthur and Harriet for dinners with various dignitaries, and had the pleasure of being with their hosts when they met the governor, Lord Willingdon, in Mumbai (Bombay). Lady Willingdon was eager to meet the Jameses and hear about the voyage since she was just a babe in arms when her father and mother had sailed *Sunbeam* around the world— the very voyage that had inspired Arthur.

From Colombo, *Aloha* would sail to Aden, Yemen, beginning the homeward-bound leg of the journey through the Red Sea and the Suez Canal, across the Mediterranean, and the Atlantic. In Colombo, the Smiths said their farewells and left by steamer for France, where they would rejoin their children.

The only downside of the trip seems to have been something that would have upset any sailor: a lack of wind during the last three months. Arthur's attraction for storms had paled. *Aloha* had cruised 10,000 miles during that time, and only 240 of those miles were made under sail, a huge disappointment for Arthur. But as Vogel concluded, "Jake has the satisfaction of having taken *Aloha* around the world without a single incident or accident of any kind, and of having given his guests an unforgettable and unique experience."

Control 12

As with everything else he did, Arthur's stock market dealings were conducted quietly. In fact, when a small, back-page news story in 1921 reported he was thought to be buying stock in the Western Pacific Railroad, the item seems to have been ignored by other newspapers. It wasn't until he had taken control of Western Pacific in 1926 that his financial dealings made the news. Then, it was big news. The *Wall Street Journal* ran this quote from Arthur: "The Burlington has been using the Denver & Rio Grande and the Western Pacific for years to make connection with San Francisco. There is no need for any more extension in that direction. But I look to see eventually the extension of the northwest lines into California. It was James J. Hill's dream when he built the Great Northern, and his visions generally come true."

In 1924, Arthur had sold the El Paso & Southwestern Railroad to the Southern Pacific, an interesting development given the fierce, unfriendly competition that had always existed between the two lines. The Southern Pacific was controlled by E. H. Harriman.

Copper prices had fallen after the conclusion of World War I, causing the El Paso & Southwestern's revenues to decrease by a third. Selling the road made sense. But as the El Paso & Southwestern's largest stockholder, Arthur had directed the railroad's president to purchase connecting lines that would take the El Paso line into Los Angeles at the same time negotiations were underway to sell the El Paso to the Southern Pacific. One can only presume the stated Los Angeles ambition was to threaten the Southern Pacific's exclusive hold on access to Los Angeles, and thereby boost the value of the El Paso line.

The credibility of the El Paso line wanting to acquire a line into Los Angeles was substantiated by Arthur's insistence that the Southern Pacific's Central Station in the city was in dire need of a big improvement. At the time, trains entering Los Angeles moved along one of the city's main arteries, Alameda Street, disrupting traffic. "Anybody who rides into Los Angeles as I did this morning," Arthur told the press, "can see for himself that the present terminal facilities of the SP here could not well be worse. Conditions so bad can't be and won't be allowed to continue indefinitely."

Those who knew Arthur Curtiss James also knew that, as a railroad man, his priorities included building proper terminals. Terminals designed for the efficient handling of freight, and for the comfort and convenience of passengers, were up there on his list of necessities learned from James J. Hill, along with with maximum 1 percent grades and 10-degree curves of track, the ratio of train-miles (expenses) to ton-miles (earnings), more powerful locomotives, and lighter cars. Those golden rules of railroading had been taught to Arthur by James J. Hill, who had also fought for "union" stations, those designed to handle any and all railroad companies servicing a city.

The timing for talking about terminals could not have been better. As Bill Bradley notes in *The Last of the Great Stations: 40 Years of the Los Angeles Union Passenger Terminal*, 1924 marked the ninth year of a pitched, divisive civic battle about the construction of a new terminal. It had begun in 1915, when several Los Angeles agencies had filed complaints for the removal of railroad grade crossings in the city. The idea of a proper terminal had become a political hot potato that was tossed among the California Railroad Commission, the California Supreme Court, and the Southern Pacific, the Union Pacific, and the United States Supreme Court. It was one of those issues that saw every business, every political party, every civic organization, both the city's major newspapers, and every citizen taking sides.

Terminals adequate to service all lines serving a metropolis (hence the term "union") had also been required by Interstate Commerce Commission mandates pertaining to the extension of various rail lines it had approved. Arthur leaned heavily on those mandates. During his negotiations with Southern Pacific, he had purchased a 40-acre property in Los Angeles ostensibly for a terminal. The struggle over Union Station would be protracted for many years. Construction would not begin until 1934.

Meanwhile, the El Paso sale went through. "I have never been associated with any piece of business that gave me more pleasure," Arthur told a *Los Angeles Times* reporter, "but it was the economic thing to do. There was no need of duplicating existing facilities if they could be brought to serve the purposes contemplated when our announcement was made of our intention to push through to the Pacific Coast. Those assurances appear to have been obtained, and this existing arrangement is the result."

The "sale" of the El Paso to the Southern Pacific appears to have been more a merger. An article in the December 4, 1924, issue of the *Magazine of Wall Street* concluded that El Paso & Southwestern had been "taken in" by Southern Pacific. That was a significant phrase coming from an insider journal like *Wall Street*, a phrase that indicated a much cozier action than a purchase. This item from the *Boston News Bureau* some years later (1928) succinctly states what seem like contradictions: "Mr. James acquired his interest in Southern Pacific in 1924, when he and his associates turned over control of the El Paso & Southwestern, receiving in part payment $28 million [$400 million today] par value of Southern Pacific stock, and $29.4 million [$421 million today] in bonds." In becoming the largest individual stockholder in the Southern Pacific, Arthur held the high card.

It's unusual when selling a company includes the seller "acquiring an interest" in the purchaser. One can't help but wonder if El Paso & Southwestern was "taken in" by Southern Pacific, or if Southern Pacific was "taken" by Arthur Curtiss James. It would seem the latter is more likely. When asked about that piece of property he had purchased in Los Angeles, the *Los Angeles Times* reported, "'At least our purchase undoubtedly hastened the accommodation which has subsequently taken place,' smiled Mr. James last night." And it was a win/win situation. Ownership of the property would certainly enhance the investment value of Southern Pacific.

Either way, it was indeed a substantial gain for Arthur. The fact that part of the deal involved T. M. Schumacher moving from president of the El Paso & Southwestern to vice president of the Southern Pacific, where he would represent Arthur's interests, contributed to the drawing-room feel of it. At the same time, as writer David Myrick points out in "The Strange Story of the El Paso & Southwestern" *Trains*, February, 1966), "the transaction also required the Espee [Southern Pacific] to construct a new line to serve Phoenix, and to provide Phelps Dodge with terminal property back in Los Angeles."

It was a strange story indeed. The word "sweet" is woefully inadequate to describe this deal. If there had been any hesitation on Arthur's part about moving ahead with establishing his control of Western Pacific, that influx of funds would have removed it.

The merger, or "intake" of the El Paso & Southwestern by Southern Pacific, can be marked as the beginning of Arthur Curtiss James's emergence as both able politician and savvy promoter. His business decisions to this point had been done quietly and efficiently, his natural style. The men he had hired had been well chosen, had proved loyal, and had performed to Arthur's high standards.

They had also been well compensated, and publicly praised for their good work. But now, with the association Arthur had brought about with the Southern Pacific, the curtain was rising on the biggest stage. There was only one person who could fill that stage, and that was Arthur Curtiss James himself. One can intuit that going public was not Arthur's favorite part of the projects he had in mind. But the projects were paramount, and Arthur was never one to ignore the details, or underestimate their critical importance. If his presence on stage was required, then he was ready.

Henry Anderson's monograph, *James Railway System*, underlines a financial move Arthur made about this time that indicates just how ready he was. He used his leverage as a large stockholder in the Great Northern and Northern Pacific Railroads—the two controlled the Chicago, Burlington & Quincy—to create a plan called *Unification of the Northern Pacific Railway Company and Great Northern Railway Company Plan and Deposit Agreement.* The new company formed was called the Great Northern & Pacific Railway Company. Its directors included a who's who of New York bankers, and Lewis Hill, son of James J. Hill.

Perhaps as a way of further enriching his ancestral line, in case anyone checked, in 1924 Arthur joined the American Revolution Institute of the Society of the Cincinnati (Connecticut). The rules for membership in this proud group are many and complex, but essentially one may join if his progenitor served as an officer in the American Revolution. Arthur's progenitor was Lieutenant Thomas Phelps, who fought in Baldwin's Artillery Regiment of Artificers in the Continental Army from 1776 to 1779. Thomas Phelps was the father of Anson Green Phelps, who started Phelps Dodge; the grandfather of D. Willis James's mother, Elizabeth Woodbridge Phelps; and Arthur's great-great-grandfather.

Arthur had one other important duty to take care of before he made the moves that would begin a period of several years when railroad business would consume a large part of his life. That was to check out the pair of new diesel engines with state-of-the-art electric drive that had been installed in *Aloha*. At the Marine Exposition in New York in the fall of 1925, the Westinghouse Company had advertised its electrical drive system as designed for *Aloha*: "Two Winton [diesel] engines, each driving a Westinghouse 175kw. generator and 30kw exciter will be installed in *Aloha*'s engine room... [Commander James] will be able to control the speed of the propeller and quickly change its direction with electric steering gear... and maneuver *Aloha* without giving orders as easily as a taxi driver maneuvers through traffic." Westinghouse said the system was based on the same theory used to propel the 600-foot battleship USS *Colorado*, and that *Aloha* was one of the first private yachts to have the electrical drive installed. The idea had appealed to Arthur, given his familiarity with similar technology involved in railroad operation. In 1909 the Great Northern had electrified service through four miles of the Cascade Tunnel. Locomotives working hard on the 1.7 percent grade through the tunnel filled the bore with coal smoke. To solve the problem, three-phase AC current had been run through the tunnel to the locomotive, then converted to DC to run the turbines. (The Long Island Railroad had begun electrification in 1905, and the New York, New Haven & Hartford had been electrified from New Haven to New York between 1907 and 1914.)

Arthur skippered his yacht for the sea trial of the new propulsion system. *Aloha* cruised from Manhattan to Coconut Grove in the spring of 1926. Representatives from consulting architects Tams & King, Westinghouse, the Winton Engine Company, and the Staten Island Shipbuilding Corporation, where the installation had been done, were on board. One log entry of the trip read: "Under one diesel engine we made better speed than under one boiler with steam, at a very much more economical consumption of fuel." Arthur observed that while the vibration was not excessive, the noise on the bridge was "impossible." He hoped the engineers could rectify that problem "so we will not have to record a mistake in having switched from steam."

* * *

What launched Arthur to the forefront of the biggest game in town was his announcement, on June 11, 1926, that he had acquired "a substantial interest" in the stock of the Western Pacific Railroad. He had purchased 48 percent of the Western Pacific's $88 million worth of preferred and common stock, becoming its chairman. The *New York Times* carried the story on its lead financial page. "I Believe in California and the Great West," was the headline. Arthur was quoted at length:

"For many years I have been a holder and believer in Great Northern, Northern Pacific, Burlington, Southern Pacific, and other Western railroads, and now have added to my railroad interests the holding of Western Pacific, having entire confidence in the ability of the territory served by Western Pacific to support an independent competing system, which shall have for its sole objective the upbuilding of the territory served by it. I believe in California and the Great West, and shall do my utmost to co-operate with the Western Pacific management in serving the public, and so helping to build up the entire region through which it passes."

Arthur was a controlling shareholder and a director of all the railroads he had named, including the Southern Pacific. He again moved his friend, T. M. Schumacher, this time from vice president of the Southern Pacific to the presidency of the Western Pacific, reminding the railroad world that Schumacher had been general traffic manager of the railroads and industrial companies controlled by Phelps Dodge from 1906 to 1909, and a vice president of the Western Pacific for two years after that. At the same time, Arthur was instrumental in moving another trusted executive—Hale Holden, who was president of the Chicago, Burlington & Quincy—to the presidency of the Southern Pacific. The third, and perhaps the most talented, of this powerful and like-minded executive team was Ralph Budd, another close associate of Arthur's, who had become president of the Great Northern after James J. Hill died.

"Budd," as Ralph Hidy writes in *The Great Northern Railway: A History*, "was omnivorous in absorbing facts, cool and detached in analysis, quick and decisive in judgment. He had the rare ability to delegate authority, but at the same time keep himself fully informed." Ralph Budd was evidently cut from the same fabric as Arthur, who not only shared the vision, the inspiration, and the prowess as a negotiator to make his acquisitions flourish, but who also had the enormous wealth required to purchase control of the various properties.

For instance, Arthur had a substantial plan on paper when he took control of the Western Pacific. It involved building a support network of small carriers: acquiring the trolley line of the San Francisco-Sacramento Railroad, acquiring the electric Petaluma & Santa Rosa Railway, and extending the Tidewater Southern south down the San Joaquin Valley to Fresno. He also wanted to obtain a direct rail entrance into San Francisco. Some of those plans would pass the critical eye of the Interstate Commerce Commission (ICC), and some would not. But all of them were laid out to support Arthur's long-term, primary goal: building what would come to be called the Inside Gateway, a new route from Klamath Falls, Oregon, to Keddie, California, a construction that would finally complete the Great Northern's transcontinental route into San Francisco. On paper, the Inside Gateway would exit the Cascades east of Klamath Falls to continue the level grade of the Great Northern extension south, on the east side of the mountains—a more competitive route than the Southern Pacific's route through the hilly foothills of the Cascades.

Arthur's selection of people showed an astute feel for the politics of various situations. His decision to move the highly regarded Hale Holden from president of the Chicago, Burlington & Quincy to the top job at Southern Pacific was typical of his powerful influence as an owner being wisely exerted. The move was seen by the railroad industry as promoting closer harmony between Southern Pacific and the Great Northern group, and also as a move that could lessen Southern Pacific's opposition to Western Pacific's intention to acquire feeder lines in California aimed at the gathering and distribution of traffic; and to its building an extension north.

Just four days after his announcement about his newly acquired control of the Western Pacific Railroad, Arthur, who was off watch in his bunk aboard *Aloha*, was startled awake by the sound of a gun being fired. The yacht was three miles southwest of Watch Hill, Rhode Island, en route from New York to Newport, proceeding slowly in heavy fog. Arthur rushed on deck as "a second shot boomed and went over the bow near First Mate Burns," according to Leonard Panaggio, writing in the *Newport Daily News*: "The shots were fired at such close range that Capt. Bezanson said he could smell the gunpowder." *Aloha* hove to for ten minutes in an uncomfortable, rolling sea. With no further shots fired, no sight of another vessel, and no hail, *Aloha* resumed course and speed for Newport.

There was no further encounter, and while it was extremely unlikely that the shots could have come from a non-military vessel, no definite proof was established. The only thing one knows for certain is that Arthur was extremely upset to have been mistaken for a rumrunner. Arthur was already known as an outspoken opponent of Prohibition. It was said that his enthusiastic support and significant financial backing of presidential candidates Al Smith in 1928 and Franklin Delano Roosevelt in 1932 were galvanized by the incident off Watch Hill. Both Smith and Roosevelt were Democrats, but for Arthur—a lifelong Republican—what mattered was both men's opposition to Prohibition. (On December 5, 1933, President Roosevelt would sign the 21st Amendment, ending Prohibition.)

Those in the business who were doggedly following Arthur's railroad moves probably didn't notice another activity of his that was mentioned in a complimentary profile of Arthur that ran in the *Denver Post* on February 1, 1927, under the extended headline, "Arthur James, New Railroad King, No Horatio Alger Hero—Rich Man's Son Has Added Fifty Million to His Inheri-

tance, But Would Have Won Had He Been a Poor Boy." Arthur's
railway prowess was compared to the Colossus of Rhodes, and
he was touted as "following not the gleam of gold or power, but
a vision of service to the country." But the most notable item
was buried toward the end of the piece. Arthur, it seems, had
been made a "Chevalier" by King Victor Emmanuel of Italy for
contributions he and his mother had made to the Italian School
of the Children's Aid Society in New York City. Arthur had contributed $300,000 ($6.8 million today) to construct a building
at Hester and Elizabeth Streets for the "academic and industrial" education of Children of Italian Descent. "Mr. James's purse
is readily opened for charities," the *Post* commented, "though
in most of his philanthropies he stipulates that the gift will be
canceled if used to obtain publicity."

By mid-1928, Arthur's activities in Northern California and
Central Oregon were being well covered by the press, and with
good reason. "He had pulled off a triple play," Henry Anderson
writes. "When his dominance passed from the El Paso & Southwestern to the Southern Pacific and Western Pacific, he benched
the competition. His role in the multi-faceted maneuver reflected
his father and James Hill capitalizing on the holdings of Great
Northern and Northern Pacific to acquire the Chicago, Burlington & Quincy, paving the way for Great Northern to link Chicago with Seattle."

The *New York Times* saw the competition between Arthur's Western Pacific and the Southern Pacific as "one of the
most interesting chapters in present-day transportation history
in the west." At stake was the rich country to the south and east
of Klamath Falls, Oregon. By having his application to the ICC
granted for building a small (2 miles) but significant link from
the town of Wells, Oregon, to connect with the Union Pacific,
Arthur had taken command of an area that would assure the
handling of traffic from Southern Idaho. That was just the beginning. Another Western Pacific application was pending for
a link from Engels, California, to Westwood, a move that was

expected to cost the Southern Pacific considerable traffic if and when a proposed (and likely) extension was built out of Klamath Falls to Alturas to access the rich lumber traffic in Northern California and Southeastern Oregon.

The railroad chessboard pondered by Arthur and his cohort (and chairman of the Great Northern executive committee) Ralph Budd, was multi-dimensional. Expansions had to be measured by the potential, sustained business that would be available in new territories; by the possibility of hooking up with tracks (and carriers) already in place; by accurately assessing the aggressiveness and leverage of the competition; by realistically forecasting the cost;

Ralph Budd (*at left*) and Arthur

and by a correct estimation of the ICC's judgment. That last item, trying to predict how the ICC would rule was perhaps the most difficult. As Richard Saunders Jr. wrote in *Merging Lines: American Railroads, 1900-1970*: "The early regulators did not have all the answers. They were individuals of honest intent who accepted the progressive notion that a perfect balance was out there... they were groping toward solutions, just as the railroads were."

It was a very crowded chessboard. Ralph Budd was also the man behind the Great Northern building the second, longer Cascade Tunnel that opened in 1929, providing a faster, cheaper route to Portland and Seattle (at 7.8 miles, in 2018 the Cascade remains the longest tunnel in the United States). Budd shared Arthur's vision of completing Hill's plan to join Seattle with San Francisco and Oakland. With Arthur James's leverage of capital, and Budd's experience, the two were unstoppable. It was not a game for the faint of heart. And while Arthur's seemingly bottomless wealth helped immensely, by itself that wealth was simply a door opener, a tool that would provide a stack of chips, and that would require nothing less than brilliant management.

One example of the complexity of the situation goes back to a battle James J. Hill and his Great Northern had had with E. H. Harriman's Union Pacific forces in the early 1900s for control of the Deschutes Canyon, located in the Warm Springs Reservation north of Bend, Oregon. Harriman had previously outmaneuvered Hill in their constant battle toward developing an "unbroken" line from the Missouri River to Portland. Hill had been hampered at the time by problems with his directors, and also had been bested on the financial front by Harriman. But, as Anderson writes in *James Railway System*, "Harriman was thwarted when Hill took control of the Spokane, Portland & Seattle Railway that ran along a more efficient route on the north bank of the Columbia River from Portland east through the Cascades."

The Great Northern and the Union Pacific had thus ended up on opposite banks of the Columbia River. When it subsequently appeared that the Deschutes Canyon was the preferred route for an extension from the Columbia River south to Bend, Oregon's geographical center, Hill had attacked with renewed vigor, using the Oregon Trunk Line he had created as a paper company some years before as his official flag bearer. The result was that both Harriman's and Hill's construction crews ended up in a race to build tracks through that formidable canyon, the sheer walls of which were 900 feet high in places. Locals called the struggle between those two powerful, uncompromising pioneers the Deschutes Canyon War, and with good reason. Rival construction gangs often had bloody clashes, wielding whatever implements were at hand.

Harriman's sudden death in September 1909, in mid-race, with construction approaching a narrowing of the canyon that afforded only one possible path for laying track, resulted in cooler heads prevailing. In the end, Hill's team won the battle. The Oregon Trunk Railway was established through the Deschutes Canyon between Wishram, Washington, and Bend, Oregon.

Then, in 1923, as Ralph Hidy relates in his history of the Great Northern, the Southern Pacific began extensive construction around Klamath Falls that opened up massive sources of lumber, provided a shorter and easier route from Portland and Eugene to an existing route at Ogden, Utah, and improved the Southern Pacific's competitive position. All that activity by the Southern Pacific, and the resulting demand from Oregonians for even more rail service, caused the Great Northern to take an interest. In response, the Southern Pacific geared up to prevent Great Northern or anyone else from exploiting what it considered its domain: namely, Western Oregon and California. The Great Northern—then run by Ralph Budd and Arthur—used the existence of the Oregon Trunk Line to gain entry to Klamath Falls, challenging the Southern Pacific's assumed exclusivity.

First, they successfully petitioned the ICC to build a line south toward Klamath Falls, a line that would hook up with Southern Pacific. But Southern Pacific refused to cooperate. So the Great Northern asked the ICC for permission to build a line from Bend through Paulina (100 miles east) and the Sprague River into Klamath Falls. The ICC agreed. There was more opposition from Southern Pacific followed by slick legal maneuvering on the part of Great Northern. By gaining permission to have the Great Northern, as parent company, representing the Oregon Trunk Line in proceedings before the ICC, the Southern Pacific "felt pressured," as Ralph Hidy wrote. For political reasons, the

Southern Pacific "could not play the Northern Pacific against the Great Northern. Finally, after prolonged and often heated negotiations, the SP acceded to Great Northern's wishes."

The Great Northern completed a line from Bend to the tiny town of Chemult in May 1928, and subsequently finished the 75 miles to Klamath Falls. Arthur's excellent vision, buoyed by his understanding of the competition's capabilities and weaknesses, his political savvy, his ability to keep disagreements among his own railroad boards to a minimum, and his keen sense of timing caused the *Times* to conclude: "As a strategist, Arthur Curtiss James, controlling owner of the Western Pacific, seems to have the upper hand in the contest with the Southern Pacific for a foothold in the new traffic territory."

The moment they knew Klamath Falls was in their grasp, Arthur and Ralph Budd had begun their campaign to build the Inside Gateway. Once again, the Southern Pacific went on a rampage against what they thought was a further intrusion into territory they felt belonged to them.

The Southern Pacific's pitched opposition to Arthur's plans remains another mystery, since Arthur was the Southern Pacific's largest individual stockholder at the time, and was said to control the company. Prior news reports had claimed that Arthur had divested himself of his Southern Pacific stock, "several years ago . . . shortly before he acquired control of the Western Pacific, which is part of an alliance of railroads in competition with SP in transcontinental traffic." Another reason the media surmised he had supposedly divested himself of Southern Pacific stock, was that the banking interest behind the Southern Pacific—Kuhn Loeb & Company of New York—was a "principle competitor and reputed antagonist" of Morgan & Company and the First National Bank of New York, banking firms with which Arthur was associated. Arthur's reported divestiture would seem to have made sense. But as the ICC hearing at which Arthur's application for the Inside Gateway would be heard drew closer, Arthur confirmed he was still fully involved with the Southern Pacific.

During a series of meetings in Portland, one of several Pacific Northwest cities that Arthur, T. M. Schumacher, and Ralph Budd visited in hopes of generating support for the Inside Gateway, the Portland *Morning Oregonian* reported:

[James's] admission yesterday that he is still the largest individual shareholder in the Southern Pacific Company is believed to be the first public refutation of a story that gained considerable credence on this coast about three years ago, and which, it is believed, had never been officially denied until yesterday.

It was reported at that time, and considerable publicity was given the report, that Mr. James, upon finding his position as major shareholder in the Southern Pacific and in the Northern Lines was a rather ticklish position, had disposed of his Southern Pacific interests and had allied himself wholly with the Northern Lines. By his own statement yesterday, he still enjoys a very strong position in the Southern Pacific organization.

At the time of the Portland disclosure, Arthur's holdings in the Southern Pacific were said to be in the $40 million range ($580 million today).

At a luncheon given for Portland civic leaders by Ralph Budd aboard a train—the Great Northern Special—Arthur was asked if construction of the Western Pacific and Great Northern link north would hurt the Southern Pacific. Writing in the *Oregonian* the next day, Harold A. Moore reported: "'Why how could it?' James replied. 'It will open a new country. It will bring about new development, a development that also will help the Southern Pacific and other coast railroads. Do you think that I, with my interest in the Southern Pacific, would advocate anything that would hurt those interests? Positively not.'

"The pleasant, bearded face of this railroad multi-millionaire broke into a reassuring smile," Moore wrote. "He knew what he knew, and that was that."

Then Arthur did some selling. "Anything that will develop

the Portland territory will develop Portland," he said, displaying his understanding of the value of a good sound bite long before those compressed, pithy utterances had a name.

While bringing the Inside Gateway to fruition provided the main impetus for Arthur's pursuit of the Western Pacific, there was another potential attraction that line held for him. Opening up a transcontinental route further south would be very productive for all five of the railroads he was heavily associated with—Great Northern, Northern Pacific, Chicago, Burlington & Quincy, Western Pacific, and Southern Pacific—and a few others with which he was not associated, including the Denver & Salt Lake, Western Pacific & Denver, and Rio Grande & Western. As the *New York Times* concluded, "Under present laws these systems could not be merged formally. However, it appears possible that their operations could be integrated to give the desired service."

The major stumbling block for this project was a debate over building the Dotsero Cutoff, a 41-mile shortcut between Denver, Colorado, and the town of Orestod (Dotsero spelled backwards), Colorado, along the western slope of James Peak in the Rocky Mountains. The cutoff would replace the old route across the Continental Divide that was a pattern of many steep switchback loops, and it would provide the missing link for the 6.2-mile Moffat Tunnel, that had been completed in 1928. Named after the Colorado financier and railroad man David H. Moffat, the tunnel was part of the Dotsero discussion. The battle to build the Moffat had raged from 1902, when it was first designed, to 1923, when construction started. The enormous cost overruns from projection ($6.62 million—$96 million today), to completion ($23.9 million —$346.4 million today) had created a financial logjam that would not be fully resolved for sixty years, and that had created law suits by the scores. The climate in Dotsero land was not exactly welcoming to the idea of taking on another extremely expensive railroad project.

The name Dotsero, by the way, came about from a survey-or's mark on a map. Dot zero, the mark (an ink dot) was called, was made at the beginning of a proposed route. Surveyors were often expected to name areas they established, a job that be-came a bother after they had exhausted their stock of relatives', friends', and pets' names. They grasped at any possible name that came along, hence Dotsero (and Orestod).

The argument for the Dotsero Cutoff was that, in conjunc-tion with the Moffat Tunnel, it would reduce the distance be-tween Denver and Salt Lake City by 173 miles, provide easier grades, and make Denver the most attractive point of inter-change for the Rio Grande. It would also provide transportation for Rocky Mountain coal deposits of incalculable tonnage. As W. W. Baldwin analyzed it in his book, *Corporate History of the Chicago, Burlington & Quincy Railroad Company and Affiliat-ed Companies*:

The significant fact was that Orestod was only 38 miles from the Denver and Rio Grande's main line at Dotsero. So how could the Rio Grande be persuaded to construct this cutoff? At the time, the Rio Grande was controlled equally by the Western Pacific and the Missouri Pacific, and there seemed little likelihood these two owners would permit the Rio Grande to short-circuit their established transcontinental route via Salt Lake and Pueb-lo. As it happened, however, the man who controlled policy on the Western Pacific was Arthur Curtiss James, long a close friend of Ralph Budd, and then a director of the C.B.& Q. Conse-quently, he shared Budd's earnest desire to develop Denver as a gateway for Rio Grande-Burlington transcontinental traffic.

So it was that Budd sought James's aid in forcing construc-tion of the cutoff... James immediately grasped the point. With-out criticizing the reasonable improvements the Rio Grande was making on its existing main line, James simply insisted that equal consideration be given to the cutoff. Shortly afterwards, the deci-sion was made to go ahead if the necessary funds could be found.

Having gotten the railroads in line, Arthur traveled to Denver to do a bit of selling. Once again, he delivered a neat sound bite. "It's up to you folks out here to build the Dotsero Cutoff," he said, as quoted by the *Rocky Mountain News*. "You'll have to settle all your Moffat Tunnel suits in court first. Then things will begin to look like business." "Up to you folks" was a made-to-order headline. *The Rocky Mountain News* loved it:

> *Mr. James gave expression to what this newspaper has been drumming for months into the public ear, that litigation will never build the Dotsero Cutoff and place Denver on a through route and cut in half the distance between the two slopes of the single state.*
>
> *The tunnel is there. It cost a whole lot more than expected, but what can be done about it?.... The sensible thing is to make the most of the situation, stop crying over spilled milk and put the tunnel to the best possible use in the public interest so as to get returns direct and indirect to the property which bonded itself for the construction of this common carrier and spearpoint in the whole Western railroad strategical situation.*
>
> *"It's up to you folks." Assuredly it is, and if "you folks" will form a vigilantes committee to look after YOUR own interests the Dotsero Cutoff will be built. If not, YOU will know the reason why.*

The Dotsero Cutoff would be built, but it would take several years before enough financial damage from tunnel construction was under control to allow various forces (including the ICC) and the necessary funding to come together to make it happen. Meanwhile, Arthur turned his full attention to the Inside Gateway. There, he had a fight on his hands, primarily from the Southern Pacific. Again, the conflict was puzzling. Some surmised that Arthur's very strong position in the Southern Pacific did not deter that railroad from standing up for what it thought was best for its future. Others thought the opposition from the Southern Pacific was offered as a distraction calculated to obviate any chance of a monopoly being suggested. The Sherman Antitrust Act was only forty years old, and the Clayton Antitrust Act (1914) had further empowered the Sherman. The lesson of the Northern Securities

Case had to still be fresh in Arthur's mind. In any event, Southern Pacific's opposition was strong and to the point. In fact it appeared to be too strong, and too well crafted to be a distraction. The Southern Pacific's main argument, in addition to stopping

other railroads from usurping "its territory," was to prevent duplication of its lines that were already in place, or extensions that were under construction. As a man with a strong financial foot in both camps, Arthur's position was that the competition would be good for passengers, freight shippers, and both railroads.

During the spring of 1929, when this conflict of interest was heating up in anticipation of the ICC hearings in the fall that would consider Arthur's (Great Northern's and Western Pacific's) application for building the Inside Gateway, the Southern Pacific was already laying track between Klamath Falls southeast to Alturas, California, and northwest from Alturas to Klamath Falls at the combined rate of six miles a day. The combined cost was $55,000 a day ($800,000 today). That connection to Alturas would connect the Southern Pacific with the Nevada/California/Oregon line that would allow Southern Pacific traffic to flow eastward. Hale Holden, the former Burlington president Arthur had helped select for Southern Pacific's top job, said his company would invoke the law to protect its investments in any territory where the entrance of another road would mean needless duplication. "The Transportation Act," Holden told the *New York Times*, "was passed to prevent construction of unnecessary railroad mileage. . . . Such duplication will be costly to the investor, and the public will have to foot the bill in the long run."

The Inside Gateway extension Arthur was proposing would in fact parallel the Southern Pacific tracks for forty miles out of Klamath before it turned south toward Bieber, and eventually be built further south to Keddie, where it would connect with the Western Pacific's tracks into San Francisco.

Holden's opposition had support. In May 1929 the *Los Angeles Times* headlined, "45 Civic Bodies Hit GN Plans." All forty-five chambers of commerce and civic organizations, including city councils, service clubs and associations, and development boards, were listed. The *Times* summation of their objections was that "the GN extension would be wasteful, unnecessary, and likely to impose a burden on the public." It was to visit these opponents in person and present the Great Northern side of the argument that Arthur, often with Ralph Budd and T. M. Schumacher at his side, traveled around the Northwest that summer to present their case.

The press was happy to finally have access to this heretofore-absent magnate of the rails, and they liked what they saw. They treated Arthur kindly, which helped. He was called a quiet gentleman, with "a well-trimmed black beard marking him as an unusual character in a beaverless world." A beard, at the time, was sometimes called a "beaver." A *San Francisco Examiner* writer commented, "You can't get away from that man's smile—the twinkle of clear brown eyes that leap out at you from

The press called Arthur (at left) "the quiet gentleman"

the ambush of his ample whiskers. . . . Other railroad kings and giants of finance have won their way with a steely glance or firm set lips. This new Gould, or Harriman, or Hill—call him what you will—wins with a smile, and parries with it too."

In a profile, the *Oakland Post Inquirer* called Arthur "a regular fellow who laughs frequently and seems to enjoy it. Long crinkles at the corners of his eyes tell of much time spent in the open. Strong teeth flash white through gray-streaked brown whiskers." In a profile of Arthur, *Post Inquirer* writer H. R. Hill related a tale Arthur had told him about James J. Hill (no relation to H.

R.), with Arthur calling James J. Hill "the most kindly man I ever knew." Arthur said as a young man he once had failed to sort out the difficulties of a railroad he had been made chairman of. He had returned to New York down in the dumps. "I ran across J. J. Hill," Arthur told writer Hill, "and he asked me what was wrong. I told him. In his office he talked to me for two straight hours. My success, or failure in this particular venture was nothing to him. It was just friendliness from him, that was all. He told me what to do and I took his advice." *Post Inquirer* writer Hill was impressed by Arthur's calm demeanor in the face of such a tension-filled, critical time. "In his Western Pacific office," Hill wrote, "James sat at a plain oak desk barren of anything related to business. Just an inkwell and a scratch pad. No letter files lining the walls. A peaceful woodland scene hung on one wall."

The Great Northern team registered wins in Seattle, Tacoma, and San Francisco. In fact the more than 4,000 members of the San Francisco Chamber of Commerce voted 3,095 to 1,162 in favor of the new line from the north coming into their city. And Arthur, Budd, and Schumacher came out of Portland feeling optimistic. There was plenty going on behind the scenes in Portland. Frederick Weyerhaeuser, who, in 1900, had founded the now-well-known lumber goliath in his name, was just one industrialist who took part in the conversation, expressing interest in how his logs might be moved to the mill in Klamath Falls. Weyerhaeuser denied he was seeking a connection with the feeder line that would provide a connection between the Klamath Basin and Medford, Oregon, a booming town created in the late 1800s by railroad expansion, and a county seat since 1927. Arthur was quoted in the Portland *Oregon Daily Journal* as saying he didn't know the source of capital behind the various feeder roads being proposed. "But we are interested," Arthur said, "in any proposition looking to real development in the Pacific Northwest."

Toward that end, Arthur's team would begin writing the lengthy application for the building of the Inside Gateway that he would present to the ICC in the fall of 1929.

Life *18*

Given the intense activity on the western railroad fronts in the late 1920s, the weight of consequences that hung on every decision, one could be forgiven for assuming that Arthur was totally consumed by the calculations, the deals, the politics, the meetings, the hearings, the media, and all the travel involved. But the fact is that no matter what was going on, or how important the major focus of his business affairs were at any given time, Arthur never neglected the private and personal aspects of his life. How he managed to accomplish this is one of the many mysteries he left for us to contemplate.

For one, from the letters that are available we learn that his correspondence with Mabel Todd never faltered. In the 1920s, the letters referred to the mental problems Mabel's husband David was suffering. Since 1917, David, Mabel, and their daughter, Millicent Todd Bingham, had been neighbors of the Jameses, in Coconut Grove, living in a house Arthur had arranged for them. That year, Amherst's board of trustees had placed David on permanent leave as his behavior grew more erratic. At the time, Arthur had written to Mabel, "you will be mighty glad to get rid of all the trouble of the establishment and the thankless task of being a public entertainer for College Parasites." In 1922, David had been institutionalized.

Arthur wrote Mabel about having had a visit with David where he was interned. "He does not seem to be at all violent," Arthur wrote, "and his hallucinations are along the same lines he had had for many years. A short talk with the doctor indicates that he also feels that there is no great improvement." Letters to Arthur from financial managers thank him for checks in the $10,000 to $20,000 range (in today's dollars) sent to a trust he had set up for the Todds. In the summer of 1928, Arthur wrote to "My Dear Mrs. Todd," saying "I am leaving for Amherst tomorrow for Commencement, but on my return next week shall look forward to seeing you."

In 1928, Arthur financed the construction of Christadora House, a seventeen-story building at 143 Avenue B, in New York's East Village. This would be the new home of the Christadora Settlement House, a refuge for impoverished women trying to subsist in the slums of the city. Christadora was founded in 1897 by Christina McColl, a YMCA-trained crusader who felt organized religion had ignored social evils born of industrialism. Their first residence was the cellar of an East Village delicatessen, a social center intended to be "tolerant, educationally effective, and conducted without evasion on a truly religious, non-sectarian basis," according to a paper on Christadora written by June Hopkins.

Harriet James had served as president of Christadora's board of managers for many years, and had taken the lead in making the new quarters into a reality. The new building, designed by Henry Pelton, the architect who had designed Riverside Church, had cost $1 million ($25 million today), and was well equipped with the latest technology, from kitchen to treatment centers.

While the railroad business was severely cutting down on the time Arthur had for sailing, his favorite pastime was always on his mind. When an opportunity to do something for sailing

David and Mabel Todd were supported by Arthur as they grew older.

in Newport arose, Arthur jumped on it. It had to do with Lime Rock, an uprising of limestone ledges 900 feet off the southeast side of Newport Harbor upon which a small lighthouse had been built in 1854. Arthur could almost see the location from his observatory at Beacon Hill House. It was only a few rocks down the shore from Aloha Landing. It was a famous lighthouse, thanks

The facilities at Christadora House—Harriet was president of the board

to a woman named Ida Lewis, daughter of the original keeper, who had made a name for herself by saving a total of eighteen unfortunate souls from drowning in the sea. Several were soldiers rowing back from Newport to Fort Adams, who were either novice at handling a boat, or (in at least one case) drunk. *Harper's*

Magazine wrote about Ida Lewis in its June 1869 issue, recounting how she would respond to mishaps in all manner of weather by launching her rowboat and pulling to the aid of the distressed. "This is a girl in her 28th year," *Harper's* reported, "slender, blue-eyed, with light brown hair, frank and hearty," and calling her heroic acts "very improving reflections upon the sphere of women."

Lime Rock Light was renamed Ida Lewis Light in 1924. By 1928, a metal tower had replaced the lighthouse, and the property had been placed on sale. According to a letter written by Mrs. Horace Beck, wife of Arthur's personal physician, a good

Woodcut of Ida Lewis rescuing two soldiers off Lime Rock

friend and a veteran of many *Aloha* cruises, her husband had heard about the impending sale of Lime Rock and remarked that it would make a very nice clubhouse for the Narragansett Bay Regatta Association. Rumors were that fishermen planned to bid for the place so they could use it for culling and cleaning their fish. Local residents feared for the odoriferous mess such activity could create. Mrs. Beck suggested that her husband contact Arthur, who might be interested. Beck did, and Arthur was interested. But he knew if he started bidding on the place, the price would skyrocket. He asked Beck to be his straw man. Now Beck had to hustle, because it turned out the sale was happening that very day. By the time Beck had reached the pier, the boat taking bidders to the rock had departed. As luck would have it, the boatman knew Beck and turned back for him.

The bidding was so enthusiastic that the price rose beyond the number Arthur had given Beck. Beck, the story goes, called Arthur. Exactly how Beck called Arthur, in 1928, from a clump

Ida Lewis Yacht Club with *Aloha* anchored in Newport Harbor

of rocks 900 feet from the beach, is not explained. Perhaps the small, two-story lighthouse structure had a telephone installed. That would have made sense. But no need to spoil a good story. Beck called Arthur. According to Mrs. Beck's letter, Arthur said to her husband, "Horace, you went out there to buy it didn't you?"

Beck won the bidding for Arthur. Lime Rock would become the Ida Lewis Yacht Club in 1929. The original structure formed the basis for the clubhouse, and a 700-foot-long pier was built

from shore to provide access. Arthur became the club's first commodore. The Ida Lewis Yacht Club's burgee is emblazoned with
eighteen stars in honor of the lives saved by its namesake, the
first female lighthouse keeper in the United States.

In 1928, Arthur was also planning to take his yacht *Aloha*
on a race to Spain that was being hosted by Queen Victoria and
King Alfonso, Spain's regents. While it's true that *Aloha* was
a fully-crewed, independently-functioning vessel, every own-
er-skipper of a yacht tends to get very involved with the many
details associated with entering any race, let alone a transatlantic race for a cup offered by European royals. Perhaps a
new sail, or two, or three, would be required, or certain pieces
of weighty cruising gear should be removed from the vessel
in the interest of increasing speed. And there were dozens of
questions, such as who would best be included among the afterguard for his navigational skills? The race involved thirteen
yachts—of which *Aloha*, at 216 feet overall, was the largest—
divided by size into two classes. The smaller yachts, racing for
the Queen's Cup, would start off the Ambrose Lightship (marking the entrance to New York Harbor's main shipping channel)
on June 30. The larger yachts, competing for the King's Cup,
would start at Ambrose on July 7.

"Aloha, Dauntless, Guinevere, Spanish yachts Among Others In The List," headlined the *New York Times* preview of the
race on May 7, 1928 [the *Times* always gave good coverage to
yachting events in those days]. That implied Arthur had been
doing strategic thinking about this race for several months, por-
ing over historical weather patterns for July as he considered
the most advantageous course across the Atlantic. It turned
out that was all for naught. On July 1, just a week before the
start, the *New York Herald Tribune* headlined, "Commodore
James Withdraws *Aloha* from Ocean Race." The subhead read,
"Inability of His Wife to Accompany Owner Causes Change
in Plan." The story went on to report that Harriet was convalescing from an appendicitis operation. "Although Mrs. James

is much improved in health," the story read, "the Commodore declined to sail his auxiliary bark without her on board."

Arthur had also taken an active role in politics in 1928. Although he was a Republican, he supported two Democrat candidates, largely because of their opposition to Prohibition. One was presidential candidate Al Smith, former governor of New York, with a campaign contribution of $25,000 ($364,000 today). Smith, whose platform also included strong economic conservatism, would lose to Herbert Hoover in 1928. It was said that anti-Catholic sentiment was the real issue behind Smith's loss. Arthur was also a participant in Franklin Delano Roosevelt's successful run for the governor of New York that year. As we have seen, when Arthur participated in anything, it wasn't just with money. He always got involved.

* * *

In reviewing Arthur's life, one doesn't encounter many instances when his feathers seem to have been ruffled. But when his half-cousin, Edward James, showed up in New York in 1929, Arthur was definitely annoyed. Edward was from the British side of the family. Both Arthur and Edward were grandsons of Daniel James, the early Phelps Dodge partner, but Edward's grandmother was Daniel's second wife, Sophia Hitchcock. His parents were William Dodge ("Willie") James, and his wife, Evelyn ("Evie") Forbes. Philip Purser, who wrote *Where Is He Now?: The Extraordinary Worlds of Edward James*, noted that Arthur had become "increasingly xenophobic over the years.... he had taken against the English branch of the family and against Edward in particular." Purser suggested that Arthur's displeasure with Edward might have come from a visit Arthur and Harriet had made to England in the early 1920s, when Edward would have been a teenager. During that visit, Purser wrote: "Poor Harriet James, who called [with American impropriety] to Edward VII as he went out with a gun, 'Good hunting Your Majesty,' was heartlessly teased, which may have contributed to the anti-British sentiments adopted by her husband. In 1923, however, Mrs. James (Evie, Edward's mother) and her unmarried daughters found the home comforts of the cousins in Newport, New York City, and Florida so agreeable they stayed for month after month."

Edward was much younger than Arthur. Born in 1907, he was only twenty-two when he first ventured to New York. But the young man's name had been bandied about high-society's drawing room circuit since his birth, when gossips whispered he was the illegitimate son of Edward VII, who was, in fact, his godfather. It is more generally accepted that his mother, Evelyn, was the daughter of King Edward. Then at age four (1912), when his father died, Edward James had inherited West Dean, a ninety-eight-room, fortress-like medieval castle on a 6,500 acre estate near Chichester, England, dating from 1085, that had long been a royal hunting park. He would not take charge of the estate until he was twenty-five. The problem was that while Edward got the estate, his sisters inherited the money. Edward lived in the gardener's cottage until, at age twenty-one, he inherited a fortune from his uncle Frank, who had been killed by one of the elephants he was hunting in Africa. As the British *Sunday Observer* remarked upon Edward's death in 1984, "He was an eccentric in the best British tradition... a poet, and a man with more than sufficient money to live out his fantasies."

Edward also had talent. He had won an art prize at age fifteen, and he would add several books of poetry to his credit along with a rather dense autobiographical novel, *The Gardener Who Saw God*, that is said to be best read with a dictionary at hand. The preface stated that "the perceptive mind of the gardener sees the futility, uselessness and absurdity of much of modern society and catches a glimpse of what life might be and should be." *Time* magazine reviewed the book in 1937: "The book will delight many with its suave philosophy, its grave absurdities, the considerable skill its first-novelist author discloses in the conduct of its curiously bifocal narrative."

Born to the purple, Edward revolted against the society he was expected to champion. Instead he chose a provocative, rebellious life, delighting in challenging the norms of the culture with far-flung views of other realities. He was known primarily for his support of the arts, surrealism in particular, and for his close affiliations with avant-garde painters like René Magritte, and Salvador Dali. Edward sometimes stayed with Arthur and Harriet when he was in New York. One can assume that both his extravagant antics in the city and his general philosophy of life did not jibe with the conservative demeanor of his hosts.

Edward James and Tilly Losch at West Dean

Edward became enamored of the lovely Austrian dancer/choreographer/painter/actress Tilly Losch, after seeing her perform. He met her on his first visit to New York in 1929. By then he had become attracted to the French surrealists. "Like them," Nicola Coleby wrote in *A Surreal Life: Edward James 1907-1984*, "James sought imaginatively to reconstruct the real and to challenge the values of society."

Perhaps that seeking was in part the motivation for Edward taking an entire floor in the Grand Hotel in Rome for his honeymoon with Losch in 1930, or when he hired a string sextet to play for them at luncheon, or when he hired a full orchestra to play for them at dinner.

Later, Edward had appeared in New York with Salvador Dali, staying at one of the more refined hotels in the city. One evening it was said the two men had freed an ostrich from its cage at the Children's Zoo in Central Park and taken it to their suite. Alcohol could have been involved. Confined to the bathroom, the large bird stomped the floor all night. When the complaints of the guests in the room below were brought to Edward's attention, he pointed out to management that they might have regulations prohibiting cats and dogs, but there was no mention of ostriches in the rules. The next day, Edward and Salvador returned the beleaguered bird to the zoo with its head protruding from the sliding roof of a taxi, much to the delight of the throngs on the avenue.

Edward James in Mexico

On a more serious note, when his marriage to Losch was failing in 1933, Edward funded a ballet company, Les Ballets, founded by none other than George Balanchine, who created two ballets for Losch. Also involved were acclaimed songwriter Kurt Weill, and his wife, the noted singer Lotte Lenya. But the ballet did not save the marriage. Edward accused Losch of having an affair. Losch said Edward was a homosexual, which wasn't the case. Edward was bisexual.

Perhaps more to the point of Arthur's discomfort with his British cousin's spendthrift way of life was this summation of Edward's philosophy, expressed by him in a letter to a friend, the American actress Ruth Ford, whose brother was the bohemian surrealist Charles Henri Ford: "So I sum up my point of view in relation to that inherited fortune by saying that money seemed to have been given to spend... but I was not simply going to give it away to some uncreative institution called a charity. I felt that I could do more to alter the face of the world, more to usher in that new world, by spending it in my own way—in particular by fostering any and all creative spirits I could meet with, who had something individually to contribute to the building of that more vivid and more living future.... Moreover, I could see hardly anyone who supported the sort of stairways to imagination which seemed to me to be so vital and necessary to the spiritual potency of this future."

It's difficult to imagine a view of how to best employ one's fortune more diverse from that of Arthur's. A telling measure of Arthur's frustration with his half-cousin was that he did not include Edward in his will. Monetarily, that would have made little difference to Edward, who had turned West Dean into an art training center for adults, and in 1945 had moved permanently to the middle of Mexico, where he amused himself by building parts of more than thirty dwellings—"follies"—that never got finished. But Arthur had made his point.

* * *

From building a settlement house for women in need in New York City, to founding a yacht club in Newport, to planning a race to Spain, to actively supporting political candidates of his choice, to dealing with the behavior of a wild and crazy cousin and the sustained, poor health of his wife, to providing a steeple for a church in Paris—all this gives testament to the immense amount of ground Arthur Curtiss James's philanthropies, personal interests, and responsibilities covered. The Japanese media's tangled translation of its appreciation of Arthur comes to mind: "Mr. James is very clever to earn money and equally clever to spend it."

The steeple Arthur had donated was for the American Church in Paris, the first American Christian church formed outside the United States. The church was founded in 1814. In the early 1920s, the church hierarchy began raising money for a handsome fifteenth-century-style Gothic cathedral that would accommodate an interdenominational, international Christian congregation of 600 people. Construction began in 1926. Joseph Wilson Cochran, known as "the building pastor," wrote a book called *Friendly Adventures*, about the drama of building this church. The book is dedicated to Arthur Curtiss James. Cochran described a fund-raising trip to "approach once more faithful friends in New York." It seems there was a shortage of $150,000 ($2 million today) needed to build the steeple on the cathedral.

The trip was not a success. Cochran had to admit that the tower was not a necessary part of church worship. He returned home, "reluctantly resigned to a towerless church." Scott Herr, currently senior pastor of the American Church in Paris, suspects that Cochran had access to Arthur through mutual friends on Cape Cod. Given Arthur's proven global interest in Christianity, Herr thinks Cochran had taken hat in hand and approached Arthur directly.

Arthur was a devoted Christian, as we have noted. When at sea on his yachts, as captain, Arthur took Sunday worship seriously, rarely missing an opportunity to lead the service himself. When in Newport, there is no indication he was a Sunday regular at the Trinity Episcopal Church (founded 1698), where he had purchased the double-sized pew 68, middle aisle, in 1912. Although John Hattendorf's history of the church (*Semper Eadem*), confirms that Arthur was an active participant in Trinity's management. In the 1920s, the church was going through typical expansion problems, and making plans to replace the parish house. "Clubs and societies clamor for the same room,"

Hattendorf wrote, "and there is constant friction. The shower rooms and locker rooms are not fit to be seen."

Arthur was a member of the Committee of Advice at Trinity. He joined another committee at Trinity formed to raise the $100,000 needed for the work. "Most of the money," Hattendorf wrote, "was donated by Arthur Curtiss James."

In New York, in addition to his (and his family's) long-standing and generous support of the Union Theological Seminary, Arthur was a leading officer of the Madison Square Presbyterian church. When that church, designed by Stanford White, was demolished in 1919 to make room for an insurance tower, Arthur was among several laymen of the church who negotiated the merger of that congregation and the congregation of the University Place Church into the First Presbyterian Church.

Steeple of the American Church in Paris

We also know that Arthur had previously contributed significantly to Christian enterprises overseas. Among them were the Doshisha School in Japan, Canton University in China, and the American Board of Commissioners, charged with exporting the Christian gospel to non-Christian nations. And Arthur, it seems, had already donated $100,000 ($1.4 million today) toward the construction of the cathedral for the American Church in Paris. In the book of correspondence between John D. Rockefeller and John D, Rockefeller Jr., titled *Dear Father, Dear Son*, John D. Jr. wrote to his father about the American Church: "Arthur Curtiss James was very much interested in the construction of the new building and we joined quite generously with him in contributing to it."

Cochran's book about building the cathedral in Paris does not indicate that he visited Arthur, but he did write that in May 1929, "with almost every vestige of hope for the tower having expired . . . came a letter from a New York friend stating that his representative would soon be passing through Paris, and would like to have a look at the progress. The visitor," Cochran continued, dutifully preserving anonymity, "was pleasant but non-committal. He ventured it would be desirable if we could build the tower high enough to afford a suitable entrance to the church. Nothing more was heard until in September, 1929, came this cablegram: Responsible anonymous party offers to underwrite cost of completed tower but cost must not exceed present bid of $150,000."

Blessed relief was followed by more drama. The media had announced the "underwriting" as an outright gift. "This was an unpardonable blunder," Cochran wrote, "making it practically impossible to enlist the interest of others in consummating this stupendous task." Cochran visited the original underwriter for a face-to-face apology. "Go ahead," the underwriter told him. Cochran called him, "the anonymous Great Heart. He said, 'Don't stop, tell them not to cease work. Whenever you need the cash let it be known and it will be forthcoming.'"

"The world is better for such men," Cochran wrote. "The pledge of anonymity is released. This book is dedicated to him." The initials "ACJ" are subtly carved above the arch from the portico facing the Church House (west) as you step out of the entrance to the sanctuary of the American Church in Paris.

Driving the Spike

The ICC hearing on the Inside Gateway proposal from the Great Northern and Western Pacific Railroads took place in San Francisco on November 13, 1929. Interstate Commerce Commissioner Charles D. Mahaffie was presiding. More than 200 "witnesses and intervenors" from eleven states had come to be heard on the application from Great Northern to lay track 88 miles south from Klamath Falls, Oregon, to Bieber, California; and for the Western Pacific to lay track 112 miles north from Keddie to Bieber. *Time* magazine, as always, provided the comprehensive view:

> *Achilles in this canto of the railroad epic is played by Arthur Curtiss James of the Western Pacific. Bearded, eye-glassed, urbane, he is known for different things to different people. To Manhattan socialites, he is the host of a huge granite mansion on Park Avenue at 69th Street. To yachtsmen, he is the able and enthusiastic skipper of the famed, square-rigged yacht* Aloha. *To many a rich old lady he is vice president of Phelps Dodge Company... but to railroad men and the general public, Arthur Curtiss*

James is the man who owns more railroad stocks than anyone else in the country. . . . Strangely, in this present battle, he is the largest stockholder of his foremost opponent, Southern Pacific.

Casting Arthur as Achilles was an interesting choice by *Time.* Surely, when it came to railroads, Arthur was indeed a great warrior. But there was no evidence to date of a fatal flaw in him, as with Achilles's problematic heel. Was *Time* just having fun, tongue in cheek, or did *Time* have exclusive, inside information? Did it have to do with the confusion over the Southern Pacific fighting against its largest stockholder? If so, *Time* was keeping mum.

The much bigger story was the fact that the stock market crash of 1929, "Black Tuesday," when a record 12.9 million shares were dumped by panicky investors who had lost confidence in the economy, had taken place just two weeks prior to the ICC hearing. As Canadian economist and diplomat John Galbraith wrote in *The Great Crash,* "the economy was fundamentally unsound." Galbraith pointed out that corporate and banking structures were unhealthy, foreign trade was unstable, and he stressed "the bad distribution of income." In 1929, the wealthiest 5 percent of the population received 30 percent of the personal income (compared with 1 percent owning more wealth than the bottom 90 percent in 2017). In his *People's History of the United States,* Howard Zinn wrote that in 1929, "the capitalist system was driven by the one overriding motive of corporate profit, and was therefore unstable, unpredictable, and blind to human needs. The result of all that: permanent depression for many of its people, and periodic crises for almost everybody." Back in 1605, the great Spanish writer Miguel Cervantes wrote in his novel *Don Quixote,* "Forewarned, forearmed," but greed renders ears deaf.

Black Tuesday was the crash that officially started the Great Depression. It's odd that *Time* didn't factor that monumental event into its story on the railroad epic being played out in San Francisco. Perhaps the deadlines that *Time* had to meet in 1930 were not flexible enough to include that stunning bit of frightening news. "Much of the industrialized world," William D. Cohan wrote in *The Last Tycoon: The Secret History of Lazard Frères & Co.*, "was thrown into a near decade-long depression."

It was reported that Arthur would lose 50 percent of his fortune in the Depression, and that even so, he had done better than most. He was said to have predicted the Great Depression, yet he did not sell his Western Pacific stock in 1928, when he could have made a profit, saying—according to Arthur L. Lloyd, writing in *The Encyclopedia of American Business*—"that selling would be directly contrary to his reason for buying the line in the first place." It gives one an idea of the depth of Arthur's wealth when, in spite of his clear view of the unstable economics that lay ahead, he was still charging forward with a railroad project that would cost him $14.5 million ($216 million today) before it was done.

Arthur was the first to testify before the ICC. He began by stating his position: "Through consolidating the El Paso & Southwestern with the Southern Pacific, I found myself the largest stockholder in the latter road, and, as far as I know, I still occupy this position." He also made it clear that he, through his Western Pacific ownership, also owned half of the Denver & Rio Grande Western. He spoke of how he had been attracted to the Western Pacific's "severe" reorganization, and its strong strategic position from the way it entered California through the friendly, 1.3 percent–maximum grades of Feather River Canyon. "After looking over the territory and taking the best railroad advice available," Arthur told Charles Mahaffie, "it was my belief that Northern California would afford sufficient business for the Western Pacific and the Southern Pacific and, in fact, there is necessity for further railroad development.... Having come to this conclusion, I bought control of the Western Pacific, not withstanding my large investment in the Southern Pacific.

"The program of expansion I had in mind we are now trying to carry out," he continued, "and if permitted to do so, California will, in my opinion, be greatly benefitted, and this benefit will be shared by all the railroads in proportion to the business they do here, and this would, of course, be especially true of Southern Pacific."

Arthur used Southern California's rail system as an example of the "constructive development" he had in mind for the north. "The development of that section has been due very largely to the fact that it has had the service of two, and then three, strong railroads in competition with each other," he said. "If the Western Pacific is supported and made a strong competitor in Northern California, and if the Great Northern also becomes a competing road there, the same result will follow as in Southern California."

Arthur was followed by Ralph Budd, who attempted to de-rail the Union Pacific's opposition in advance, saying: "Its north-western interests are secondary to its central and southwestern interests. Thus the interests of the Union Pacific are more closely allied with the policy of keeping southern Oregon and northern California bottled up for the Southern Pacific."

Following Budd were a string of "pro" witnesses who spoke of everything from Western Pacific's reliance on freight interchange points for survival, to new revenues predicted from the proposed route between Klamath Falls and Bieber, to auditors with figures that promised timely loan payoffs, to engineers who applauded the natural adaptability of railroad construction in Northern California, to those in the lumber trade who loved the whole idea.

The hearing went on for nine days, with testimony filling many hundreds of pages. The *Seattle Times* called it "one of the epic battles of modern railroading." In the end, the ICC granted the application to build the Inside Gateway, based on its belief in the "benefits of competition."

It's interesting to note that initial reconnaissance surveys for both ends of the Inside Gateway project had begun in February 1929, nine months before the ICC hearing took place. The commencement of that work was either a calculated show of Arthur's fierce determination, an indication of his confidence about the positive outcome of the ICC hearing, his desire to be prepared to move quickly if the hearing was decided in his favor, or perhaps all of the above. It helped that he was able to finance the costly surveys that were, as the building of a railroad line goes, comparatively inexpensive.

T. L. Phillips, Western Pacific's principle assistant engineer at the time, described the Keddie-to-Bieber survey in an article he wrote for *Railway Age* in 1932. The 112-mile route was divided in thirds, with a team of thirty men working on each section. A dozen camps were built. They were considered plush, with electricity and heat, a far cry from the rough camps that had preceded them wherein violent drinking and prostitution were rampant. The terrain being surveyed was mountainous, thick with virgin timber growing out of decomposed lava beds. Most of the project was done by automobile, but saddle horses were used at times, and some of the survey had to be done on foot. Phillips wrote:

The located line was projected on the contoured prelimi-nary maps and from this projection a complete, detailed profile was made, showing ground and grade lines, curvature, drainage openings, bridges, tunnels, and highway crossings, excavation, embankment, and clearing quantities and estimated classifica-tion.... By accurate scaling, careful calculation, and instrumen-tal surveys, the projected line was established on the ground and was fully located by the latter part of October, 1929.

The ICC decision on the application was not forthcoming un-til June 20, 1930. It only took two months for construction con-tracts to be finalized. In a spot so thickly timbered that the men struggled to find a path wide enough to drag the steam shovel into place, the first shovelful of dirt was lifted on August 16, 1930.

Three days before this seminal moment, Arthur had left with Harriet for a vacation in Europe. This information was gleaned from an exchange of letters Arthur had with Mabel Todd, who wrote to him on the letterhead of Camp Mavooshen on Muscongus Bay in Bremen, Maine. Camp Mavooshen is on Hog Island, 15 miles northeast of Boothbay Harbor. Mabel Todd had bought 330-acre Hog Island in 1908, to save it from being clear-cut by the logging industry. Today, Hog Island is an Audubon Camp.

In a letter dated August 9, 1931, Mabel wrote to Arthur about a dream she'd had about him:

When I found you had been to Bar Harbor and not here, I was so disappointed that I spent the whole night following in a dream. It seemed to me it was hours long! Here is the dream: I seemed somehow to be examining all the great halls and corridors and different rooms in a huge capital building. I had several ladies, friends, with me. We very soon came across my old friend Arthur James, dressed in magnificent colours like the costume of a Seminole chief, wonderful horizontal stripes in many gorgeous colors—red and yellow, green, brilliant blue, in a coat like a pajama jacket, and short trousers under a skirt, all dizzying colours. His hands were full of tickets; I said "Arthur, we have come to get tickets for the ball," to which he replied, "Yes, I have them here," and gave me three for my friends.

Then modestly I asked "please may I have two more." "Who for," said Arthur. "Why for David and me," I said. Whereupon he looked tremendously solemn and dignified, and said "I don't know about that, I'll have to see about that." "But," I said, "I have got a good dress, you won't be ashamed of me." But he turned away, to give tickets to the next applicant. For a long time it seemed to me I followed him about, always expecting my tickets, but never getting them. Those in my hand grew very limp and hot, and I got no more.

Suddenly exclaiming "Oh my stomach!" Arthur seized his abdominal protuberance with both hands and fled, where I did not know; but I followed the brilliant colours disappearing through the marble corridors as fast as I could, and examined more corridors than I could possibly count, finally penetrating into the enormous convention hall where presidents are made.

I gave the three tickets to the friends to whom I had prom-
ised them, so I never had any myself. I never found Arthur again.
I was so grieved and disappointed that I woke up.
And the sun was shining into my little window.
So you see, I sometimes think of you!

Given the delivery time of mail from Maine to New York in the 1930s, Arthur's reply dated August 12, 1931, was no doubt written upon receipt:

My Dear Mrs. Todd:
Thank you for your good letter of August 9 and your dream
was certainly an involved one, and I am sorry that my tickets for
the grand ball with its magnificent coloring, myself as a Seminole
Chief and various other appendages, ran out and you did not get
them. However, I don't think you should go to such frivolous
performances and I am glad you woke up even through you were
grieved and disappointed at not being able to play Cinderella.
We went to Bar Harbor arriving at 9:30 pm and sailing at
11 o'clock the next morning simply for the run at sea, and as I
had to be in New York at the beginning of the week could not
stop at your island, although we thought of you as we passed the
entrance to your bay about 60 miles out to sea.
We are sailing for Europe today on the Mauretania for a
short vacation, and will be back about the middle of September.
Very sincerely yours,
(signed) A C James

No announcements had been made about breaking ground for the Inside Gateway, but word got out. A crowd of some 300 people gathered the morning of August 16, 1931, to witness the opening ceremonies. At its peak, construction on the Western Pacific extension involved twenty-seven power shovels and draglines and all the cars, trucks, compressors, machinery and equipment, and men needed to support them.

Clearing the heavily forested territory was a huge job. A total of 10.5 million feet of timber was cut into logs and shipped to lumber mills. It was an extraordinary project. The survey had indicated eleven tunnels would be necessary, but two were eliminated when it was found that blasting and excavating an open cut would do the job. Writing in *Locomotive Engineers Journal* in 1932, James William Fraser described the "big shot" that made one particular tunnel unnecessary. Miners had worked for seventy days digging powder tunnels and "shot pockets" prior to the firing of the blast.

Seven main tunnels, each 1,115 feet long, including cross cuts, 43 pockets and 13 down holes were drilled from the surface. Fifty tons of black powder were tamped into the holes, and an additional two tons of dynamite caps placed for detonators. The pockets were connected by 2,500 feet of wire, then by a field wire to the battery position on the slope some 500 feet above the drilling.

The crowd moved back to the safety zones a quarter mile away. The shot firer leaned his weight on the plunger. An instant later there was a dull, muffled roar and the mountain side became as a living thing. One hundred seventy-five thousand tons of rock, earth, and trees rose in one vast cloud. When the dust settled there was a great scar across the landscape 400-feet long, 140-feet wide, and from 75- to 100-feet deep.

The nine remaining tunnels required for the railroad ranged from 400 to 1,070 feet in length, and they were all built by the same crew. Eight major bridges ranged from 150 to 900 feet in length and from 30 to 225 feet in height. Steel for bridges and materials for track were brought in by rail as the tracks were laid.

Arthur wasn't on hand for this excitement. After his trip to Europe, he'd returned to have a look at the progress of construction, then traveled back east for a week or two of tending to business and also pleasure. The fact that Arthur had "surfaced," that he had become someone who responded in a friendly and articulate way to press inquiries, had elevated him on the media's list of people to watch. That meant the privacy he had treasured and cultivated all his life had been compromised. In early October 1931, when his yacht *Aloha* had a scrape with the passenger steamer that ran between Providence, Rhode Island, and Block Island, 10 miles offshore, it was well publicized. *Aloha* was leaving Newport. The steamer *Sagamore* was inbound. *Aloha* sounded one horn, indicating a pass to starboard. *Sagamore* answered with two horns (a pass to port). Confusion ensued. *Aloha*'s Captain Zarno put the engines full-astern, avoiding a catastrophe, but in the maneuvering, *Aloha*'s bowsprit tore away *Sagamore*'s stern awning, causing considerable fright on the steamer, but no injuries.

The Great Northern extension south from Klamath Falls to Bieber was a less formidable part of the job, but the construction process was similar. What took everyone by surprise was how the project was completed in a few days more than sixteen months. When that first scoop of dirt was lifted in August 1930, engineers estimated the completed line would go into service in the summer of 1932. That both construction teams were rolling into Bieber, California, in early November 1931 was thanks in part to the modern machinery being used—10-yard hydraulic dump excavators, electric tunnel locomotives, and dragline excavators—and to the capability and urgency of the engineers and men on the job.

Little Bieber, population 312 in 2010, is truly in the middle of nowhere. Settled about 1877, the old, classic cow town is located on the banks of the Pit River in the center of an expanse of flat, sandy land of 100 or more square miles, elevation 4,175 feet. Sparse patches of pine grow here and there. The snow-capped Warner Mountains rise on the northeast horizon, some 50 miles distant. The wind from any direction sweeps across downtown Bieber at will, and on November 19, 1931, when the ceremony featuring the driving of a golden spike was to be held—the spike symbolizing the final fastening needed to join the two extensions—it was windy and cold. For the 2,000 people sitting in the bleachers that had been constructed for the occasion, it was tough duty.

Dignitaries were present in abundance, including Ralph Budd; T. M. Schumacher; Harry Adams, president of the Western Pacific; J. S. Pyeatt, president of the Denver & Rio Grande Western; F. E. Williamson, president of the New York Central; J. Cannon, president of the Missouri Pacific; Fred B. Houghton, vice president of the Santa Fe System; and a raft of other railroad executives. There is no indication that Harriet James was in attendance. Arthur's speech was brief. Here it is in its entirety:

Hanging in my office in New York is a lithograph which has been used by the Great Northern as a background for their annual calendar. In a small insert at the bottom is an excellent picture of James J. Hill. Beside this is one of the little locomotives of about 1899, and discernable in the mist and haze in the background is one of the mammoth locomotives of the present day. This illustrates the dream of James J. Hill, the great empire builder.

Today we come here to celebrate the fruition of Mr. Hill's dream and in loving reverence for his memory it is my pleasant duty to drive the golden spike symbolizing the dream which has required more than two generations to accomplish.

We, of this generation, pledge ourselves to use our best endeavors to carry out the dreams of our fathers to make this highway of commerce an efficient aid in helping to develop this great country which we all love so well.

There were a few other speeches, including similarly brief remarks by Ralph Budd, who also praised James J. Hill, saying, "it was his wish and his unending effort to serve these communities in the way that would make the territory most happy, most fruitful, and most prosperous for them." Budd pledged that the Great Northern would "carry on the spirit of the Empire Builder in the service which we bring to you."

Then, without further ado, Arthur stripped off his overcoat and suit jacket. Standing strong against the brisk November day in vest and shirtsleeves, he took the unwieldy 10-pound spike maul that was handed to him, smartly choked up on the handle like a man intending to bunt, and with a series of accurate, shortened strikes, drove home the golden spike. He straightened up, removed his hat and held it toward the heavens. His hoot of exultation triggered the roar of the spectators.

Several songs were written about it. Edward Murphy of San Francisco wrote these new words to "There's a Long, Long Trail A-Winding":

There's a long, long train a-winding
From the land where Bieber lies
Where the golden spike is waiting
To be hammered in the ties

It's not clear who had the idea to use the planks of the bleachers to build a roaring fire against the elements, but soon a teepee of planks had been constructed and the fire was catching hold nicely. No doubt there was hell to pay to the bleacher company, but the aptly named bonfire not only provided much needed warmth but added a cheerful, celebratory touch to the proceedings. The extra added attraction was a train of 100 freight cars carrying Shevlin pine lumber from northern California and Oregon to San Francisco that came rolling through shortly after Arthur had driven the spike. Arthur had organized the train just in case anyone needed a reminder of this new line's value.

The next day, George T. Cameron used his privilege as publisher of the *San Francisco Chronicle* to rave about the Inside Gateway in a column, "What a Few Miles of Rail Do." He wrote about how the Gateway had connected his city to a 13,000-mile network of railroads. "This great gridiron of rails over seven states," Cameron wrote, "tapping as many more and extending into Canada, has been something remote from San Francisco. Yet only 203 miles of new road was necessary to bring it into this city. . . . Between Klamath Falls and Keddie, the Great Northern taps the metropolitan cities of St. Paul, Minneapolis, Winnipeg, Vancouver, Seattle, and Portland. Its network of lines spreads over Minnesota, North and South Dakota, Montana, Idaho, Washington and Oregon, and now penetrates California." Cameron pointed out that through the Great Northern's half-owner-ship of the Chicago, Bur-lington & Quincy, San Francisco was connected to 9,000 more miles of railroad through Wy-oming, Utah, Colora-do, Nebraska, Iowa, Missouri, Kansas, and Illinois.

THE GOLDEN SPIKE IS HAMMERED HOME: ARTHUR CURTISS JAMES, Said to Be the Country's Largest Individual Owners of Railway Stocks, Just After Driving the Last Spike of the New 200-Mile Line Linking the Great Northern and the Western Pacific Systems at Bieber, Cal.

Newspaper writers with a sense of history reminded readers it had been Secretary of War Jefferson Davis who had first initiated sur-veys for a transcontinen-tal railroad as early as 1853. Six survey teams had crossed the United States that year, explor-ing virgin territory and often fighting bloody skirmishes with Na-tive Americans in their quest to find the preferred route. Before the Civil War, no railroad company wanted to risk the immense cost of building cross-country. During the war, when the priority for a transcontinental route became obvious, the federal government decided to back five carriers: Union Pacific; Central Pacific; Atchison, Topeka, & Santa Fe; Southern Pacific; and Northern Pacific. The Pacific Railroad bill, an act aiding the construction of a line from the Missouri River to the Pacific Ocean, was signed into law on July 1, 1862, and the competition had begun.

Those in the travel business were enthusiastic about the new connection to San Francisco. They were quick to point out the many national parks that would be more easily available when passenger service was initiated, including Yellowstone, Glacier, Mount Rainier, Crater Lake, Yosemite, Mesa Verde, Grand Canyon, and Rocky Mountain, and the new recreational possibilities that had been opened up. As it turned out, passenger service on this route would always be secondary to freight.

In the days following the celebration at Bieber, the press had descended on the man who had driven the golden spike. Arthur didn't disappoint them. Unaccustomed as he was to being in the public eye, he took the opportunity to speak out about a few issues that were bothering him, like Prohibition: "It may be an unpopular statement," he told Miller Holland of the *Sacramento Bee*, "but I am of the opinion that modification of prohibition would help materially in bringing back better times. It would not only help revive industries, and give employment to many now idle, but it would halt the terrible wave of lawlessness and crime which has swept the country." As sensible as it was, Arthur's strong, anti-Prohibition stance was not a popular one at the time. But whenever the opportunity arose, Arthur spoke out against what historians have concurred was a "noble experiment" that failed miserably. In 1930, he had donated $25,000 ($375,000 today) to the Association Against Prohibition.

As for the Great Depression, Arthur said: "We mustn't let down. It will be a long pull before conditions are normal. Everyone will have to take their coats off and go to work." As for future financial calamities, Arthur said, "We shouldn't allow drunken speculation to prevail again as we did in 1928."

Railroads continued to be his primary focus: "Railroads will be the backbone of America's transportation system for decades to come. I say this despite the ever-increasing competition of bus and air transport. It will be a long time before either buses or airplanes carry the bulk of the nation's freight."

For all his deference to James J. Hill, and his efforts aimed at fulfilling Hill's transcontinental dream, Arthur was now in control of more railroads and track than Hill—or Harriman or Gould for that matter—had ever commanded. His track holdings were said to be one-seventh of the country's total, or 40,000 miles. And as the *Omaha World-Herald* reported on November 21, 1931, "James is reputed to be the largest holder of railroad stocks in the world."

In fact his railroad securities investments at the time were, in a round figure, $350 million ($6.36 billion today). The James System included the Chicago, Burlington & Quincy out of Chicago, with one prong to Minneapolis, the other to Denver. The Minneapolis prong was carried by the Great Northern and Northern Pacific to Seattle, then south along the Inside Gateway to San Francisco. The Southern Pacific, in which he remained a controlling investor, was a successful competitor in that region. The Denver prong was picked up by the Denver & Rio Grande Western from Denver to Salt Lake City; and the Western Pacific from Salt Lake to Sacramento. The electrified Sacramento-San Francisco Railroad (owned by Arthur) carried the James line into Oakland. "It is good for the territory served," The *New York Post* pointed out, "that [James's] controlling influence is beneficent, as it is more or less. If it were not, that would be a menace to social existence in a quarter of the country's area."

The immense control Arthur had attained, the incredible wealth he had accumulated, seemed to make no difference in how this man comported himself. That *Omaha World-Herald* article cited above, from November 21, 1931, just a couple weeks after Arthur had driven the golden spike in Bieber, was headlined, "Just a Rail Magnate," and was subheaded, "Reputed World's

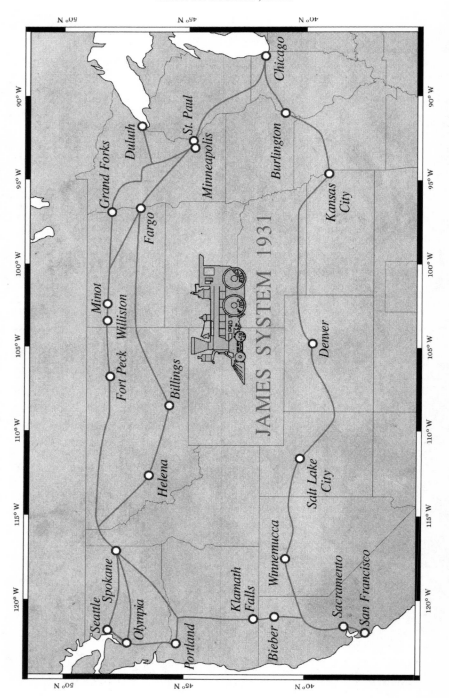

JAMES SYSTEM 1931

Greatest Holder of Stocks Travels Unobtrusively, Alone." It was about Arthur arriving at Los Angeles' Union Station on his way home to New York. The article read:

A middle-aged man of medium stature, his face and tiny red bow tie almost hidden by his full beard, attracted the attention of train men and passengers as he strode briskly through the waiting room of the Union Station Friday evening, puffing in jerks on a half-smoked cigar.

But no one except newspaper men and the Superintendent of the Station recognized the man in the slightly-worn, velvet-collared overcoat as Arthur Curtiss James.

He sent a telegram and then inquired the direction of a mail box.... He was on his way to New York to be with his wife, who is ill, following a nervous breakdown.

After much persuasion, he consented to pose for a photograph outside the Station door where so many people wouldn't be watching. To most questions, he was non-committal as usual.

He showed interest, however, when he was told the stock market had had another sinking spell Friday, and some of the rail issues sank to the lowest point of the decline which began more than two years ago.

Journeying 15 Onward

A nervous breakdown...

Harriet had a history of health issues. She had suffered a bout with typhoid fever after the voyage to Japan on *Coronet* in 1896. In the early 1900s, Arthur's letters to Mabel often indicated that Harriet was indisposed. The twenty-one days Harriet had spent taking the healing waters at Carlsbad back in 1914 had seemed excessive unless there was some ailment in particular that she was trying to cure. There was the appendectomy in 1928. Then there is Joan Malkovich's remark that as a child growing up on the Beacon Hill estate she frequently interacted with Arthur, but hardly ever saw Harriet, leading Joan to consider that poor health might have been the reason for Harriet's reclusiveness. But a nervous breakdown was another matter.

A letter from Arthur to Mabel Todd on December 11, 1931— less than a month after he had driven the golden spike—indicates it was an ongoing problem: "Harriet is going through a regular attack of nervous prostration. The doctors assure me she will eventually come out of it in good shape, but do not give me any idea as to when, so we can form no plans about Florida. Of course

if she gets well, or improves sufficiently we will make a bee line for the south, but it is too early to make any plans yet."

At the time, Mabel was living in Coconut Grove, Florida. The Todds had fallen upon hard times in the 1920s after David had been eased out of his professorship at Amherst. Prior to that (1913) Mabel had suffered a stroke that had ended much of her writing and lecture tours. Arthur had come to the Todds' rescue with both emotional and financial support.

Now Arthur was confronted with his wife's emotional decline.

In the *Boston Medical and Surgical Journal* of 1883, nervous prostration had been defined by Professor Roberts Bartholow, MD, LLD, of the Jefferson Medical College of Philadelphia faculty, as "a state of debility in which nervous derangements predominate. A man... finds himself unequal to his daily tasks; he suffers odd sensations in his head; his digestion is disordered; he is weak; wakefulness, mental depression, and a thousand and one new sensations of strange character and fearful portent are superadded.... Physicians often say 'neurasthenia,' or 'hypochondria' according to their habits or mind or to their training.... Sometimes the condition is called the 'American disease.'"

Dr. Philip Hirsh, a psychiatrist (retired) and, as it happens, a Jefferson alumnus, says terms like neurasthenia and psychasthenia are holdovers from the nineteenth century. "But," Hirsh says, "they all imply anxiousness, weakness (the core issue, the 'asthenia') leading to prostration, and a collection of symptoms including Obsessive Compulsive Disorder, phobias, constant worry, fear, emotional lability, and intractable inability to escape the clutches of a host of other disabling vagaries, all highly resistant to intervention no matter how drastic."

Another letter from Arthur to Mabel on January 18, 1932, just a month after he had written her about Harriet's initial diagnosis, suggests the seriousness of his wife's condition. Harriet was being treated at the James House in Tarrytown, but there is no reason that can be found why she was moved there.

Arthur wrote: "The doctors do not expect her to be anywhere near well before April or May. They are planning to move her to Florida early in February, but she has got to go there as an absolute invalid and Fourway Lodge will be completely closed to visitors or guests of any kind, as the doctors insist that she shall not see anyone outside of her nurses and myself for many weeks to come."

In mid-July that year, Mabel, now in her seventy-third year, wrote to Arthur from Camp Mavooshen, Maine, inquiring about Harriet. Mabel was busy. She had been persuaded to work on an enlarged version of the *Letters of Emily Dickinson*, which she had edited and published in 1894, but her tone indicated she was disappointed in the direction her life had taken:

At the very end of August they take poor David to observe the eclipse [an eclipse of the sun on August 31, 1932]. I do hope he will be happy. The whole country seems to be coming to New Hampshire, and many of his old friends will see him. I am very busy writing some Emily Dickinson stuff, and taking a rest after every morning's work. I do not seem to be of any real use in this world, but still hope on for a return of the original me before I have to journey onward to—? I always think of you with affection.

Cordially yours, Mabel L. Todd

As usual, Arthur responded directly:

I'm glad to tell you that during the last ten days a distinct improvement has taken place in Harriet's condition, and the doctors now feel that the corner has been turned and that convalescence, while sure to be slow, is reasonably certain to be steady.

My social doings are entirely nil. Under doctor's orders, I spend the first three days of the week in Tarrytown with Harriet, and the weekends at Newport, taking up some of my old cronies like Pete [Alford] and John Miller as often as possible. Passing

through a period like this lets one know who one's friends are,
and fortunately, I seem to have a whole lot who stand by me.
With best wishes, believe me,
Very sincerely yours, AC James

Harriet would be an invalid the rest of her life.

Mabel Todd would "journey onward." Another stroke took her life six months later, on October 14, 1932, at Camp Mavooshen. She was survived by her husband David, who would live in an institution until his death at age eighty-four in 1939, and their one child, daughter Millicent (Mrs. Walter Van Dyke Bingham, of New York). Three days later, Mabel's funeral was held in Amherst. Dr. Stanley King, then president of the college, was among the pallbearers. Arthur Curtiss James was not.

* * *

That bit of news about another decline in the value of railroad stocks passed onto Arthur by the journalist who had recognized him at Union Station in Los Angeles, came as no surprise. His comment to the press about the Depression—that it would be a long pull before conditions returned to normal—was the insight of a man whose railroads were struggling to keep tens of thousands of employees on the job. Railroad traffic continued to shrink as factories went out of business. Many railroads went bankrupt.

The Western Pacific felt the pinch, but it continued to upgrade. In 1933, according to Arthur Lloyd, "a six-year program of improvement of the Western Pacific mainline between Salt Lake City and Oakland, California, was completed." This was designed not only to make freight traffic more efficient, but also to improve the Western Pacific's attraction for passengers. It was all for naught. That same year, 25 percent of the US workforce was unemployed. Wages had fallen by a startling 43 percent. Neither the freight nor the passenger traffic was there.

It was, by all accounts, a deteriorating situation that portended dire financial consequences. While Arthur had to be preparing for difficult days, he continued to advance his vision of the future. He knew the Depression couldn't last forever. While the nation's rail system would be taking its lumps along with everything else, Arthur's conviction that the future of the nation's economy was dependent on railroads was unshakable. Regardless of the severe economic collapse the country was suffering, rail had to be ready when the need returned. Like James J. Hill before him, Arthur believed in testing and assessing his own product. For many years Arthur's personal goal had been to log 50,000 miles a year on his passenger trains. He continued to advance his campaign for faster passenger service, saying that could be accomplished in part by the manufacture of lighter equipment. In 1933 he wrote to D. A. Steel, then associate editor of *Railway Age* magazine: "It is my personal belief that the Century of Progress Exposition in Chicago will be a splendid eye-opener for some railroad men, particularly along the lines of reducing weights of passenger cars. The trend is already in that direction for the dead weight per passenger on the Royal Scot in England in just about half what it is on first-class American trains. The Pullman company is evidently alive to this situation and its new lightweight car and streamline design is the beginning of a radical change in our ideas in this country."

No question Arthur was right about the future look of railroads. But before such progress could be enjoyed, there was the matter of surviving the Depression, or to use the more clinical term used by economists, the "economic contraction" that had started in October 1929. "Short-term" had already amounted to several years, with more to come. On May 1, 1935, the Western Pacific had defaulted on its bond interest. The Reconstruction Finance Corporation (RFC), which had loaned several million dollars to the Western Pacific in hopes of preventing such a default, immediately called for a reorganization plan to be submitted by the officers of the company.

The RFC had been created by an Act of Congress approved by President Herbert Hoover at the beginning of 1932. It was designed to restore confidence in the banking system, which was in a shambles. The RFC made loans to banks, large businesses like railroads, and, on occasion, to promising projects that were providing jobs, like $3.5 million ($64 million today) to the Dotsero Cutoff that was being built in Colorado. By being charged with mitigating problems with the economy, and by being given generous funds to do so, the RFC was essentially handed the power to make national policy. As James Butkiewicz, professor of economics at the University of Delaware, has written about the RFC on EH.net: "While the original objective of the RFC was to help banks, railroads were assisted because many banks owned railroad bonds, which had declined in value, because railroads had suffered a decline in their business. If railroads recovered, the increase or appreciation of bond prices would improve the financial condition of the banks holding these bonds."

Of several railroads that had been asked for reorganization plans, the Western Pacific was the first to deliver. Its plan, reported in the *New York Times* on June 23, 1935, was to "cut down fixed interest charges by two thirds," to $1.081 million ($20 million today). Western Pacific said that would be accomplished through recapitalization, which would increase the par value of bond issues from $49 million ($890 million today) to $70 million ($1.3 billion today).

That reorganization plan, which also needed to be approved by the ICC because it was for a railroad, was not accepted by the RFC. It would be three years, four different plans—one of which was written by Chairman James himself—and two heart attacks, before a Western Pacific plan would be accepted by the RFC and the ICC. In fact, the plan for Western Pacific reorganization that was finally accepted was written by the ICC. The extreme nature of it created a ripple of anxiety throughout the rail and financial worlds. But the Federal Bankruptcy Act of 1933 had given the ICC power to supervise or rewrite these organization plans, after which railroads would be allowed to continue operating with their debts temporarily in limbo.

The problem was that, since 1929, Western Pacific had not earned enough to cover its fixed charges. That did not bother Arthur, who had apparently been willing to make up the annual difference of several million dollars. In a petition filed by Western Pacific with the Northern District Court of California, Southern Division, at the time of Western Pacific's failure to meet its bond interest payments, four creditors were listed. One was the A. C. James Company, whose loans of $5 million were double those of the Railroad Credit Corporation, and nearly double those of the RFC. Arthur knew Western Pacific was being well-managed, and was simply slogging through the Depression as best it could. He knew when financial stability returned, the railroad would regain its strength.

Perhaps ICC overseers had chosen to temporarily overlook this unusual arrangement wherein the controlling stockholder would double as the principle creditor, but when Western Pacific had defaulted on paying its bond interest, the ICC took action. The question is why, if Arthur was meeting the annual fixed charges himself, did he stop? Perhaps he too thought it was time to reorganize. Or perhaps the ICC had let him know that enough was enough.

The plan finally written by the ICC reduced Western Pacific's capitalization by 30 percent and reduced fixed charges by a whopping 85 percent, from more than $3.5 million to around $500,000. The ICC accomplished this by wiping out the equity of stockholders and claims of unsecured creditors, making them bear most of the loss. As owner of 40 percent of Western Pacific stock, Arthur bore the brunt of the ICC plan. In round numbers, it cost him $30 million ($530 million today).

In its coverage of the ICC's harsh action, *Time* magazine, October 1, 1938, did not hold back: "This sort of forthright organization is almost unprecedented in US railroad history," *Time* noted, going on to report that "Western Pacific was the fourth Class I railroad shoved through the wringer in four months."

But *Time* gave the ICC the last word: "If," a statement issued by the ICC read, "reorganization is to be successful, the capital structure of the reorganized company must be realistically related to its actual earning power."

According to G. H. Kneiss, in his article about Western Pacific's first fifty years, the $18 million program started by Arthur to restore the railroad to first-class condition in the 1920s, when he took control, had been derailed by the Depression. "In 1936," Kneiss writes, "a three-year rehabilitation program was initiated with RFC funds. It was actually a delayed continuation of the James plan." That plan included the installation of more-durable, creosoted ties and heavier-weight rails; the addition of more powerful locomotives, air-conditioned passenger cars, and improved freight cars; the establishment of shops in the stations; and the rebuilding of locomotive turntables to handle larger capacity.

In 1935, the writer Arthur D. Howden Smith began a series of articles in the *Philadelphia Record* called "Men Who Run America," a series that included Arthur Curtiss James. The articles would be compiled into a book by the same name, the subtitle of which was *A Study of the Capitalistic System and Its Trends Based on Thirty Case Histories*. Smith's introduction has an all-too-familiar ring for our twenty-first-century audience, some eighty-two years later: "It constitutes the first intelligent attempt to trace the outstanding economic phenomenon of the past generation: the abnormal concentration of power over vested wealth in the hands of a dramatically limited number of persons. . . . Capitalism allowed to run wild can be as dangerous to the fabric of a democracy as any other system."

In the prologue of the book, Smith explained how his initial list of 50,000 nominees was reduced to 1,500, then to a "master list" of 300, before the final cut to 30 was made. "They were singled out as typical of various phases of capitalism, good, bad, and in between," Smith wrote. "The only other touchstone employed was that each should represent the element of power, in a national sense, rather than mere wealth."

It is quickly evident that Arthur D. Howden Smith considered Arthur Curtiss James to be one of the good ones. Referencing Arthur's remarks upon his purchase of control of Western Pacific in 1926, in which he praised the quality of the territory served by the railroad, and stated his belief "in California and the

MEN WHO RUN AMERICA

ARTHUR C. JAMES

Arthur C. James Is Unsung King of Western Rails

One of 10 Richest in U. S. — Also Sea Skipper

By ARTHUR D. HOWDEN SMITH

Copyright, 1985, by New York Post, Inc.

You hear a lot about the Van Sweringens. You hear very little about Arthur Curtiss James. Yet he is said to be the largest individual owner of railroad securities in America, and he is the last man in our generation to create what is called a "railroad empire."

James is a kindly sort of person, with a reddish beard gone gray, and quizzical eyes behind glasses. He represents the third generation of a family that has possessed wealth and yet has generally managed to dodge publicity. His grandfather was one Daniel James, who founded in 1828 what is now the Phelps-Dodge Corporation, lords of copper, and popularly identified with the names it bears—the Jameses have always managed to get along without thrusting the names forward.

His father, D. Willis James, became a partner in this firm in 1848, and made a reputation as one of the outstanding metallurgical pioneers of the the Southwest.

ARTHUR CURTISS JAMES

cutoff which saved 170 miles or more on the route to the Coast.

The setup was: the Burlington from Chicago to Denver, the Denver & Rio Grande from Denver to

Pacific and other Western railroads, and have now added to my railroad interests the holding of Western Pacific. I have entire confidence in the ability of the territory served by the Western Pacific to support an independent competing system which shall have for its sole objective the upbuilding of the territory served by it. I believe in California and the Great West, and shall do my utmost to co-operate with the Western Pacific management in serving the public and so helping to build up the entire region through which it passes."

He Doesn't Strut

The above may be accepted as the James creed in public relations, his conception of his responsibility to the public for the use he makes of his millions, and as such it is an interesting exposition of capitalistic philosophy at its best. Egocentric and not egotistical. And startling in its revelation of the power one man may obtain over the lives of millions

Great West," Smith had this to say: "Those remarks may be accepted as James's creed in public relations, his conception of his responsibility to the public for the use he makes of his millions, and as such it is an interesting exposition of capitalistic philosophy at its best." Smith went on to say this about Arthur:

He has to the fullest extent the ideal of what might be called "the complete capitalist," that is, service of personal wealth... he wants to put what he has to work for the benefit of others.... Without any of the strutting which characterized the performances of Hill, Harriman, the Goulds, and Commodore Vanderbilt, he has mobi-

lized one of the country's principle transportation blocs.... He is probably one of the 10 or 12 richest men in America... his Phelps Dodge holdings by themselves, it is fairly certain, would entitle him to that description. His railroad holdings are potentially richer, allowing for the decrease in values which has accumulated since 1929. With a return of prosperity, they should increase by hundreds of millions.

It was not until 1944, three years after Arthur's death, that the courts would finally approved the stringent ICC reorganization plan. When Arthur had bought controlling interest in the Western Pacific in 1926, the stock was listed at $38 a share. During the height of the Depression, it had sunk as low as 56 cents. Thanks to the boom of business stimulated by World War II, by mid-1945 Western Pacific stock had grown to $43 a share. A year later it would crest at $53.

* * *

The heart attacks were Arthur's. Rare footage of the skipper taken aboard *Aloha* in the summer of 1934 depicts a robust older salt puffing happily on a cigar. On September 1, 1935, when work had begun on the second reorganization plan, Arthur had suffered his first seizure. There is no indication that the two were related, but stress had to be a factor. It's likely that Arthur had his first heart attack in Newport, since sailing there is excellent in the fall.

The archives of Amherst College contain letters from Arthur's longtime associate, a man named William W. Carman, who had worked for Arthur's father, as well as letters from Arthur to George Plimpton, a textbook publisher who was then president of Amherst's board of trustees. Letters from both men were also written to Margaret Hitchcock, who was then Amherst's curator of memorabilia. Arthur did not know "Peggy" Hitchcock, whose family had served Amherst over three generations. But he obviously felt comfortable writing to her. So did Carman, who wrote on September 25, 1935, saying "the doctors have issued strict orders that Mr. James is to be kept from all visitors and correspondence."

Early in November 1935, Carman wrote: "Mr. James continues to improve... but he is still not out of the woods.... Doctors are hopeful that he will come through this without any permanent injury to his heart, but it is going to be a very long, drawn-out convalescence."

A month later Arthur had been moved to New York, presumably to be closer to better medical care. On December 2, 1935, he wrote to Peggy Hitchcock: "I was allowed out of the hospital... now practically out of the woods. Write to 39 East 69th Street as I am not allowed to go to the office."

As soon as he was sufficiently recovered, on January 25, 1936, he traveled by train to Fourway Lodge in Coconut Grove, Florida. In February he suffered his second attack.

In mid-March he wrote Peggy:

It is now just a month since I had my second heart attack, and I am again using my crutches to a small extent and my wheel chair in the afternoon, but I have not yet graduated to the point where I was before when they let me wash my face and clean my own teeth.... Dr. Frissell reported that my heart was doing as well as could be expected and that now the only trouble that he can see is the swelling of my feet.

This headline from the *Newport Mercury and Weekly News*, on April 24, 1936, said as much as any folder of medical reports about Arthur's prognosis following his heart ailments: "*Aloha* May Be Laid Up This Summer—Present Plans Indicate James's Houseboat *Lanai* Will Be Used By Family." The short news item on page eight of the *Mercury* reported that while *Aloha* was in New York, having undergone a twenty-five-year overhaul as required by marine insurance, *Lanai* was en route from Miami to Newport. This was the second houseboat designed by Trumpy named *Lanai*, which Arthur and Harriet had acquired in 1928 for use in Biscayne Bay. At 85 feet overall, this yacht was 15 feet longer, and had more powerful engines than the first *Lanai*.

The summer of 1936, Arthur and Harriet were back in Newport. Both were ailing. That summer, *Aloha* had remained tied up to J. K. Sullivan's dock at the end of Pelham Street in Newport, where Arthur had a sail loft. (That building would become the Black Pearl Restaurant in 1967.) Arthur did go for a cruise that summer, but on a steamship.

Arthur spent a lot of time thinking about *Aloha*, namely what would become of his pride and joy. His epitaph for the first *Aloha*, the brigantine, had been brief, matter of fact. But this boat was different, a member of the family for more than two decades. He noted he had put 60,000 miles under his famous bark's keel, including the world cruise in 1921. Once he'd driven her from Sandy Hook, at the entrance of New York Harbor, to Gibraltar in a bit more than sixteen days. These days, like so many other possessions, boats come and go. Owners tend to be fickle. New designs catch the eye, technological wrinkles promise to make life more comfortable aboard, or more fun. Trading up, or even sideways, is easy to do in an active, mass market. In the 1930s and on into the 1960s, boats' names were as solidly linked with their owners as Daimler is linked with Benz. During those years, and before, the family vessel was traditionally passed on and sailed with pride by successive generations. One would sooner trade in the family dog than give up the handsome schooner, the robust yawl, or even the treasured little day-sailer.

In his reduced physical condition, Arthur had to know the glorious days of him putting the massive *Aloha* through its rigorous paces were done. His master's certificate was no longer posted in the wheelhouse because he had been unable to take the physical required for renewal. His captain's certificate was posted, which was intolerable, unacceptable. For a man with his passion for the sea, losing control of *Aloha* had to be devastating.

One of his first thoughts was to scuttle the yacht, take her out into very deep water and sink her. He was certainly not the first man to have such a dire, albeit romantic, thought about a love object, although the advanced degree of obsession required to carry out such an extreme act had not heretofore been a characteristic of Arthur. Knowing that he was considering such an end for the yacht provides new insight into what a toll it must have extracted from Arthur to share *Aloha* with the US Navy. To sink her would have been to confirm he could not abide the thought of anyone else sailing and possibly enjoying her. And yet, in the interest of national defense, he had allowed her many charms to be violated with gray paint from stem to stern, her name changed to a number, herself displayed as a target for any enemy submarines on the prowl (like *U-53* that had so boldly visited Newport in 1916), and run by a gang of military personnel who treated the yacht without respect for her exalted lineage. And don't forget, after the navy spent months painstakingly removing all that gray paint and putting *Aloha* back in shape for Arthur, he had put her in the yard for several more months to bring her up to his lofty standard of what was proper.

It was said there were one or two wealthy gentlemen who would have been interested in acquiring *Aloha*, but of course the money involved was not a consideration for Arthur. And who among those pretenders would have had both the means and the taste required for keeping her in the manner to which she had grown accustomed, the manner that she deserved? The yacht had recently been overhauled. She was fit, in Bristol condition. Better to sink her in her prime than let her languish and deteriorate under anything less than Arthur's loving care.

But cooler heads prevailed. One can only guess who those cooler heads might have been. Harriet? Pete Alford, Arthur's longtime friend from Amherst days and a regular aboard *Aloha*? The captain and officers of the yacht? John Matheson, another regular? In any case, Arthur recanted, made the decision to have the art removed—the carved panels and other work by von Rydingsvärd—gather all the books and many personal items, many of which are at Mystic Seaport Museum, and have *Aloha* broken up for her metal.

In Newport, where *Aloha* had been as much of a fixture in the harbor as Ida Lewis Light, news of the yacht's impending demise was greeted with shock, and sadness. "She has been part of us over those years," the *Newport Mercury* writer eulogized, speaking for this seafaring town that was silently sharing Arthur's grief: "just as she has been part of the life of her owner, Arthur Curtiss James. Now as much as we regret to learn of her passing, we can bear with him in his decision to allow her to sail no more. . . . She will be missed from her moorings in Brenton Cove in summer months, and from her berth at the foot of Pelham Street in winter. Where else will a fir tree be hoisted to a mast top as a symbol of Christmas among seafaring men in the future?"

On Friday, October 16, 1937, the *Mercury* headline read, "Yacht *Aloha* Towed to Fall River." The article explained that Arthur had sold *Aloha* to the General Scrap Iron Company of Providence and Fall River. It did not mention the price—a reported $25,000 ($430,000 today). The company had sent a tugboat down to pick up the yacht. A *Mercury* reporter happened to be crossing the Mount Hope Bridge, which joins Aquidneck Island (where Newport is located) with the mainland, as *Aloha* approached under tow. He stopped his car to watch the bark's masts slip under the bridge with barely two feet of clearance. The *Mercury* also ran this letter from Newport resident Lewis Ledoux:

When the yacht Aloha *was backed out of her berth at J. K.'s dock yesterday, there was something of sadness about it all. The once pride of the Atlantic going on her last trip on the towline. Her majestic masts seemed so rigid and bare, the absence of her yards and furled canvas, made one feel peculiar and sad. All will miss* Aloha, *but her owner, Commodore Arthur Curtiss James, gives up the greatest yacht he ever possessed, and the greatest ever afloat. Farewell,* Aloha.

His great yacht might have been gone, but only death itself can end lust for the sea among those who are stricken. Though his days aboard even the most accommodating vessel were numbered, Arthur had to have a capable yacht standing by. The first of the following year, he bought a 126-foot motor yacht designed by Cox & Stevens, a lovely vessel palatially finished. He called it *Aloha Li'i*, or "tiny" *Aloha*. The yacht had been built in 1931 by the Defoe Shipbuilding Company in Bay City, Michigan. It was much larger and a lot more comfortable than the 50-foot runabout *Mauna Loa*, and with a 16-knot cruising speed considerably faster than either of the houseboats named *Lanai*. *Li'i* was also a beauty, with a nearly plumb bow, a subtle sheer line that complemented the yacht's low profile, and a handsome, tapered overhang at the stern.

No logs or other documents can be found to indicate that Arthur made any cruises on his new yacht the summer of 1938. But for a sailor, just having a vessel of choice standing by is reassuring, be it a dinghy or a gold-plater.

The letters to Peggy Hitchcock continued. In September 1938 Arthur wrote from Newport: "I was not able to go to the tennis as there are too many stairs to be negotiated." He also wrote about a complication, an encounter he'd had with fleas, of all things: "The bites turned out to be pretty bad. The doctors refuse to let me go to Florida on Friday as I anticipated, but now expect to leave Monday."

A month later, he wrote Peggy from Fourway Lodge: "We got down here very comfortably, Mrs. James standing the trip about as well as usual, and I am gradually improving. I can now get on my left slipper and can walk a few steps without too much discomfort."

The two heart attacks had taken their toll. At age seventy-two, Arthur was in decline, and he knew it. On November 4, 1939, he resigned his position as chairman of the board and a director of the Western Pacific Railroad, having served in those capacities for thirteen years. "In taking this action," *Railway Age* reported, "Mr.

James explained that this was merely one of a series of such resignations from other companies in which he is deeply interested, owing to his desire to lighten the burden of business activities, adding that he has not disposed of any part of his investment in the Western Pacific, and has no intention in doing so." Arthur's resignation would become effective on December 31, 1939.

A few weeks after he resigned, Arthur wrote to Peggy, his confidential pen pal at Amherst whom he had never met. "I arrived in Miami a week ago yesterday. . . . Since arrival have been pretty badly knocked out, but apparently have gotten through and am now in about the same condition as usual."

The "same condition" was not a very active one, but Arthur enjoyed the balmy Florida weather, and he spent some time on the new motor yacht. He also maintained an interest in his portfolio of philanthropies, including small additions he made that included a fellowship for a member of Amherst's class of 1940. The *Springfield Union* of March 14, 1940, elaborated: "A member of the class interested in social work will receive a fellowship of $500 [$9,000 today] through the generosity of Arthur Curtiss James, '89, for a year of study and work in New York City. The fellowship requires that the recipient shall live and work in the Christadora Settlement House... and shall enroll in at least two of the courses offered by the New York School of Social Work."

In the spring of 1941, Arthur and Harriet were at home at 39 East 69th Street in New York. On May 15, Harriet suffered a heart attack and passed away. While her demise had not been unexpected, considering that she had been incapacitated and bedridden for nearly ten years, the end of life never fails to stun.

The death of his wife had a debilitating effect on Arthur. In a letter to Peggy Hitchcock on May 21, 1941, Talbot Lewis, an office-mate of Arthur's at Phelps Dodge, reported: "I regret to tell you that Mr. James is not being allowed to see his friends."

A few days later Arthur was admitted to Harkness Pavilion at Columbia Presbyterian Hospital. He passed away a week later, on June 4, 1941, just twenty days after Harriet. His cause of death was listed as pneumonia. At his deathbed was William Carman; Harriet's niece, Harriet DeForest Manice and her husband William; and a friend, Mrs. Marshall Price.

MRS. JAMES LEFT FUND FOR CHARITY

Christodora House and Y. W. C. A. Get $100,000 Each Under Terms of Her Will

SMITH COLLEGE $50,000

Sister, Mrs. Ferry, and Niece, Harriet Manice, Receive $700,000 Each

Mrs. Harriet Parsons James, wife of Arthur Curtiss James, New York industrialist, who died last Thursday at her home, 39 East Sixty-ninth Street, after an illness of ten years, named as her principal legatees her sister, Mrs. E. Hayward Ferry of 944 Fifth Avenue, and her niece, Harriet F. Manice of Old Westbury. L. I.

According to the *Springfield Union*, Harriet left an estate will of $2.7 million ($45.8 million today). She left substantial gifts to several institutions, schools, municipalities, and charities, and a total of more than half a million (today's dollars) to various employees. She left the Northampton house to her sister, Mrs. Hayward Ferry, along with a substantial trust. Mrs. Ferry, along with Harriet DeForest Manice, were named to share "equal residuary interests," and to receive $700,000 each ($11.5 million today).

That was fortunate for Harriet Manice, because alongside Edward James, Harriet was the other close relative whom Arthur had deleted from his will. In the absence of children,

Harriet James's niece, Harriet DeForest Manice, was written out of Arthur's will for being openly critical about his womanizing.

niece Harriet was a logical heir apparent, but Arthur had taken umbrage at her outspokenness about his behavior with women. Many years later, Joan Malkovich was not all that surprised to learn about that. "So he kept her out of the will," Joan said. "That's interesting. What a rascal."

When Newport resident Robert Manice contemplated that situation, he shook his head. "Shucks," he said, "that's too bad, wouldn't it have been nice! My grandmother Harriet was quite righteous about his womanizing, his interest in the ladies, a roaming eye, if you will. He had companionship, I'm sure, and I think for whatever reason she couldn't help it, she had to get it out. His message to my grandmother was, I'm not going to leave you anything. I'm going to disinherit you."

The newspaper obituaries were lengthy and complimentary. "Industrialist, One of Nation's Richest Men, Victim of Pneumonia—Gave Millions to Charity—Liberal in Politics, He Fought Prohibition—Yachting His Favorite Pastime" read the *New York Times* headline. Glowing tributes mixed with heartfelt sadness came from Amherst, Hampton, Union Theological Seminary, and the many other organizations whose boards of directors Arthur had graced. Funeral services were held at the church Arthur had attended and supported, the First Presbyterian Church on Fifth Avenue at 12th Street in Manhattan. The Reverend Henry Sloane Coffin, president of Union Theological Seminary, and moderator of the Presbyterian Church in the United States—and at the time the most prestigious minister in the country, according to the cover of *Time*, November 15, 1926—offered an eloquent prayer for Arthur Curtiss James during the service. Coffin prayed, in part:

We praise Thee for his fidelity in the discharge of a weighty trust; for his modesty who sought no praise from man; for his single-mindedness who wished only to be wisely useful; for his outgoing sympathies and his stalwart devotion to things true, just, and honorable... for his readiness to spend and be spent in causes which enlisted his enthusiasm; for his dedication to himself and to Thy church, and for all that he has meant as comrade and fellow worker to those at his side through the years. Rise up, we humbly beseech Thee, in the oncoming generation of men of like public spirit and Christian consecration to carry forward the institutions which he saved and to guide and strengthen Thy church with like sense of obligation.... Grant us joy for him in his relief from confining weakness, and thankfulness for a well-fought fight and a life-work well done.

Arthur was buried at Green-Wood Cemetery in Brooklyn, New York, a 478-acre Revolutionary War historic site that was turned into a cemetery in 1838. It has become a final resting place for many notable figures from all walks of life. Arthur's parents, Daniel Willis James and Ellen Stebbins Curtiss James, had been buried there along with their first son, Daniel Willis Jr., who was born three years before Arthur. The boy had died at age ten months for unknown reasons. Arthur had placed a monument on the James plot in 1907, when his father died. In the early 1920s, Arthur had commissioned a redesign of the monument by the Boston architectural firm of Allen & Collens, the firm that had designed the Union Theological Seminary, as well as Arthur's house on East 69th Street. The monument is semicircular, 25 feet across. A 30-foot Corinthian column, with the word "JAMES" carved into its base, rises from the center. On the flat side of the monument's layout is seating, backed by a thick hedge of privet. On the curved side are four sarcophagi, with the initials DWJ / DWJ Jr., ESC, ACJ, and HEP carved into the marble tops.

Legacy

Arthur Curtiss James left an estate of $35.5 million, $603 million in today's dollars. Nearly four-fifths of the estate was set aside for the creation of the James Foundation, the income from which was to be used "to aid charitable, religious, and educational institutions." One-tenth of his estate was directed to the United States Trust Company, executor of Harriet James's estate, with directions that it be distributed as part of her personal estate under the terms of her will. It seems that, after tax appraisal, Harriet's charitable bequests had exceeded her funds. Eighteen cousins had shared in this bequest from Arthur.

In a codicil to his will, Arthur singled out Margaret and Marshall Price of Miami, "Two friends," he wrote, "who have meant much to me in the difficult later years of my life. They have shown me a self-sacrificing and thoughtful helpness which is given to few men. Even before the beginnings of my own illness they gave me comfort and support beyond all measure, and during the worry of my wife's illness. I wish to express the deep gratitude I feel for them, and, as a symbol of this gratitude and affection rather than for any pecuniary value represented, I give and bequeath [to them] all my personal jewelry." In addition, he left the Prices $50,000. He left similar financial legacies to several friends, business associates, and relatives, including Pete Alford, and William Carman. More than 100 of his employees who had been with him for five years or more, including *Aloha* crewmen, received cash or annuities. And Harriet's niece, Harriet DeForest Manice, wasn't totally forgotten. While not granted the role of heiress, Harriet was left $150,000.

Arthur's charge to the James Foundation, initially chaired by William Carman, which Arthur specified would be "organized for a term of twenty-five years," was clear: "I desire that said foundation apply each year a sum equal to approximately one-half of the income of the principle funds... to such ends, and that such sum be divided into twenty-eight equal shares and distributed as follows:"

Three shares to Union Theological Seminary.

Two shares each to Hampton Normal and Agricultural Institute [now Hampton University]; The American Board of Commissioners for Foreign Missions; Christadora House; The First Presbyterian Church (Manhattan); the Children's Aid Society; Amherst College; Metropolitan Museum of Art; the Presbyterian Hospital; the American Seamen's Friend Society.

One share each to The Board of Home Missions of the Presbyterian Church; the Newport R.I. Hospital; the New York Public Library; the Tuskegee Normal and Industrial Institute; the American Museum of Natural History.

One-half share each to the American University of Beirut, Syria; Society for the Promotion of the Gospel Among Seaman of the Port of New York.

Having listed those in line for annual gifts, Arthur added this: "Nothing herein contained is intended to limit or control the authority of the board of directors... to discontinue distributions to any of the institutions hereinabove specified." The statement clearly reflected Arthur's confidence in the foundation's board to do the right thing: to either drop or add institutions as they saw fit. It was so like Arthur to specify that the board should number five members; to say each should be chosen from the directors of his three private companies—A. C. James Company, Curtiss Southwestern Corporation, and Curtiss Securities Company; to actually name the five initial board members; to set out general guidelines; and then to rely on these men to make good decisions on his behalf. It was an approach that had worked well for him all his life, and it worked again with the foundation. In 1943, the foundation purchased the bonds held by the Western Pacific Railroad Corporation, the holding company for the railroad. As Henry Anderson writes in his monograph, "The executors rationale was that the Foundation, rather than the legatees, would be in a more secure position to preserve potential value of the debt instruments by riding out the revival of the Western Pacific, and therefore best insure they would ultimately have the values that Arthur Curtiss James had envisioned." As we have seen, just a year later Western Pacific stock would hit new highs.

Ten years later, in May of 1951, the James Foundation board reported that it had distributed a total of $12 million. The foundation's assets at the time were $31.276 million. William Carman died in 1952. Robert Coulsen, one of the original trustees and an executor of the James estate, replaced Carman as president at that time.

By 1964, when it came time to dissolve the foundation by making a final disbursement, the assets had soared to $96.35 million ($776 million today), thanks in part to inflation, and even more to a productive investment strategy. The foundation reported that since its inception in 1941, it had made grants of more than $42 million. In a statement to the *New York Times*, Donald McKinnon, who was president of the foundation at the time, singled out early investments in IBM and American Natural Gas as reasons for the Foundation's ability to issue so many generous grants.

The final disbursement was shared among ninety-two recipients. In its final report, published in 1965, the board wrote:

"With the broad discretionary powers granted to them by Mr. James, the Trustees endeavored to effectuate what they believed would have been his wishes and objectives in the light of current conditions in a changing world.... The Trustees believe that Mr. James will be remembered as a humanitarian whose deeds rather than his words were his contribution to society." The grants ranged from $15 thousand to $5.5 million. Institutions receiving a million dollars or more were:

American Museum of Natural History – $2,728,635
American University of Beirut – $1,250,000
Amherst College – $3,500,000
National Missions of the United Presbyterian Church – $1,000,000
The Boy's Club of New York – $1,000,000
Brown University – $2,500,000
Catholic Charities of the Archdiocese of New York – $1,466,209
Children's Aid Society, New York – $3,731,347
Columbia University – $3,000,000
Cornell University – $2,500,000
Dartmouth College – $2,500,000
Federation of Jewish Philanthropies, New York – $1,466,209
Federation of Protestant Welfare Agencies, New York – $1,466,209
Hampton Institute – $3,000,000
Harvard University – $4,000,000
Lincoln Center for the Performing Arts – $1,300,000
Menninger Foundation – $1,000,000
Metropolitan Museum of Art – $3,500,000
Mt. Sinai Hospital, New York – $1,250,000
Society of the New York Hospital – $2,000,000
New York Public Library – $2,572,503
New York University – $1,500,000
Newport Hospital, Newport, Rhode Island – $1,500,000
University of Pennsylvania – $1,500,000
Presbyterian Hospital, New York – $4,000,000
Theological Seminary of the Presbyterian Church – $1,000,000
Princeton University – $2,500,000
Roosevelt Hospital, New York – $1,000,000
St. Luke's Hospital, New York – $1,500,000
Salvation Army, New York – $1,000,000
Seamen's Church Institute, New York – $1,000,000
Tuskegee Institute – $2,500,000
Union Theological Seminary, New York – $5,502,981
United Church Board for World Ministries – $2,500,000
Yale University – $3,000,000

In many cases, funds to colleges were earmarked for their medical schools. Also, the following additional colleges received an average of $500,000 each: Barnard, Berea, Bowdoin, Bryn Mawr, Colgate, Cooper Union, Episcopal Theological School, Haverford, Fordham, Johns Hopkins, Lehigh, Mount Holyoke,

Portrait of Arthur Curtiss James in Amherst's chapel

Polytechnic Institute of Brooklyn, Pratt Institute, Radcliffe, Protestant Episcopal Theological Seminary in Virginia, Smith, Swarthmore, Trinity, Union, Vassar, Wellesley, Wesleyan, and Williams.

Talk about gifts that keep on giving. Yale provides the best example, since that university is habitually ranked among the top managers of academic endowment funds. In 1964, the James Foundation's gift of $3 million to Yale was divided in four parts: $500,000 to the medical school; $500,000 to the divinity school; $1.75 million to the college; and $250,000 to the law school. Today's inflated value of $500,000 in 1964 is $4 million. But the current principle value of the gifts to the medical and divinity schools is currently three or four times larger than that. Each of them produces interest of more than a half a million annually. The $1.75 million that was given to the college in 1964 is currently worth around $45 million, and produces around $2 million annually, all thanks to conservative management and a very successful investment policy. Arthur would be extremely pleased to know that his money is still contributing to the higher education of doctors, medical researchers, theologians, engineers, scientists, and teachers.

It's difficult to imagine the amount of possessions involved—art, books, furnishings, and the trinkets—from five gorgeously appointed homes. In all the towns and cities where the Jameses' houses were located, literally hundreds of small, often insignificant items from the houses are gathering dust in attics or sitting forgotten on many mantelpieces, and tables. That's especially true in Newport, because Beacon Hill House had sat dormant for so many years, and because *Aloha* was broken up nearby in Fall River, Massachusetts.

In New York, Parke-Bernet Galleries conducted a three-day sale of the artistic contents of 39 East 69th Street. The sale was held at the mansion, and it brought in a total of $45,834 ($800,000 today). It involved paintings, Gothic tapestries, Gothic and Renaissance sculpture pieces, furniture, silver, and carpets. Highlights of the sale were a Kirman cypress carpet that was purchased for $1,300 ($22,000 today); and a late-fourteenth-century sculptured-marble Spanish effigy of an armored knight for $800 ($13,500 today).

The Wounded Bunkie by Frederic Remington

The Parke-Bernet catalog, *Arthur Curtiss James Art Collection*, holds only one surprise other than the expected Persian carpets, eighteenth-century European furniture, Chinese carpets and porcelains, English silver, and British paintings. Like other wealthy Americans living in the Gilded Age, the Jameses had bought from the best galleries and shops, and the most important international dealers. Some questions will never be answered. Was the collection something the couple developed together? Did they have agents acting on their authority? But it is tempting to contemplate what the collection would bring on today's market. The Gothic tapestries alone, mostly from Brussels and all from the fifteenth century, would surely bring astronomical sums. Two of them now hang in the Musée de Cluny in Paris, along with other treasures from the Middle Ages.

Only eight of the forty artworks in the catalog were by Americans. But the sculpture, *The Wounded Bunkie* by Frederic Remington (1896)—this is the surprise. The bronze shows two

US Cavalry soldiers on horseback, galloping away from unseen pursuers. One soldier is wounded, unsteady in his saddle. The other props up his bunkmate as the two men gallop for their lives. It was Remington's second sculpture. Fourteen copies of *The Wounded Bunkie* were sand-cast during the artist's lifetime. Arthur had purchased number four.

The Wounded Bunkie is a compelling piece of work. As he manages his flying steed and steadies his distressed friend, the uninjured rider casts a wary look back at his pursuers. The two horses look frantic. It helps that the frozen, anxious moment of Remington's horses and riders is suspended, anchored lightly to the ground by only parts of two hooves. One simply cannot look at this piece and look away. To look is to become involved. The viewer finds himself staring, anxious, pulling for these soldiers who are in obvious peril. It is a very Kiplingesque moment, bringing to mind those lines from the poet's "The Ballad of East and West," as the colonel's men contemplate the danger of going after Kamal, who has stolen the colonel's mare: "There is rock to the left, and rock to the right, and low leaf thorn between, and you may hear a breech bolt snick, where never a man is seen."

Arthur may or may not have thought about Kipling, but for sure this Remington piece had to recall for him the early exploits of his old friend and associate James Douglas, the chemist hired by his father to go west and evaluate the mining situation in Arizona in the 1880s. Douglas was an impressive man, as physically strong as his faith-based, humanitarian leadership qualities that would eventually propel him to the presidency of Phelps Dodge. Douglas set out on that initial evaluation assignment with full knowledge of the murderous attacks that had been made by Apaches along the very routes he would have to travel.

For Arthur, *The Wounded Bunkie* had to have brought back a vivid memory of the fate of the Western frontier, the collateral destruction of a culture caused by the railroads that were leading the charge to expand the economic vitality of the nation. Rarely is there progress without damage. In 1889, Andrew Carnegie had written that "we must accept, and welcome... the great inequality of environment, the concentration of business... in the hands of a few, and the law of competition between these as being not only beneficial, but essential for the future progress of the race." Certainly Arthur had read that message from one of the few men in America whose wealth equaled, or perhaps exceeded, his, and surely he was a believer. While the major changes to the frontier had been perpetrated long before Arthur had gotten into the game, he had driven the golden spike that had galvanized 13,000 or so miles of railroad track. That Arthur would be one of the first to buy this Remington, and display it in his home, speaks volumes about his awareness, and his acceptance of the negative, as well as the positive civic consequences of his actions.

The mansion at 39 East 69th Street would be turned into offices for the James Foundation for several years. Joan Malkovich lived there as a teenager with her father, Douglas Shewring, who managed the house. In 1958, the house was torn down to make way for a twenty-story apartment building. Bearing screwdrivers and pry-bars, a jolly wrecking crew of more than 300 people—many of them interior decorators, antiques dealers, or wealthy homeowners—cruised the rooms removing everything from marble sinks, doorknobs, sconces, and carved oak paneling, to soap dishes. As they left, they paid for the items they had selected.

Life tenancy of the house built by Arthur at 82 Round Hill Road in Northampton was left by Harriet to one of her sisters. After her sister died, the house was passed on, as Harriet had desired, to the Clarke School for the Deaf. In 2011, Mr. and Mrs. Robert Beede purchased 82 Round Hill Road as their home. Mrs. (Fraser) Beede reports that while the infrastructure restoration they did was extensive, the exterior was preserved, as were the architectural details of the rooms.

The North Tarrytown (now Sleepy Hollow) house is part of the Phelps Memorial Hospital complex. Like 39 East 69th Street, Fourway Lodge in Coconut Grove was razed to make room for more compact development. But the saddest tale is that of Beacon Hill House in Newport, completely gutted and burned to the ground by vandals.

The problem with the large estates built in the pre-income-tax days of the early 1900s is that when their owners died in the 1930s and '40s, there were very few people or institutions capable of taking them on. Just ask the Preservation Society of Newport County, with its hands full maintaining the lineup of mansions on Bellevue Avenue that are under its aegis. Arthur was the largest taxpayer in the county, don't forget. Add that to all the other maintenance that was required at Beacon Hill, beginning with 100 gardeners working every day, and the working farm with its dairy, and the property presented a financial "mission impossible" for potential buyers and recipients alike.

As we know, Arthur was a Presbyterian. He also belonged to Trinity Episcopal Church in Newport. Neither organization was big enough to take on such a large, demanding property accepted as a gift. Beacon Hill was given to the Roman Catholic Diocese of Providence, Rhode Island. Christopher "Toby" Pell, a retired museum director and bond salesman, who with his partner, Barclay Douglas, bought 34 acres of the Beacon Hill property in 1976, said his father, Claiborne Pell, had the same problem dispensing his estates in Fishkill, New York, and Newport when he was sent to Portugal by President Franklin Delano Roosevelt in 1937. (Clairborne Pell would go on to become a Democratic Senator from Rhode Island for thirty-six years. The Newport Bridge is named after him.) "He gave both estates to Catholic Dioceses," Toby Pell says. "They were the only organizations big enough to handle those large properties. My guess is it was the same with Beacon Hill."

The Providence Diocese's approach to caring for Beacon Hill was not encouraging. They used it as a resource, removing all the capping stones from the walls of the estate to build a monastery in Lincoln, Rhode Island. The walls deteriorated after that. Unattended, save for a lone supervisor who lived in a detached garage apartment, the house gradually fell into further disrepair, becoming a hangout for vagrants, vandals, and kids on larks. An attractive nuisance, long vacant, Beacon Hill House was a disaster waiting to happen, and on the night of Friday, May 5, 1967, arsonists struck. A previous fire at Beacon Hill had been extinguished with only minor damage. This one consumed the entire house. According to the *Newport Daily News*, one observer drawn to the enormous blaze who was standing amid the mass of broken marble, glass, collapsed fire hoses, and mud was heard to comment: "Well, I guess that decides what the Bishop is going to do with this place."

You'll recall that Harriet James's niece Harriet and her husband William DeForest Manice had been living in the Edgehill house on the Beacon Hill property. Upon their deaths, their children, Mr. and Mrs. William DeForest Manice Jr., had continued to live there. Their nephew, Robert Manice, said his aunt and uncle had been treated like their own children by Arthur and Harriet. Robert said his uncle often went sailing with Arthur.

But in 1973, William Manice Jr. and his brother tore down Vedimar, the house Arthur had built for his doctor, to avoid taxes. They weren't the only ones making what seemed like rash decisions in those days. Newport had suffered a severe financial setback in 1973 when the US Navy suddenly pulled its destroyer fleet, air base, and Seabee Center out of the area. The loss of 17,000 military and 6,000 civilian jobs virtually crippled the town, and it had a serious effect on the country's smallest state. Real estate values plummeted. For example, Hammersmith Farm, where Jacqueline Bouvier (Mrs. John F. Kennedy) had grown up—75 handsome acres of waterfront a few hundred yards from Beacon Hill—was sold in 1976 for a paltry $750,000. That same year, Surprise Valley Farm had been sold for $675,000 to a Providence group that would establish the Edgehill Alcoholic Rehabilitation Center.

Meanwhile, 34 acres of the Beacon Hill property had been sold to a developer who planned to put 275 condominium units on the hilltop. When the developer was stymied by problems with the city over installing a sewer line to the property, Newport's Old Stone Bank foreclosed. Enter Telegraph Hill Associates, namely Christopher Pell and Barclay Douglas, who purchased the 34 acres for $375,000 in 1976. "We saved it," Toby Pell says of the property. "Foundations had been poured, a lot of plywood was up." The land was under four-acre zoning. Once Pell and Douglas had selected their house sites, they looked for others who might be interested in building houses on the former James property. One couple who bought in was Mr. and Mrs. Earl Powell. Mr. Powell, better known as Rusty, an art historian and museum director, would be named director of the National Gallery of Art in 1980.

Excavation began for the foundation for the Powell house. Then it stopped. A structure of some sort had been encountered by the machine operator, who was sensitive enough to stop. Shovels were broken out. Careful handwork began to reveal a large, rectangle of concrete and stone. "We knew it was the Blue Garden," Nancy Powell says, "but we weren't sure what that was." The Powells began doing the research while workers began clearing pools that had been buried by thick, thorny underbrush. It became an archeological dig. Orders were issued to save anything solid that was encountered. It took the Powells two years of hand-scrubbing decorative elements they had found, and fitting them back in place, to restore three of the Blue Garden pools and fill them. They never did figure out the pumping system Arthur had installed to keep the pool water moving and fresh. "In 1980, no one in the state could figure out the system Arthur and his team had worked out in 1914," Nancy Powell says.

The next activity on the James property was in 1998. The Edgehill Center's mortgage had been issued by the US Department of Housing and Urban Development (HUD). The center defaulted on the loan, and HUD held a foreclosure auction. The property consisting of Edgehill and the model farm, approximately 28.5–acres, was purchased by Carol Ballard and her husband, Leslie Ballard, a Texas oilman, and their "cordial acquaintance," the late Mrs. Dorrance Hamilton. Mrs. Hamilton was the Campbell's Soup heiress, a philanthropist well known for her interest in preservation. Known widely as "Dodo," Mrs. Hamilton had long been a force in Newport. In a "fair division" determined by a partition commissioner assigned by the court, the Ballards got Edgehill house, a carriage house, and an undeveloped parcel of the land. Dodo Hamilton got the farm that she named Swiss Village. She had begun total restoration of the farm, which she planned to use for the preservation of rare and endangered breeds of livestock. The relationship between the two owners would sour. They would spend nearly eighteen years in court battling over details involving the sewer system and an access road.

With the Swiss Village Farm project up and running, Mrs. Hamilton would purchase another section of the James property known as the East Lawn to build a house of her own. When the abutting property (including the Powells' house), where the Blue Garden had been located, became available in 2012, she purchased that as well with a total rebuild in mind. That daunting, carefully researched task was begun almost immediately. Like the original, the restoration project took two years to complete. Today, the Blue Garden is "private and not open to the public." However, legitimate recognized organizations can request an appointment for a group of its members by email. Those who are admitted will experience an ultimate example of formal landscaping. They'll first view a video of the reconstruction, followed by a prolonged ramble among the blue flowers, pools, pergolas, waterfalls, and wrought-iron gates of the painstakingly replicated Blue Garden. Unlike when Arthur owned it, the Farm is run as an exclusive enterprise. It is open to visitors one day a year.

Another enduring element of the Jameses' presence in Newport, in addition to the Ida Lewis Yacht Club, is Aloha Landing, Arthur's boathouse, which was purchased and renovated by Sam Mencoff. Mencoff is cofounder and co-CEO of Madison Dearborn Partners, a Chicago investment firm. He is also chancellor of Brown University. The exterior of the Landing has been meticulously restored, stone by stone. But the interior will never again see a wet sail bag. It's been converted into an elegant, small dwelling, with kitchen and living room upstairs, bedroom and storage downstairs, all varnished teak, glass, and stainless. There's also an ample dock that doubles as a comfortable waterfront porch, with floats to accommodate small boats. The turntable for cars, now electric, is in working order.

Mencoff, who with his wife, Ann, gave Brown University's medical school a gift of $50 million in February 2018, was mentioned in *Barron's* as one of several "ultra-high-net-worth" Americans who have increasingly devoted themselves to philanthropy. Arthur Curtiss James would approve of Aloha Landing's new owners.

All of Arthur's boats are either gone, or lost to us, hidden away under other names. Except for the "houseboat" *Lanai* (now *Argo*), and *Coronet*, of course. It's going on twenty-three years since *Coronet* was taken over by the International Yacht Restoration School in Newport, fourteen years since a building was constructed around the remains of the big schooner at the IYRS campus, and twelve years since *Coronet* Restoration Partners (Dr. Robert McNeil and Jerry Rutherford, principles) took over the project. The work has been sporadic, dependent on funds available. At this writing, it's been more than a year since another plank was fastened to the hull. Those who know how much money has gone into this project aren't saying.

The current goal is to complete hull and deck sometime in 2020 so *Coronet* can be launched. After so many years, that may sound like wishful thinking, but there is no one even remotely involved with this project who doesn't think it will be completed. It has that kind of grandeur, that kind of overpowering presence. All agree it will be worth the wait. One thing is certain: when sail is raised again on that amazing vessel, there will not be a more perfect living memorial to Arthur Curtiss James.

It's too bad Arthur's not around. It's his kind of project. He'd have *Coronet* finished and sailing in the twinkling of an eye.

Acknowledgments

Thanks to Harry Anderson for his life-long research on his cousin Arthur Curtiss James, research that inspired this book and the companion documentary, *Of Rails & Sails*. To Joseph Daniel, filmmaker and book producer, for the design and production of this book, and for envisioning and producing *Of Rails & Sails*, a project that would lead to this book. To Annie Kiker, field producer of the film, for casting, locations, costumes—the whole nine yards—and for research. To Elizabeth Cameron for her errorless proofing services, and Ben Smith for his maps and cover design.

And to those who contributed research: Bert Lippincott, Newport Historical Society, RI; Bishop Joel Marcus Johnson, Easton, MD; Bob MacKay, SCYC; Dylan Gaffney, Forbes Library, Northampton, MA; Edward Singer, Washington, DC; Francis Hester, IYRS Newport, RI; Gordon Creed, Washington, DC; Janet Gross, Forbes Library Northampton, MA; Julie Gaffney, Forbes Library; Kate Malcolm, Madison Historical Society, NJ; Kip Requardt, Oxford, MD; Michele Hughes, Freeport-McMoRan, Phoenix, AZ; Mike Kelly, Amherst College Archives, Amherst, MA; Vanessa Cameron, NYYC.

ACKNOWLEDGMENTS

And to the following for their assistance, encouragement, and contributions: Beth Detmold, Northampton, MA; Bert Lippincott, Newport Historical Society, RI; Bill Lynn, Herreshoff Marine Museum, RI; Carol Mowrey, Mystic Seaport, CT; Chris Eareckson, Talbot County Free Library, MD; Christopher Williamson (Capt., *Argo*); Dana Clough, Herreshoff Marine Museum, RI; Denise Meagher (mate, *Argo*); Dyer Jones, Newport, RI; Jeff Fellows, Oxford, MD; Earl and Lisa Stubbs, Newport, RI; Fraser Beede, Northampton, MA; Fred Kaplan, author; Gary Jobson, Annapolis, MD; Gloria Pierce, Ransom Everglades School, FL; Jay Serzan, Newport, RI; Jeanne Gamble, Historic New England; John Rousmanier, NY; John Mecray (1937 – 2017) marine artist; Leah Rousmanier, Union Theological Seminary; Phillip Connell, Newport, RI; Rev. Canon Anne Marie Richards, RI; Terry Nathan, IYRS, Newport, RI; William (Gary) Bennett, Houston, TX

- RV

The Newport Daily News

$1.00
NewportDailyNews.com   NEWPORT ◆ MIDDLETOWN ◆ PORTSMOUTH ◆ JAMESTOWN ◆ TIVERTON   Friday
September 1, 2017

Filmmakers lift the veil from the life and times of Arthur Curtiss James

By Sean Flynn
Staff writer

Dave Hansen | Staff photographer
Roger Vaughan, left, the writer for the documentary film 'Of Rails and Sails,' and director Joseph Daniel stand outside the Jane Pickens Theater in Newport, where the film will premiere on Sept. 14.

NEWPORT — "Of Rails and Sails" is a new documentary film that lifts the curtain on Arthur Curtiss James, the railroad baron who owned the Beacon Hill estate and the Aloha boathouse in this city and the Coronet yacht now being restored at the International Yacht Restoration School.

Director Joseph Daniel and writer Roger Vaughan were in the city Wednesday making preparations for the upcoming premiere at the Jane Pickens Theater on Sept. 14.

James, who lived from 1867 to 1941, was a very private person who shied away from publicity. There is not a lot of readily available information about him, although he had controlling ownership of about 40,000 miles of railroad track — about one-seventh of the entire network in the country — when he died. He was among the 10 wealthiest people in the country.

Daniel and Vaughan have spent the past two years researching James' life and have uncovered some amazing resources that can be seen in the documentary, including film footage of him and his wife, Harriet Parsons James. How the old film was found is among the stories the filmmakers told during an interview with The Daily News on Wednesday.

James left his estate on Brenton Road to the Diocese of Providence. After he died, the James Foundation of New York oversaw the property until it was transferred to the diocese 10 years later.

The main estate home was demolished after a fire in the late 1960s, but the Sisters of St. Joseph of Cluny established a convent in the former guesthouse of the estate, across from the site where Cluny School was built. The sisters founded the school in 1957. The former convent was sold in 2012.

In the top part of a bedroom closet of the guesthouse, the nuns found three cans of 16-mm film and turned them over to the International Yacht Restoration School.

The Manice family, friends of the James family, shot the film and there is footage of Arthur Curtiss James and his wife playing tennis, going on a buggy ride and swimming at Bailey's Beach. Two of the films were railroad films centered on the Great Northern transcontinental railroad route that James was instrumental in completing.

Daniel and Vaughan received the film from IYRS, had it converted to digital format, and excerpts can be viewed in the documentary

FILMMAKERS A7

The sequence is supposed to be book, then film. We all know that. But at first, a book about this very private man seemed beyond one's grasp. We began making the film. Little by little the doors started to open, material appeared, people surfaced, and lo and behold, the book also began to take shape.

Appendix One – Associations of Arthur Curtiss James

Director

Chicago, Burlington and Quincy Railroad Co.
Colorado & Southern Railway Co.
Copper Queen Consolidated Mining Co.
El Paso & Southwestern Railroad Company
First National Bank, NY
Great Northern Railroad Co.
Hanover National Bank, NY
Morenci Southern Railway Co.
Nacozari Railroad Co.
Northern Pacific Railroad Co.
Northern Securities Co.
Old Dominion Co.
Phelps Dodge Corp.
Picacho Mining Co.
Rock Island
Southern Pacific Railroad Co.
Stag Canyon Fuel Co.
Western Pacific Railway Co.

Trustee

Amherst College
Children's Aid Society
Hampton Normal and Agricultural Institute
Madison Public Library
New York Trust Co.
Union Theological Seminary
United States Trust Co, NY

Member (*organizations and societies*)

American Geographical Society
Institute of Mining Engineers
L'Union Interalliee, Paris
Merchants Society of New York

American Museum of Natural History
Chamber of Commerce, NY
Charity Organization Society
Council on Foreign Relations
English-Speaking Union
Italian Historical Society
Japan Society

Metropolitan Museum of Art
New York Historical Society
New York Zoological Society
NY, NJ Port and Harbor Development Co.
Royal Geographical Society
Society of the Cincinnati, Connecticut

Member: (*religious, fraternal, clubs*)

Alpha Delta Phi
Amherst Association of New York
Amherst Club of New York
Atlantic Yacht Club
Broad Street Club
Century Association
Chicago Club
Down Town Association
Eastern Yacht Club
First Presbyterian Church, NY
Hampton Association of NY
Ida Lewis Yacht Club

Metropolitan Club
New York Botanical Gardens
New York Yacht Club
Pacific Union Club
Park Avenue Association
Riding Club
Seawanhaka Corinthian Yacht Club
Sleepy Hollow Country Club
St. Francis Yacht Club
Trinity Church, Newport
University Club
YMCA

Honors

Commodore – Seawanhaka Corinthian Yacht Club 1901–1905
Commodore – New York Yacht Club 1909–1910
Commodore – Ida Lewis Yacht Club 1929–1932
Commandatore of the Crown of Italy
Commander of The Order Leopold II

Other Associations of Arthur Curtiss James

American Brass Co.
Ansonia Clock Co.
Burro Mountain Copper Co.

Curtiss Securities
El Paso & Northeastern Co.
United Globe Mines

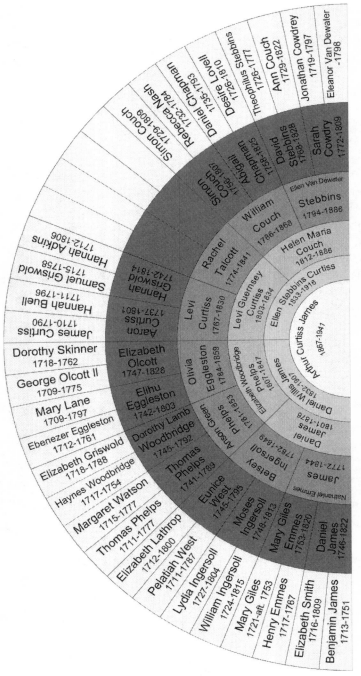

Arthur Curtiss James' Genealogy Fan Chart

Appendix Two – Genealogy

Ancestors of Arthur Curtiss James

Generation 1

Arthur Curtiss James, son of Daniel Willis James and Ellen Stebbins Curtiss, was born June 1, 1867, in New York, NY. He died June 4, 1941, in New York, NY. He married Harriet Eddy Parsons April 23, 1890, in Northampton, MA. She was born September 6, 1867, in MA. She died May 15, 1941, in New York, NY.

Generation 2

Daniel Willis James, son of Daniel James and Elizabeth Woodbridge Phelps, was born April 15, 1832, in Liverpool, England. He died September 13, 1907, in Carroll, NH. He married Ellen Stebbins Curtiss February 7, 1854, in New York, NY.

Ellen Stebbins Curtiss, daughter of Levi Guernsey Curtiss and Helen Maria Couch, was born December 21, 1833, in New York, NY. She died April 28, 1916, in New York, NY.

Generation 3

Daniel James, son of Nathaniel Emmes James and Betsey Ingersoll, was born April 17, 1801, in Truxton, NY. He died November 27, 1876, in Lancashire, England. He married Elizabeth Woodbridge Phelps March 24, 1829, in New York.

Elizabeth Woodbridge Phelps, daughter of Anson Green Phelps and Olivia Egleston, was born August 22, 1807, in Hartford, Hartford, CT. She died June 21, 1847, in Lancashire, England.

Levi Guernsey Curtiss, son of Levi Curtiss and Rachel Talcott, was born December 18, 1803, in Granville, MA. He died August 7, 1834, in Saint-Jean-sur-Richelieu, Montérégie Region, Quebec, Canada. He married Helen Maria Couch March 5, 1833, in New York, NY.

Helen Maria Couch, daughter of William Couch and Ellen Van Dewater Stebbins, was born October 16, 1812, in New York, NY. She died August 15, 1886, in Maplewood, NH.

James/Phelps/Dodge Relationship

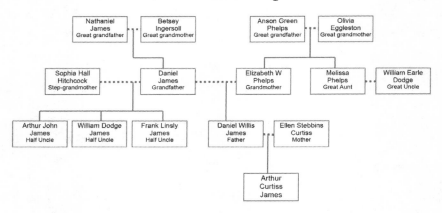

Generation 4

Nathaniel Emmes James, son of Daniel James and Mary Giles Emmes, was born July 2, 1772, in Bristol, RI. He died June 14, 1844, in Truxton, NY. He married Betsey Ingersoll in 1799 in New York.

Betsey Ingersoll, daughter of Moses Ingersoll and Eunice West, was born April 10, 1782 in Lee, Berkshire County, MA. She died February 17, 1849 in Truxton, Cortland County, NY.

Anson Green Phelps, son of Thomas Phelps and Dorothy Lamb Woodbridge, was born March 24, 1781, in Hartford, CT. He died November 30, 1853, in New York City, NY County, NY. He married Olivia Eggleston October 26, 1806, in Hartford, CT.

Olivia Eggleston, daughter of Elihu Eggleston and Elizabeth Olcott, was born March 30, 1784, in Middletown, CT. She died April 24, 1859, in New York, NY.

Levi Curtiss, son of Aaron Curtiss and Hannah Griswold, was born November13, 1767, in Granville, Hampden, MA. He died September 19, 1830, in Granville, Hampden, MA. He married Rachel Talcott.

Rachel Talcott was born in 1774. She died September 16, 1841, in Graville, Hampden County, MA.

William Couch, son of Simon Couch and Abigail Chapman, was born May 8, 1786, in Southport, Fairfield County, CT. He died September 7, 1868, in Southport, Fairfield County, CT. He married Ellen Van Dewater Stebbins December 11, 1810, in New York, NY.

Ellen Van Dewater Stebbins, daughter of David Stebbins and SarahCowdry, was born August 19, 1794, in New York. She died August 14, 1886, in New York, NY.

Generation 5

Daniel James, son of Benjamin James and Elizabeth Smith, was born September 29, 1746, in Bristol, Bristol, RI. He died September 25, 1822, in Truxton, Cortland, NY. He married Mary Giles Emmes October 21, 1769, in Bristol, RI.

Mary Giles Emmes, daughter of Henry Emmes and Mary Giles, was born October 13, 1753, in Bristol, RI. She died February 18, 1820, in Weybridge, Addison, Vermont.

Moses Ingersoll, son of William Ingersoll and Lydia Ingersoll, was born July 14, 1748, in Great Barrington, Berkshire, MA. He died September 9, 1813, in Lee, Berkshire, MA. He married Eunice West December 28, 1769, in Stockbridge, MA.

Eunice West, daughter of Pelatiah West and Elizabeth Lathrop, was born April 30, 1745, in Tolland, Tolland County, CT. She died November 19, 1795, in Lee, Berkshire County, MA.

Thomas Phelps, son of Thomas Phelps and Margaret Watson, was born July 17, 1741, in Simsbury, Hartford, CT. He died February 28, 1789, in Simsbury, Hartford, CT. He married Dorothy Lamb Woodbridge.

Dorothy Lamb Woodbridge, daughter of Haynes Woodbridge and Elizabeth Griswold, was born November 13, 1745, in Simsbury, Hartford, CT. She died in 1792, in Simsbury, Hartford, CT.

Elihu Eggleston, son of Ebenezer Eggleston and Mary Lane, was born August 1, 1742, in Middletown, Middlesex, CT. He died April 10, 1803, in Hartford, Hartford, CT. He married Elizabeth Olcott May 31, 1772, in Hartford, CT.

Elizabeth Olcott, daughter of George Olcott II and Dorothy Skinner, was born September 24, 1747, in Hartford, Hartford, CT. She died May 26, 1828, in New York, NY County (Manhattan), NY.

Aaron Curtiss, son of James Curtiss and Hannah Buell, was born September 9, 1737, in Durham, Middlesex, CT. He died May 30, 1801, in Granville, Hampden, MA. He married Hannah Griswold May 11, 1763, in Granville, Hampden, MA.

Hannah Griswold, daughter of Samuel Griswold and Hannah Adkins, was born April 22, 1742, in Durham, Middlesex, CT. She died February 21, 1814, in Granville, MA.

Simon Couch, son of Simon Couch and Rebecca Nash, was born May 18, 1756, in Westport, Fairfield, CT. He died November 8, 1807, in Fairfield, CT. He married Abigail Chapman November 25, 1779, in Fairfield, CT.

Abigail Chapman, daughter of Daniel Chapman and Desire Lovell, was born October 10, 1758, in Fairfield, CT. She died December 18, 1825.

David Stebbins, son of Theophilus Stebbins and Ann Couch, was born October 7, 1768, in Ridgefield, CT. He died April 3, 1828, in Ridgefield, Fairfield, CT. He married Sarah Cowdry October 29, 1793, in New York, NY.

Sarah Cowdry, daughter of Jonathan Cowdrey and Eleanor Van Dewater, was born February 26, 1772, in Ridgefield, Fairfield, CT. She died December 11, 1809, in Ridgefield, CT.

Generation 6

Benjamin James, son of John James and Eunice Stetson, was born in 1713, in Bristol, Bristol, RI. He died October 14, 1751, lost at sea. He married Elizabeth Smith July 6, 1738, in Taylor, Florida.

Elizabeth Smith was born March 15, 1716, in Bristol, Bristol, RI. She died in 1809 in Stockbridge, Berkshire, MA.

Henry Emmes, son of Nathaniel Emmes and Hannah Grafton, was born January 6, 1717, in Boston, Suffolk, MA. He died February 24, 1767, in Newport, RI. He married Mary Giles July 7, 1743, in Boston, Suffolk, MA.

Mary Giles, daughter of William Gyles and Mary Codner, was born March 15, 1721, in Boston, Middlesex, MA. She died in Bristol, Bristol, RI.

William Ingersoll was born April 1, 1724, in Springfield, Hampden, MA. He died August 10, 1815, in Lee, Berkshire, MA. He married Lydia Ingersoll December 11, 1746, in Great Barrington, Berkshire, MA.

Lydia Ingersoll was born October 1, 1727, in Great Barrington, Berkshire, MA. She died June 2, 1804, in Lee, Berkshire, MA.

Pelatiah West, son of Francis West (Deacon) and Mercy Minor, was born September 3, 1711, in Stonington, New London County, CT. He died July 11, 1787, in Lee, Berkshire County, MA. He married Elizabeth Lathrop December 5, 1734, in Tolland, CT.

Elizabeth Lathrop was born January 20, 1712, in Barnstable, Barnstable, MA. She died March 17, 1800, in Lee, Berkshire, MA.

Thomas Phelps was born July 27, 1711, in Windsor[Poquanock], Hartford, CT. He died September 25, 1777, in Canton, Hartford, CT. He married Margaret Watson November 23, 1737, in West Hartford, Hartford, CT.

Margaret Watson was born June 7, 1715, in West Hartford, Hartford, CT. She died January 9, 1777, in Canton, Hartford, CT.

Haynes Woodbridge was born October 15, 1717, in Simsbury, Hartford, CT. He died April 12, 1754, in Simsbury, Hartford, CT. He married Elizabeth Griswold December 29, 1742, in Simsbury, Hartford, CT.

Elizabeth Griswold was born August 3, 1718, in Simsbury, Hartford, CT. She died in March 1788, in Simsbury, Hartford, CT.

Ebenezer Eggleston was born April 4, 1712, in Middletown, Middlesex, CT. He died April 28, 1761, in Middletown, Middlesex, CT. He married Mary Lane November 15, 1733, in Middletown, Middlesex, CT.

Mary Lane was born December 30, 1709, in Middletown, Middlesex County, CT. She died October 9, 1797, in Bloomfield, Hartford, CT.

George Olcott II was born in 1709, in Hartford, Connecticut Colony. He died February 25, 1775, in Hartford, Connecticut Colony. He married Dorothy Skinner May 28, 1741, in Hartford, CT.

Dorothy Skinner was born March 30, 1718, in Hartford, CT. She died June 27, 1762, in Hartford, CT.

James Curtiss was born April 1, 1710, in Durham, Middlesex, Conecticut. He died January 13, 1790, in Durham, Middlesex, CT. He married Hannah Buell September 12, 1734, in Durham, Middlesex, CT.

Hannah Buell was born December 7, 1711, in Killingworth, CT. She died September 17, 1796, in Durham, CT.

Samuel Griswold was born December 12, 1715, in Simsbury, Hartford, Connecticut Colony. He died December 3, 1758, in Guilford, New Haven, CT. He married Hannah Adkins February 8, 1734, in Guilford, New Haven, CT.

Hannah Adkins was born October 12, 1712, in Middletown, Connecticut Colony. She died December 18, 1806, in New Haven, CT.

Simon Couch, son of Thomas Couch and Sarah Gideon Allen, was born April 5, 1729, in Fairfield, CT. He died April 25, 1809, in Redding, Fairfield, CT. He married Rebecca Nash January 27, 1753.

Rebecca Nash, daughter of (Capt.) Thomas Nash and Rebecca Hull, was born November 18, 1732, in Fairfield, CT. She died January 12, 1784, in Redding, Fairfield, CT.

Daniel Chapman was born in 1735 in Green's Farms, Fairfield, CT. He died April 11, 1793, in MA. He married Desire Lovell October 4, 1750, in Stamford Darien, Fairfield, CT.

Desire Lovell was born May 9, 1726, in Barnstable, Barnstable, MA. She died November 17, 1810, in Greens Farms, Fairfield, CT.

Theophilus Stebbins, son of Benjamin Stebbins and Sarah Mead, was born May 16, 1726, in Ridgefield, Fairfield, CT. He died March 10, 1777, in Ridgefield, Fairfield, CT. He married Ann Couch July 7, 1750, in Ridgefield, Fairfield, CT.

Ann Couch was born May 9, 1729, in Ridgefield, Fairfield, CT. She died September 22, 1822, in Ridgefield, Fairfield, CT.

Jonathan Cowdrey was born in 1719, in Reading, Middlesex, MA. He died in 1797 in New York City, NY. He married Eleanor Van Dewater November 6, 1771.

Eleanor Van Dewater was born in New York City, NY. She died March 15, 1798, in New York, NY.

James/Anderson Relationship

Harry Anderson has a raft of illustrious ancestors, including Aaron Burr, but the one he admires above all is his distant cousin, Arthur Curtiss James. Coincidently, both men were commodore of the New York Yacht Club, and the Seawanhaka Corinthian Yacht Club.

Henry H. "Harry" Anderson Jr.

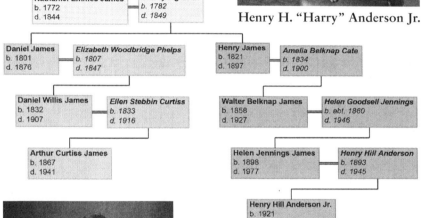

Nathaniel Emmes James b. 1772 d. 1844	=	Betsey Ingersoll b. 1782 d. 1849			

Daniel James b. 1801 d. 1876	=	Elizabeth Woodbridge Phelps b. 1807 d. 1847	Henry James b. 1821 d. 1897	=	Amelia Belknap Cate b. 1834 d. 1900

Daniel Willis James b. 1832 d. 1907	=	Ellen Stebbin Curtiss b. 1833 d. 1916	Walter Belknap James b. 1858 d. 1927	=	Helen Goodsell Jennings b. abt. 1860 d. 1946

Arthur Curtiss James b. 1867 d. 1941			Helen Jennings James b. 1898 d. 1977	=	Henry Hill Anderson b. 1893 d. 1945

Henry Hill Anderson Jr. b. 1921

For many years Harry has been determined that the very private James should be recognized for his extraordinary accomplishments in the railroad business, and for his prowess not only as master of his own vessels, but as a worthy contributor to their design and construction. This book and the companion documentary film are testament to Harry's persuasion.

– RV

Selected Bibliography

Aloha Around the World, by Karl Vogel
Austin & Mabel: The Amherst Affair and Love Letters of Austin Dickinson and Mabel Loomis Todd, by Polly Longsworth
Bisbee: Queen of the Copper Camps, by Lynn R. Bailey
The Blue Garden: Recapturing an Iconic Newport Landscape, by Arleyn A. Levee
Clinton Crane's Yachting Memories, by Clinton Crane
"The Consecrated Eminence": The Story of the Campus and Buildings of Amherst College, by Stanley King
The Commodore's Story: The Early Days on Biscayne Bay, by Ralph Middleton Munroe and Vincent Gilpin
Corona and Coronet, by Mabel Loomis Todd
Coronet: "Conquering and to Conquer," by Tim Murray
Coronet Memories, by F. Tennyson Neely
Dear Father, Dear Son: Correspondence of John D. Rockefeller and John D. Rockefeller, Jr.
Episodes in the Life of a Publisher's Wife, by Florence Doubleday
Friendly Adventurers: A Chronicle of the American Church of Paris, by Rev. Cochran
Gilded: How Newport became America's Richest Resort, by Deborah Davis
The Gilded Age: A Tale of Today, by Mark Twain and Charles Dudley Warner
The Gods of Newport, by John Jakes
The Golden Summers: An Antic History of Newport, by Richard O'Connor
Gondola Days: Isabella Stewart Gardener and the Palazzo Barbaro Circle, by Elizabeth Anne McCauley, Alan Chong, Rosella Mamdi Zorzi, Richard Lingner
The Gospel of Wealth, by Andrew Carnegie
Great Houses of New York, 1880–1930 by Michael C. Kathrens
The Great Northern Railway: A History, by Ralph W., Muriel E. Hidy, and Roy V., with Don Hofsommer Hidy
Great Yachts of Long Island's North Shore, by Robert B. MacKay
High Road to Promontory, by George Kraus

A History of Phelps Dodge 1834–1950, by Robert Glass Cleland

A History of the Endowment of Amherst College, by Stanley King

A History of the Northern Securities Case, by B. H. Meyer

Interesting People: 80 Years with the Great and Near Great, by Corinna Lindon Smith

James Douglas: A Memoir, by H. H. Langton

The Last of the Great Stations: 40 Years of the Los Angeles Union Passenger Terminal, by Bill Bradley

Legendary Yachts, by Bill Robinson

A Life in Full Sail, by Anson M. Beard, Jr.

Long Island Country Houses and Their Architects, edited by Anthony Baker, Robert B. MacKay, and Carol A. Traynor, foreword by Brendan Gill

Los Angeles Union Station: Tracks to the Future, by Bill Bradley

The Man Who Found the Money: John Stewart Kennedy and the Financing of the Western Railroads, by Saul Ehgelbourg and Leonard Buskkoff

Merging Lines: American Railroads 1900-1970, by Richard Sanders, Jr.

Milepost 100: The Story of the Development of the Burlington Line 1849–1949, by R. C. Overton

Newport: A Lively Experiment, 1639–1969, by Rockwell Stensrud

Newport in Flower: A History of Newport's Horticultural Heritage, by Harriet Jackson Phelps and Michael Hales

Notes on the Development of Phelps, Dodge & Co's Copper and Railroad Interests, by James Douglas, LLD

A People's History of the United States, 1492–Present, by Howard Zinn

Railroad Consolidation West of the Mississippi River, by Stuart Daggett

The Railroad Station, by Carroll L. V. Meeks

Seawanhaka Corinthian Yacht Club: The Early 20th Century, 1897–1940, by John Parkinson, Jr.

Semper Eadem: A History of Trinity Church, by John B. Hattendorf

A Summer of Hummingbirds: Love, Art and Scandal in the Intersecting Worlds of Emily Dickinson, Mark Twain, Harriet Beecher Stowe, and Martin Johnson Heade, by Christopher Benfey

A Surreal Life: Edward James 1907–1988, by Nicola Coleby

The Sense of Newport, by Henry James

The Strenuous Life of Harry Anderson, by Roger Vaughan

Tales of the Phelps-Dodge Family, by Phyllis D. Dodge

This Was My Newport, by Maud Howe Elliott

Vision & Enterprise: Exploring the History of Phelps Dodge Corporation, by Carlos A. Schwantes

Wanderings of Aloha, from the journals of J.S.L., F.L.S., & F.B.C.

Index

A. Carey Smith & Ferris, 152
"A Plea for Our Railroads" (ACJ), 124, 235
Adams, Charles Francis, II, 203
Adams, Harry, 315
Adamson Act, 234
Adirondack Cottage Sanitarium, 116
Adirondack-Florida School (now Ransom School), 195–96, 198
Ainu tribespeople, 70
Al Smith, 275, 298
alcohol, 68, 84, 140, 144, 256, 301
alcoholism, 53, 353
Alden Designs, 104
Alfonso, XIII, King of Spain, 297
Alford, Andrew P. "Pete," 53–54, 256, 335, 344
Alger, Horatio, 40, 279
Allen & Collens, 189, 342
Allied Chemical, 116, 157
Aloha Around the World (Vogel), 256, 258, 265–66
Aloha Landing, 158, 172, 294, 355–56
Amazon, 151
America, 33
America's Cup 33, 37, 117, 203
American Board of Commissioners for Foreign Missions, 165, 259, 304, 344

American Church in Paris, 303–305
American Geographical Society Building, 148
American Geographical Society, 132
American Institute of Mining, Metallurgical, and Petroleum Engineers, 87
American Museum of Natural History, 156, 157, 344
American Natural Gas, 345
American Protective League, 232
American Seamen's Friend Society, 344
American University of Beirut, 344
Amherst College alumni friends, 52, 53, 55, 166–67, 258, 332, 335, 338
Amphitrite, 185
Anderson, Henry H. "Harry," Jr., 35, 36, 42, 198–199, 208, 210, 271, 276, 280, 345, 358, 370
Anderson, Robin and brother Donald, 243
April Fool's Day, 52
Aquidneck Island, 145, 151,336
Argo. See Lanai
Armstrong, Samuel C., 19
Association Against Prohibition, 319
Astor, Caroline (Mrs. William Backhouse), 140, 141, 144
Astor, John Jacob, 116

Atterbury, Grosvenor, 199
Audubon, 311
Austin & Mabel: The Amherst Affair and Love Letters of Austin Dickinson and Mabel Loomis Todd (Longsworth), 28–29, 75, 159

Balanchine, George, 301
Baldwin, W. W., 285
Balfour, Arthur James, 223
"Ballad of East and West, The" (Kipling) 29, 350
Baltimore Stock Exchange, 148
bankruptcy, 102, 109, 216, 217, 235, 326
Barrack-Room Ballads, 24
Barron's, 356
Bartholow, Roberts, 324
bas-relief, 202, 263, 265
Bayley, Stephen, Taste 139
Bays, Daniel, 165
Beaconsfield House, 130, 148
Beard, Anson, Jr., 60, 62
Beck, Horace and wife, 295–96
Beede, Mr. and Mrs. Robert, 351
Bell, Alexander Graham, 50
Bell, Mabel, 50
Bellevue Avenue, 138, 139, 145, 170, 190, 352
Belmont, Alva. See Vanderbilt, Alva
Belvoir. See under James, Arthur Curtiss: Real Estate
Benfey, Christopher, 26
Bennett, James Gordon, Jr. 170
Bentinck, Venetia, 22
Berthold, Andrew, 82–83
Berwind, Edward, 139
Bezanson, Captain Peleoman, 113, 119, 130, 152, 164, 256
Bingham, Millicent Todd (Mrs. Walter Van Dyke Bingham), 26, 291, 326
Bisbee: Queen of the Copper Camps (Bailey), 86, 92, 224, 226, 233
Black Tuesday, 307
Blue Garden, restoration of, 354–55. See also under James, Arthur Curtiss: Real Estate
Blue Garden, The (Levee), 149–50, 173
Board of Home Missions of the Presbyterian Church, 344

Boston Globe, 164
Boston Medical and Surgical Journal, 324
Boston News Bureau, 269
Boston Public Library, 179
Boyd, Edith, 22
Boyd, Edward, 22
Boyd, Xandra, 22
Bradley, Bill, 268
Brassey, Lady Anna, 256
Breakers, The 139, 178
Brooklyn Museum, 35–36
Brooklyn Navy Yard, 222
Brooks, David, 121
Browning, Robert, 179
Budd, Ralph, 273–274, 277, 280–283, 285, 289, 290, 309, 315
Burns, First Mate, 275
Burr, Aaron, 199, 370
Bush, Rufus T., 36
Butkiewicz, James, 328
Byrkit, James W., 227, 233

Cable, George Washington, 18, 144
California Railroad Commission, 269
Calvin, John, 41, 249
Cameron, George T., 316–18
Camp Mavooshen, 310–11, 325, 326
canalboats 57
Cannon, J., 315
Canton Christian College, 165, 167
Cape Horn, rounding, 36, 52, 55, 77, 78
capitalism, 330
Captain Candy, 170
Carlsbad Medical Spa, 126–27, 322
Carman, William W., 332–33, 339, 344, 345
Carnegie, Andrew, 350
Cascade Tunnel, 64–65, 272, 280
Cate, Anna P., 69
Century Club, the, 134
Cervantes, Miguel, 307
Chateau sur Mer, 178
Children's Aid Society, 134, 276, 344, 346
Chong, Alan, 181
Christadora House, 292, 344
Christianity: influence on Phelps, Dodge, and James families 41–42
promoting abroad 144, 165–167, 169, 258. See also Calvin, John

Chrysler, Walter P., 116
Civil War, 26, 58, 79, 142, 318
Civil War, 26, 79, 142
Clarke School for the Deaf, 351
Clayton Act, 194, 287. See also Sherman
    Antitrust Act
Cleland, Robert Glass, 40–42, 86, 90–93,
    99–100, 227
Cleveland, Grover, 16, 125
Coates, Dudley, 22
cocaine, 68
Cochran, Joseph Wilson, 303, 305
Coffin, Rev. Henry Sloane, 341
Cohan, William D., 308
Coleby, Nicola, 300
Coleridge, Samuel Taylor, 56
Colorado, USS, 272
Colt, Caldwell Hart, 36
Congress, 220, 232
Conrad, Joseph: reading at ACJ's, 248–52
    also mentioned, 120, 209, 263
"Conrad's American Speeches and His
    Reading From Victory" (Schwab), 250, 252
"Consecrated Eminence, The" (King), 125
Cooper, James Fenimore, 53
Corona and Coronet (Todd), 63, 67, 69, 70,
    74, 78, 159–60
Coronet Memories (Neely), 62, 160
Coronet: Whither Away? (Murray), 39
Corporate History of the Chicago, Burl
    ington & Quincy Railroad Company
    and Affiliated Companies (Baldwin),
    285
Coulsen, Robert, 345
Country Life in America (Miller), 195
cowcatcher, 87
Cox & Stevens, 337
Crane, Clinton, 104, 104–108, 115
Crane, Richard T., 203
"crime of the century," 148
Crosby, Captain, 45, 46, 54, 82
Crosslinked: A History of the Red Cross
    and South Florida (Parks and Pincus),
    252
Croton Reservoir, 134
Cunard, 132, 220
"cure, taking the" 126
Cymric, SS, 119

Daggett, Stuart, 210, 217
Dali, Salvador, 300, 301
Darbyshire, construction engineer, 99–100
Dauntless, 36, 297
Davis, Deborah, 140, 141, 143, 185
Davis, Jefferson, 318
Dawson, James, 149
De Medici, Cosimo, 182–83
Dear Father, Dear Son (Rockefeller) 305
decompression sickness, 120
Denver Post 275–76
Deportation, Bisbee, 227–32
depression of 1893, economic, 50
Depression, Great, 307–08, 319, 326–27,
    329–30
Deschutes Canyon War 281
Detroit Copper Company, 97
Dickinson, Austin, 28, 29, 56, 159, 244
Dickinson, Emily, 26, 28, 325
Dickinson, Ned, 28
Dickinson, Susan, 28
Dickinson, William, 28
Dodge, Cleveland H., 191
Dodge, Phyllis B., 132, 191
Dodge, William E. "Earl," Jr., 90–91, 92, 97
Dodge, William, 41
Dodge, William, Jr., 43
Dole, Sanford, 69
Don Quixote (Cervantes), 307
Doshisha Girls' School, 258
Doshisha University, 167, 258, 304
Dotsero Cutoff, 284–86, 328
Doubleday, Florence, 250, 252
Doubleday, Frank N., 250, 252
Douglas, Barclay, 352, 354
Douglas, James, 350
Douglas, James: at Phelps Dodge, 43, 85,
    91–92, 96–102, 224, 230–31
    mentor to ACJ, 88, 96
Douglas, Walter, 99–101, 225–231
Downtown Club, 134

Eakins, Thomas, 156
earthquake, 72. See also tsunami
Ebina, Danjo, 258
Eddystone Light, 129
Edward VII, King of Great Britain 22, 299
Elms, The 139, 178

Ely, Constance Jennings, 253–54
Emmons, Robert W., II, 203
Encyclopedia of American Business, The (Lloyd), 308
Endeavour, 35
Engineering and Mining Journal, 225
Episodes in the Life of a Publisher's Wife (Doubleday), 250
Erie Basin and Drydock Company, 106
Ernest M. Skinner Organ Company, 194
Espionage Act, 232
Eugenie, Victoria, Queen of Spain, 297
excess, wretched. See Newport

Federal Bankruptcy Act, 328
Federal Reserve, 208
"Feet of the Young Men, The" (Kipling), 197
Ferry, Amelia, 169, 339
Ferry, Hayward E., 169
Fife, William, 104
"Fifty Candles for Western Pacific" (Kneiss), 211, 212, 214, 330
First National Bank, 282
First Presbyterian Church, 304, 341, 344
Fish, Marion "Mamie," 140, 178
foot-binding, 167
Forbes, Evie, 22, 298
Forbes, John Murray, 109
Ford, Charles Henri, 302
Ford, Ruth, 302
Fore River Shipbuilding Company, 152, 167
Foreign Missionary Movement in the 19th and early 20th Centuries, The (Bays), 165
Forging the Copper Collar (Byrkit), 227, 233
Francis, Arthur, 45
Fraser, James William, 313
Fraser's Remedy, 67
Freeman Thomas, Marie (Brassey), Marchioness of Willingdon, 266
Freeman-Thomas, Major Freeman, 1st Marquess of Willingdon, 266
Friendly Adventures (Cochran) 303, 305
Frissell, Lewis, 170
Frissell, Vareck 170

Galbraith, John 307
Gardener Who Saw God, The (James) 299
Gardner, Isabella Stewart, 179
German shepherds, 171
Gilded Age, 60
Gilded Age: A Tale of Today, The (Twain and Warner), 139
Gilded: How Newport Became America's Richest Resort (Davis), 140, 141, 143, 185
Gill, Brendan, 138–39, 144, 190
Gleam, 105
Goelet, Ogden, 139
Gold Coast. See North Shore
Gondola Days: Isabelle Stewart Gardner and the Palazzo Barbaro Circle (Chong), 181
Gothic art and architecture, 192, 236, 303, 348–49
Götterdämmerung, 256
Gould, George Jay, 39, 116, 210, 212, 216, 217, 331
Gould, Jay, 210, 212, 289, 319, 331
Grant, Ulysses S., 58
Great Crash, The (Galbraith) 307
Great Houses of New York, 1880–1930 (Kathrens), 190
Great Northern Pacific Steamship Company, 66
Great Northern Railway: A History, The (Hidy), 274, 281–82
Greatorex, Dorothy, 243
Greatorex, John, 150–51, 176, 202, 237, 243
Greatorex, Robina, 237
Green-Wood Cemetery, 342
Grenfell, Sir Wilfred, 170
Grounds and Building Committee, 160
Gubelmann, Walter S., 116
Guernsey Association, 244
Guthrie, Sybil Waters, 239–40

Hamilton, Alice, 233
Hamilton, Dorrance Hill, 354–55
Hammersmith Farm, 353
Hampton Institute (now Hampton University), 16, 19, 136, 156, 259, 262, 341, 344, 346
Hanover National Bank, 169

Harper's Magazine, 142
Harper's Magazine, 294–95
Harrigan, Margaret Borman, 244–45
Harriman, Edward Henry: as rival, 109–14,
    123, 143, 211–12, 280
    death, 210, 281
    merger with ACJ, 267
    railroad pioneer 57, 66, 100, 319, 331
Harriman, William Averell, 210
Harvard Club, 232
Harvard Medical School, 233
Hattendorf, John, 303–304
Heade, Martin Johnson, 26, 28
Heart of Darkness (Conrad), 248
Hepburn Act, 234
Herreshoff Manufacturing Company, 104,
    246
Herreshoff, Nathanael, 196, 203
Heyst, Alex (character), 249, 263
Hidy, Ralph, 274, 281–82
Hill, H. R., 289–90
Hill, James J.: death, 218–19
    golden rules of railroading, 215, 268
    mentor to ACJ, 96, 289, 315, 327
    railroad titan, 44, 58–59, 109, 122–23,
    167, 207–8, 267
    rivalry with Harriman, 143, 280
Hill, Lewis, 271
History of Phelps Dodge, A (Cleland),
    40–42, 86, 90–93, 99–100, 227
History of the Endowment of Amherst
College, A (King) 125
History of the Northern Securities Case, A
(Meyer), 110–12, 123–24
Hitchcock, Margaret "Peggy," 332–33, 337,
    338
Hitchcock, Sophia, 41, 130, 298
Hitchcock, Tommy, 41
Holden, Hale, 273, 288
Holland, Miller, 318
Holy Lands, 37
Hoover, Herbert, 298, 328
Hopkins, June, 292
Houghton, Fred B., 315
Howdy, 118
Howells, John Mead, 148
HUD, 354
Hunt-Douglas method, 90

Hunt, Thomas Sterry, 89
Huntington, Collis Potter, 211, 212
IBM, 345
ICC (Interstate Commerce Commission),
    234, 269, 274, 277, 281–90,
    306–310, 328–332

Iconography of Manhattan Island (Phelps
    Stokes), 148
Ida Lewis Light, 294–95, 335
Inside Gateway, 274, 282–84, 286, 288,
    290, 306, 309, 312, 319
Interesting People: Eighty Years with the
Great and Near-Great (Smith), 180, 188,
    263, 265–66
IWW (Industrial Workers of the World),
    224–232
IYRS (International Yacht Restoration
    School) 32–37, 356

J. N. Robins & Company, 106
J. P. Morgan & Company, 223, 282
Jackson, Harriet Phelps, 173
James Art Center (formerly Memorial
    Library), 168
James, Arthur Curtiss:
    Character
        affability, 24, 198, 289 283
        art collector, 156, 157, 348–51
        comparisons to mythical figures, 276,
           307
        "cool," 121, 207, 221, 247, 290–91,
           302, 32
        "cool," losing, 120, 167, 298, 304
        generosity, 131, 188, 243, 245
        good with children, 243, 248
        gossip about, 22, 244
        hobbies, 194, 245
        love of Hawaii, 68, 171, 258
        "loyal friend," 108
        private nature, 86, 145, 237, 267,
           314
        respect for employees, 237–238
        student at Amherst, 15–20, 23, 44,
           125, 208
        values, 137, 298
    Relationships
        with parents, 43–44

with mentors: Cable, George Washington, 18
Douglas, James, 88–90
Hill, James J., 59, 96
with Harriet: marriage to, 19, 22–23
romantic gestures to, 75, 78, 108, 199
strong commitment to, 178, 243–44, 321
childlessness of, 126, 191, 231
mourning of, 338
with Mabel Todd: first meeting 15, 47, 68
correspondence with, 71, 158–61, 291–93, 310–12, 322, 324–26
likelihood of affair with, 244
with other women, 244, 340–41
with extended family, 191, 298–302, 339–41
Railroad Titan
beginnings, 40, 125
initial railroad jobs, 97, 99, 208
mentored, 59, 88–90, 96
made director of Copper Queen, 40
dreaming of transcontinental line, 59, 66, 96, 109, 208–9, 219, 267, 319
focusing Phelps Dodge on mining, 85
first mine tour, 94
made vice president of EP&SW, 99
battle with Harriman, 99–101, 109–13, 123
Northern Securities Case, 110–13, 122–25, 194, 287
made director and vice president of Phelps Dodge, 136
Feather River route, 209–17
Bisbee strike, 223–33
merger with SP, 267–71
Inside Gateway, 274, 276–90
golden spike, 306–10, 313–18
WP reorganization, 327–32
press coverage, 124, 223, 234, 254, 273, 275–76, 282, 286, 321, 330–32, 341
business acumen, 136, 195, 262, 271
stock portfolio, 208–209, 216, 267–68, 273, 283, 307–8, 319
companies 208, 329, 345

depth of wealth, 136, 308
Philanthropy
anti-Prohibition, 319
children's aid, 134, 223, 276, 346
Christianity, 134–35, 165–69, 258–59, 303–305, 343–46
education, 31, 47, 125, 136, 158, 160, 195, 259, 262, 276, 332, 338, 343–47
the arts, 168–69, 343–49
the Todds, 292–93
war widows, 223
yacht community, 152–53, 294–97
Sailor
love of the sea, 103–04, 120–21, 143, 335
master of the yacht, 46, 118, 125, 138, 157
Coronet: history, 36–37
purchase of 37, 39
interior decoration 46
lifeboat design 104–105
cruises to West Indies, Nova Scotia, St. Lawrence, Japan, Iceland, 45–56, 67–83, 113–14, 156
restoration of 32–36, 356
Aloha I: building of 106–8
cruises to West Indies, Iceland, Europe, 113–15, 118, 128–31
racing, 116–17
collision, 119
sinking, 162
Aloha II: building and decoration of, 152–58
maiden voyage to Europe 162–64
cruises to Egypt, Israel, Spain, 176–77, 297
turned over to navy, 220–22, 231
returned to ACJ 222
cruise around the world, 256–66
installation of diesel engines 271–72
shot at, 275
collision with Sagamore, 314
last sail, 333–36
Lanai I, 117–18

Lanai II, 171–73, 333–34
Mauna Loa, 222, 337
Aloha Li'i, 337
gales, 45, 47, 114, 118, 119, 131, 138, 164
Real Estate
Newport's largest taxpayer, 245
Beacon Hill: building of, 144–51, 171, 177–78
Edgehill, 168–70
Blue Garden, 173–76, 178–88
Surprise Farm, 199– 203
Vedimar, 170, 353
Zeerust, 170
staff memories of, 240–45
Fourway Lodge, 196–98, 239, 252
39 East 69th Street, 190–95, 248–52, 306
James House, 192, 236–40
Death
heart attacks, 328, 332, 337
loss of Harriet, 338
hospitalization and death, 338–39
Times obituary, 341
Legacy
art collection, 157, 349
James Foundation, 343–458
to friends and relatives, 343–44
to schools and organizations, 346–48
James Douglas: a Memoir (Langton), 91
James Foundation, 344, 345–46, 351
James, Daniel (grandfather), 40, 41, 298
James, Daniel Willis, Jr. (brother), 41, 342
James, Daniel Willis: acquisition of Copper Queen, 91
death, 131
immigration to America, 42
mentor to ACJ, 40
philanthropy, 15, 18–19, 43, 125, 132–35, 165, 194
railroad stockholder, 43, 136, 208
religious, 43
rivalry with Harriman, 143
runnings Phelps Dodge, 15–16, 39
wealth, 16, 23, 132
James, Edward 298–302
James, Elizabeth Woodbridge Phelps (grand mother), 40–41, 236, 271

James, Ellen Stebbins Curtiss (mother), 18, 41, 342
James, Frank, 22
James, Harriet Parsons: causes and clubs, 69, 144, 223, 243, 252–53, 265, 339, 343:
death of, 338
designing Blue Garden, 173–176
fear of swimming, 253–254
illnesses 126, 159, 243, 297–298, 322, 325–26
inability to conceive, 126, 191, 231
loss of father, 20
marriage to ACJ, 19
nervous breakdown, 140, 321–326
relationship with Mabel, 74, 87
social personality, 52–53, 143, 178, 183–84, 298
travel writings, 63–65, 68, 71, 74, 78, 87, 94, 96
James, Henry, 141–42, 179
James, John Arthur, 21
James, Sophia, 21
James, Walter B., 22, 116
James, Walter B., Mrs. (Helen Goodsell Jennings), 22
James, William Dodge, 21–22, 298
Jekyll Island Club, 208, 253
Jenkins, Ashby, 245
Jennings, Walter, 253
Jones, plain Mr. (character), 263
Justice Department, 122, 232

Kaikilanialiiwahineopuna, High Chieftess, 141
Kathrens, Michael C., 190
Keddie, Arthur, 209–12, 217
Keeley Institute, 53
Kennedy, John S., 60, 208
King, Stanley, 125, 326
Kingdom, The, an apocalyptic sect, 37
Kingsley, William, 45
Kipling, Rudyard, 24, 29–30, 197, 350
Kneiss, G. H., 211, 212, 214, 216, 330
Knowles, Frederick, 151
Koehler, Hans J., 150
Kronprinz Wilhelm, SS, 127
Kuhn Loeb & Company, 282

Langton, H. H., 91

Larkin, Diana Wolfe, 180

Last of the Great Stations: 40 years of the Los Angeles Union Passenger Terminal, The (Bradley), 268

Last Tycoon: The Secret History of Lazard Frères & Co., The (Cohan), 308

Law of Necessity, 233

"law of the apex, the," 93

Ledoux, Lewis, 336

Legendary Yachts (Robinson), 162–63

Lena (character), 251–52, 263

Lenya, Lotte, 301

Les Ballets, 301

Letters of Emily Dickinson, 28, 325

Levee, Arleyn A., 149–50, 173

Lewis, Ida, 294–95

Lewis, Talbot, 338

Life in Full Sail, A (Beard), 60, 62

Lime Rock Light. See Ida Lewis Light

Lincoln, Abraham, 58

Lindbergh, Charles, 248

Lipton, Sir Thomas, 39, 203

Livingston, Captain and family, 51

Lloyd, Arthur L., 308

Lloyd's Register of American Yachts, 197

Locomotive Engineers Journal, 313

Long Island Country Houses and Their Architects (Gill, foreword), 138–39

Longsworth, Polly, 28, 29, 75, 159

Los Angeles Times, 269, 270, 288

Losch, Tilly, 300, 301

Lubin, C. Owen, 191–94

Lusitania, RMS: ACJ on 164, 165 sinking of, 220

Lyall, Archibald, 139

Lynn Bailey, 86, 92, 224, 226, 233

MacKaye, Percy, 180, 188

MacKaye, Steele, 180, 181

Madison Eagle, 165

Magazine of Wall Street, 269

Magritte, René, 300

Mahaffie, Charles D., 306, 308

Malkovich, Joan Shewring, 240–43, 244, 322, 340, 351

Manice, Harriet DeForest, 339–40, 344

Manice, Harriet Ferry, 247

Manice, Oliver, 247–48

Manice, Robert DeForest, 169–170, 340, 353

Manice, William DeForest, 170, 247, 339, 353

Manice, William DeForest, Jr., 170, 247, 353

Marble House, 139, 178, 190

Marine Exposition, 1925, 271–72

Marlow, Charles (character), 248

Masque of the Blue Garden, The, 181, 188

Matheson, William J. "John," 116, 157, 195–97, 256, 335

Mathis Yacht Building Company, 171

Mauretania, RMS, 312

McBurney, Robert Ross, 69

McCabe, Lida Rose, 200, 202

McClintic, F. M., 151–52

McColl, Christina, 292

McKim, Charles, 179

McKim, Mead & White, 144, 168

McKinnon, Donald, 345

McNeil, Robert, 356

Mecray, John, 35, 81

Mediation Commission, 233

"Men Who Run America" (Smith) 330–332

Merging Lines: American Railroads, 1900–1970 (Saunders), 277

Metropolitan Club, the, 134

Metropolitan Museum of Art, 132, 179, 344

Meyer, B. H., 110–12, 123–24

Meyer, Elizabeth, 35

Miller, Wilhelm, 195

mine conditions, early 91–92, 96, 225

miners, unionization of, 93, 223–32

Miyako Maru, SS, 71

Modern Philology, 250, 252

Moffat, David H., 284

Mohican, 117

Moncrieff, Audrey, 22

Moncrieff, Willie, 22

Montgomery, Antoinette, 170

Moore, Harold A., 283–84

Morgan, J. P., 39, 60, 109, 112, 116, 122, 203

Morley, Christopher, 252

Morning Oregonian, 283

Moro people, 262

Motor Boating, 171
Munroe, Kirk, 196
Munroe, Ralph M., 196–97
Murphy, Edward, 316
Murray, Tim, 39
Musée de Cluny, 349
Myrick, David, 270
Mystic Seaport Museum, 336

Narrows, the, 45
National Academy of Design, 134
National Arts Club, 134
National Gallery of Art, 354
National Register of Historic Places, 168
nationalization of railroads, 234–36
Native Americans, 63, 84, 88, 90, 209, 259, 318
Neesima, Joseph, 166–67, 258
Neptune, 114
New York Herald Tribune, 297
New York Herald, 197
New York Nautical College, 44, 54
New York Post, 321
New York Public Library, 344
New York Sun, 187
New York Times: on Hill, James J., 218
    on railroads, 226, 232, 276, 284, 288, 328
    on sailing, 36, 106, 297
    also mentioned, 121, 345
    see also under James,
Arthur Curtiss
New-York Tribune, 173
Newport Daily News, 185, 187, 221, 275
Newport Harbor Guide, The (Rafael), 200
Newport Historical Society, 358
Newport Hospital, 245, 344
Newport in Flower (Jackson), 173
Newport Mercury and Weekly News, 333
Newport Mercury, 140, 336
Newport Naval Station, 221
Newport Reading Room, 170
Newport: A Lively Experiment 1639–1969 (Stensrud), 138, 139
Newport: adultery, 140
    lavish society parties, 138–141, 143, 181–182
    of yesteryear, 142

opulent mansions, 138, 139
    port of, 138, 141, 143
Nigel Burgess Yacht Brokers, 104
Norse literature, 156
North Shore society, 115, 138
Northampton Gazette, 23
Noyes, Florence Fleming, 185–87

O'Brien, Melvin, 164
O'Conner, Dennis, 181, 182
Oakland Post Inquirer, 289–90
Ocean Drive 138
Oceanic, RMS, 130
Ochre Court, 139
Oelrichs, Theresa Fair, 130
Of Rails & Sails, 199, 358
Ogden, Robert Curtis, 18, 156–57
Olmsted Brothers, 149–50, 174–76
Omaha World-Herald, 319, 321
Onassis, Jacqueline Kennedy, née Bouvier, 353
opium, 68, 166
Oregon Daily Journal, 290

Panaggio, Leonard, 275
Panic of 1907, economic, 217
Parke-Bernet Galleries, 348
Parks, Arva Moore, 252
Parliament, 223
Parsons, Amelia, 169
Parsons, Cornet Joseph, 19
Parsons, Samuel, 23
Parsons, Sydenham Clark, 19–20
Peary, Robert, 156
Pell, Christopher "Toby," 352, 354
Pell, Claiborne, 352
Pelton, Henry, 292
penal farm, luncheon at, 262
Pennsylvania Academy of Fine Arts, 156
Pennsylvania Station, 144
People's History of the United States, A (Zinn), 307
Perkins, Charles, 109–110
Phelps Dodge and Company: battle with Southern Pacific, 99–101, 110
    battle with union, 223–33
    building railroads, 96–99, 216
    formative stages, 40–41
    ownership of Copper Queen, 40, 84

production and shipping, 16, 20
struggles, 85
takeover of Bisbee, 93–94, 225
Phelps Memorial Hospital, 237
Phelps Stokes, Isaac Newton, 145, 148
Phelps, Anson (great-uncle), 40, 41, 42, 236
Phelps, Anson Green, Jr., 236, 271
Phelps, Jane and her unmarried sister Helen, 236
Phelps, Melissa, 41
Phelps, Stowe, 199
Phelps, Thomas (great-great-grandfather), 271
Philadelphia Record, 330
Phillips Andover Academy, 166, 167
Phillips, T. L., 310
Pincus, Laura, 252
Poillon, Cornelius, 34
Poillon, Richard, 35
polo, 41, 170
Powell, Earl "Rusty," 354
Powell, Nancy, 354
Pratt Institute, 87
Preparedness Movement, 220
Preservation Society of Newport County, 352
Price, Margaret, 339, 343–44
Price, Marshall, 343–44
Prohibition, 275, 298, 318, 319, 341
Pulitzer, Joseph, 116
Purser, Philip, 298–99
Pyeatt, J. S., 315

Queen's Cup, 297

race, subject of 16–18, 157
Raceabouts, Seawanhaka, 115–18
Rafael, Anita, 200
railroad conditions, early 57–58
Railroad Consolidation West of the Mississippi River (Daggett), 210, 217
Railroad Control Act, 234
railroads, building, cost and romance of, 209
Railway Age, 310, 327, 337–38
railways: Arizona and South Eastern, 87, 99, 216 (see also El Paso & Southwestern)
Atchison, Topeka & Santa Fe 58, 96, 318

Atlantic & Pacific, 96 (see also Atchison, Topeka & Santa Fe)
Baltimore & Ohio, 56
Canadian Pacific, 58
Central Pacific 57
Chicago, Burlington & Quincy 62, 109, 136, 208, 271, 273–76, 284, 285, 318–19
Chicago, Rock Island & Pacific, 102
Denver & Rio Grande, 212, 216, 267, 308, 315, 319
Denver & Salt Lake, 284
El Paso & Southwestern 97, 99–102, 110, 216, 228, 267–70, 276, 308
Grand Trunk 56
Great Northern 31, 58–59, 62–66, 109–112, 122, 136, 167, 170, 194, 208–209, 217–19, 267, 271–77, 280–84, 288–90, 306, 309, 314–19
Long Island 115, 272
Minneapolis & St. Cloud 208
Missouri Pacific, 285, 315
New Mexico & Arizona, 97
New York Central, 56, 315
Northern Pacific, 58, 66, 109–13, 122–23, 136, 169, 271, 273, 276, 282–84, 318–19
Oregon Trunk, 280–81
Oroville & Virginia City, 210
Petaluma & Santa Rosa, 274
Philadelphia & Reading 50
Rio Grande & Western, 284
Sacramento–San Francisco 321
Santa Fe System, 97, 99, 315
Southern pacific 58, 65–66, 84, 96–101, 209–12, 216, 267–71, 273–74, 276–77, 281–88, 307–309, 318–19
St. Paul, Minneapolis & Manitoba 208
Tidewater Southern, 274
Union Pacific Railroad 57, 210–12, 318
Western Pacific & Denver, 284
Western Pacific 57, 216–17, 267, 270, 273–276, 282–85, 288–90, 306–12, 315, 319, 326–32, 337–38, 345
Ramabai Association, 169

Read, Albert C., 245–46
Red Cross Society, 252–53
Remington, Frederick, 349–51
Renaissance art and design, 177, 180, 191, 348
Resolute, 203
Revolutionary War, 342
RFC (Reconstruction Finance Corporation), 327–30
Riding Club, 134
Rime of the Ancient Mariner (Coleridge), 56
Robinson, William W. "Bill," 162–63
Rocky Mountain News, 286
Roman Catholic Diocese of Providence, 352
Roosevelt, Franklin Delano, 275, 298, 352
Roosevelt, Theodore, 116, 122, 220, 232
Rose, Hans, 221
Rosecliff, 139, 140
Rosengren, Harold, 35
Rothschild, Baron Nathaniel de, 150
Rudder, The, 151–52
Rutherford, Jerry, 356

S. Rajaratnam School of International Studies, 181
Sacramento Bee, 318
Sagamore, 314
San Francisco Chronicle, 316
San Francisco Examiner, 289
Sappho, 33
Sargent, John Singer, 148, 179
sati, 169
Saturday Evening Post, 124, 235
Saunders, Richard, Jr. 277
scenario, 15, 23, 29, 108, 120, 230
Schumacher, Thomas Milton, 216, 270, 273, 283, 289, 290, 315
Schwab, Arnold, 250, 252
Schwantes, Carlos A., 100
seasickness 46, 52, 67–68, 129
Seattle Times, 309
Semper Eadem (Hattendorf), 303–304
Shamrock IV, 203
Shawmut, USS, 246
Sherman Antitrust Act, 122–23, 194, 286
Sherman, William T., 58
Shewring, Douglas, 240–43

Sloan, Alfred P., 116
Smith College, 19, 144, 169
Smith, Arthur D. Howden, 330–32
Smith, Corinna Putnam, 180, 188, 263, 265–66
Smith, Joseph Lindon, 179–182, 184, 188, 189, 193, 200, 202 263, 265
Smithsonian Institution, 157
Snook, John Butler, 236
Society for the Promotion of the Gospel Among Seaman of the Port of New York, 344
Society of Natural History, 134
Spaulding, George, 78–83
Springfield Union, 338
St. Joseph Lead Company, 105
Standard Oil, 36
Staten Island Shipbuilding Corporation, 272
Steel, D. A., 327
Stensrud, Rockwell, 138, 139
Sterns, Charles Falconer, 53
Stevenson, George, 57
Stokes, Bessie, 54
Stokes, Edith Minturn, 148
Stokes, Frank Wilbert, 156
Sullivan, Florence S., 256
Sullivan, J. K., 334
Summer of Hummingbirds: Love, Art and Scandal in the Intersecting Worlds of Emily Dickinson, Mark Twain, Harriet Beecher Stowe, and Martin Johnson Heade, A (Benfey) 26
Sunbeam, 256, 266
Sunday Observer, 299
Supreme Court, California, 269
Supreme Court, United States, 122–23, 234, 269
Surreal Life: Edward James 1907–1984, A (Coleby), 300

Tales of the Phelps Dodge Family (Dodge), 132, 191
Tams & King, 272
Tams, Lemoine & Crane, 152
"There's a Long, Long Trail A-Winding," 316
Thompson, sailor, 55

Tiffany Studio, 181
Time, 248, 299, 306–307, 329–30, 341
Tjandi Boroboedoer, 263
tobacco monopoly, French, 129
Todd, David: at Amherst 25, 26, 47, 75,
    161, 291, 324
  "Henpecked," 160, 255
  institutionalized, 75, 292
  meeting ACJ, 29–31
  philandering, 29
  travels with ACJ, 31, 68, 73–75
Todd, Mabel: affairs, 28–29, 56, 75, 244
  at Amherst 26, 28, 56, 75, 326
  charisma, 25–28, 30
  relationship with ACJ, 71, 158–61,
    291–93, 310–12, 322, 324–26
  relationship with Dickinsons, 28, 325
  travels with ACJ, 56, 63, 66–75, 86–88,
    94
ton-miles 60, 368
Toombs, Elizabeth, 145, 146
Town & Country, 145, 177, 191–92, 200
Townsend, William, 32
train-miles 60, 268
Trains, 270
Tres Hermanes, 229
Trinity Episcopal Church, 303–4, 347, 352
"Troopin'," (Kipling), 24
Trudeau tuberculosis clinic. See Adirondack
    Cottage Sanitarium
Trumpy, John, 171, 333
tsunami, 72–73
Turks Head Building, 148
Tuskegee Normal and Industrial Institute,
    344
Twain, Mark, 18, 139
12-Meter, 105
21st Amendment, 275

Umbria, RMS, 132
Unification of the Northern Pacific Railway
    Company and Great Northern Railway
    Company Plan and Deposit Agreement, 271
Union League Club, 208
Union Theological Seminary 18, 134–35,
    157, 189, 194, 259, 304, 342–46
United States Railroad Administration, 234
United War Work Campaign, 223

van Rijn, Rembrandt, 129
Vanderbilt, Alva, 116, 139, 140–41, 190
Vanderbilt, Cornelius, 130, 139, 203, 331
Vanderbilt, Harold S., 203
Vanderbilt, William K., 139, 190
Veblen, Thorstein, 139
Victory (Conrad), 249–52, 263
Viking sagas, 156
Vision & Enterprise: Exploring the History
    of Phelps Dodge Corporation
    (Schwantes), 100
Vogel, Karl M., 256, 258, 265–66
von Rydingsvärd, Karl, 156, 336
Vos, Eleanor Kaikilani Coney, 141, 258
Vos, Hubert, 141, 258
Voyage in the Sunbeam, A (Brassey), 256

Wacouta, 62
Wagner, Richard, 183
Wainwright, Stuyvesant, 118
Wall Street Journal, 267
Wall Street, 112, 143,
Wallin, Brian, 221
Walter, Henry, 203
Wanamaker, John, 157
Warner, Charles Dudley, 139
Waters, Charles, 237
Waters, Helen, 237, 239
Weetamoe, 105
Weill, Kurt, 301
West Indian Swizzle, 47
Western Federation of Miners, 223–224,
    227
Western Pacific Company Magazine, 211
Westinghouse Company, 272
Weyerhaeuser, Frederick, 290
Wheeler, Sheriff Harry, 227–28
Where Is He Now?: The Extraordinary
    Worlds of Edward James (Purser), 298–99
White Star Line, 119
White, Stanford, 145, 148, 304
Whitehead, Ben G. and wife, 168
Whitney, William Payne, 116, 203
Williamson, F. E., 315
Willingdon, Lord and Lady. See Freeman-
    Thomas
Williston Weekly State, 168
Williston, North Dakota 63, 167–68

Wilson, Howard, 53–54
Wilson, Woodrow, 220, 232, 233, 234
Winslow, Cameron McRae, 221, 222
Winton Engine Company, 272
Wounded Bunkie, The (Remington), 349-51

Xiaoqinxian, Empress Dowager "Cixi" of
   China, 141

yacht clubs: American 118
   Atlantic 39
   Beverly 115, 116, 117, 118
   Biscayne Bay 196
   Cold Spring Harbor 116
   Hempsted Harbor 116
   Huntington 116
   Knickerbocker 116

Manhasset Bay 116
Narragansett Bay Regatta Association 295
New York Yacht Club 36–38, 106, 116,
   130, 134, 137, 151, 152, 162
Port Washington 116
Sea Cliff 116
Seawanhaka Corinthian 37, 38, 105,
   116, 157, 342
Yachting Memories (Crane), 105, 117
Yale University, 78, 158, 167, 195, 346, 348
YMCA, 19, 69, 151, 169, 223, 243, 252,
   253, 265, 292

Zarno, Captain, 314
Zinn, Howard, 307
Zorn, Anders, 179
Zoroaster, SS, 120

Made in the USA
Columbia, SC
23 January 2022

54649807R00231